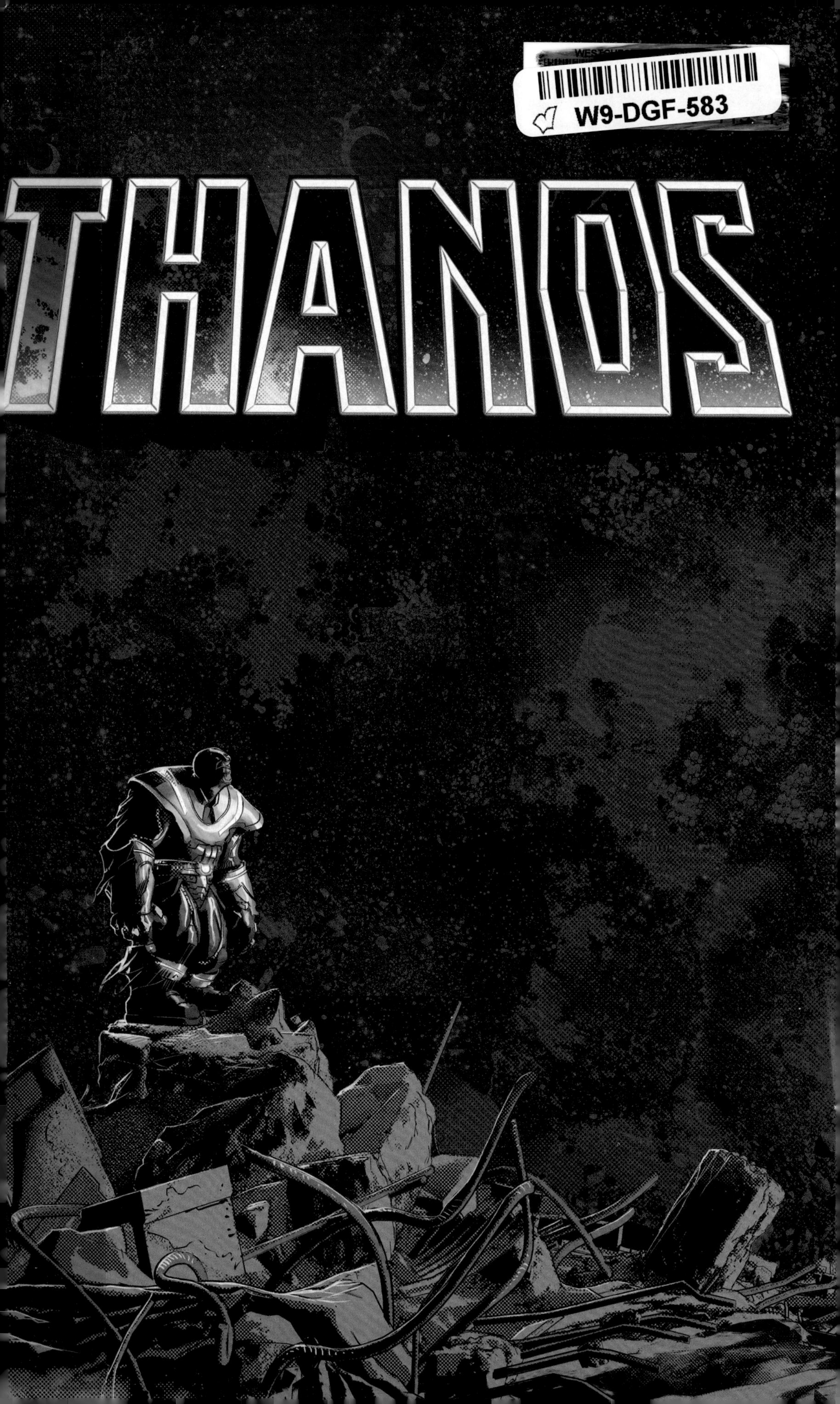
THANOS

THANOS IS DYING. SEARCHING FOR A CURE, HE HAS RAGED ACROSS THE UNIVERSE, BUT FOUND NO SUCCOR. MANY ACROSS TIME AND SPACE WOULD GLADLY SEE THANOS DEAD, INCLUDING HIS SON, THANE. UNDER THE GUIDANCE OF DEATH, THANE BETRAYED HIS FORMER ALLIES, STARFOX, NEBULA, AND TRYCO SLATTERUS, IN ORDER TO HARNESS THE POWER OF THE PHOENIX FORCE AND EXACT TOTAL REVENGE UPON HIS FATHER.

USING THE PHOENIX FORCE, THANE BLASTED THANOS WITH ALL THE RAGE AND POWER AT HIS DISPOSAL, THEN USURPED HIS FATHER'S THRONE, CURSING THANOS TO EKE OUT HIS REMAINING DAYS AS A MORTAL. THE MAD TITAN IS NO MORE.

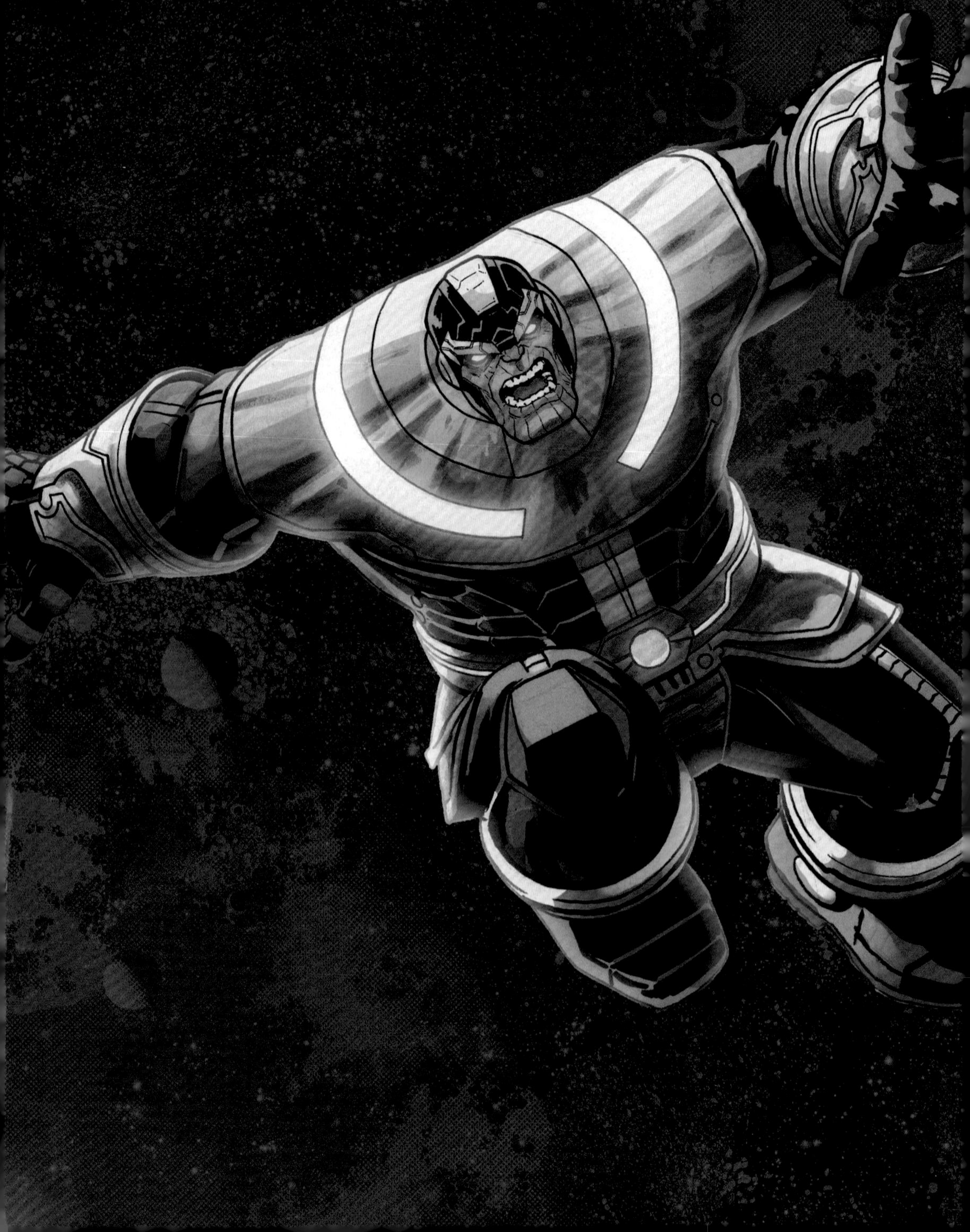

THANOS

THE GOD QUARRY

JEFF LEMIRE
WRITER

GERMÁN PERALTA
ARTIST

RACHELLE ROSENBERG
COLOR ARTIST

VC's CLAYTON COWLES
LETTERER

MIKE DEODATO JR.
WITH **FRANK MARTIN** (#7) & **RAIN BEREDO** (#8-12)
COVER ART

KATHLEEN WISNESKI, CHARLES BEACHAM & ALLISON STOCK
ASSISTANT EDITORS

DARREN SHAN
ASSOCIATE EDITOR

JORDAN D. WHITE
EDITOR

COLLECTION EDITOR **JENNIFER GRÜNWALD**
ASSISTANT EDITOR **CAITLIN O'CONNELL**
ASSOCIATE MANAGING EDITOR **KATERI WOODY**
EDITOR, SPECIAL PROJECTS **MARK D. BEAZLEY**

VP PRODUCTION & SPECIAL PROJECTS **JEFF YOUNGQUIST**
SVP PRINT, SALES & MARKETING **DAVID GABRIEL**
BOOK DESIGNER **ADAM DEL RE**

EDITOR IN CHIEF **AXEL ALONSO**
CHIEF CREATIVE OFFICER **JOE QUESADA**
PRESIDENT **DAN BUCKLEY**
EXECUTIVE PRODUCER **ALAN FINE**

THANOS VOL. 2: THE GOD QUARRY. Contains material originally published in magazine form as THANOS #7-12. First printing 2017. ISBN# 978-1-302-90558-3. Published by MARVEL WORLDWIDE, INC., a subsidiary of MARVEL ENTERTAINMENT, LLC. OFFICE OF PUBLICATION: 135 West 50th Street, New York, NY 10020. Copyright © 2017 MARVEL No similarity between any of the names, characters, persons, and/or institutions in this magazine with those of any living or dead person or institution is intended, and any such similarity which may exist is purely coincidental. **Printed in Canada.** DAN BUCKLEY, President, Marvel Entertainment; JOE QUESADA, Chief Creative Officer; TOM BREVOORT, SVP of Publishing; DAVID BOGART, SVP of Business Affairs & Operations, Publishing & Partnership; C.B. CEBULSKI, VP of Brand Management & Development, Asia; DAVID GABRIEL, SVP of Sales & Marketing, Publishing; JEFF YOUNGQUIST, VP of Production & Special Projects; DAN CARR, Executive Director of Publishing Technology; ALEX MORALES, Director of Publishing Operations; SUSAN CRESPI, Production Manager; STAN LEE, Chairman Emeritus. For information regarding advertising in Marvel Comics or on Marvel.com, please contact Jonathan Parkhideh, VP of Digital Media & Marketing Solutions, at jparkhideh@marvel.com. For Marvel subscription inquiries, please call 888-511-5480. **Manufactured between 11/3/2017 and 12/5/2017 by SOLISCO PRINTERS, SCOTT, QC, CANADA.**

10 9 8 7 6 5 4 3 2 1

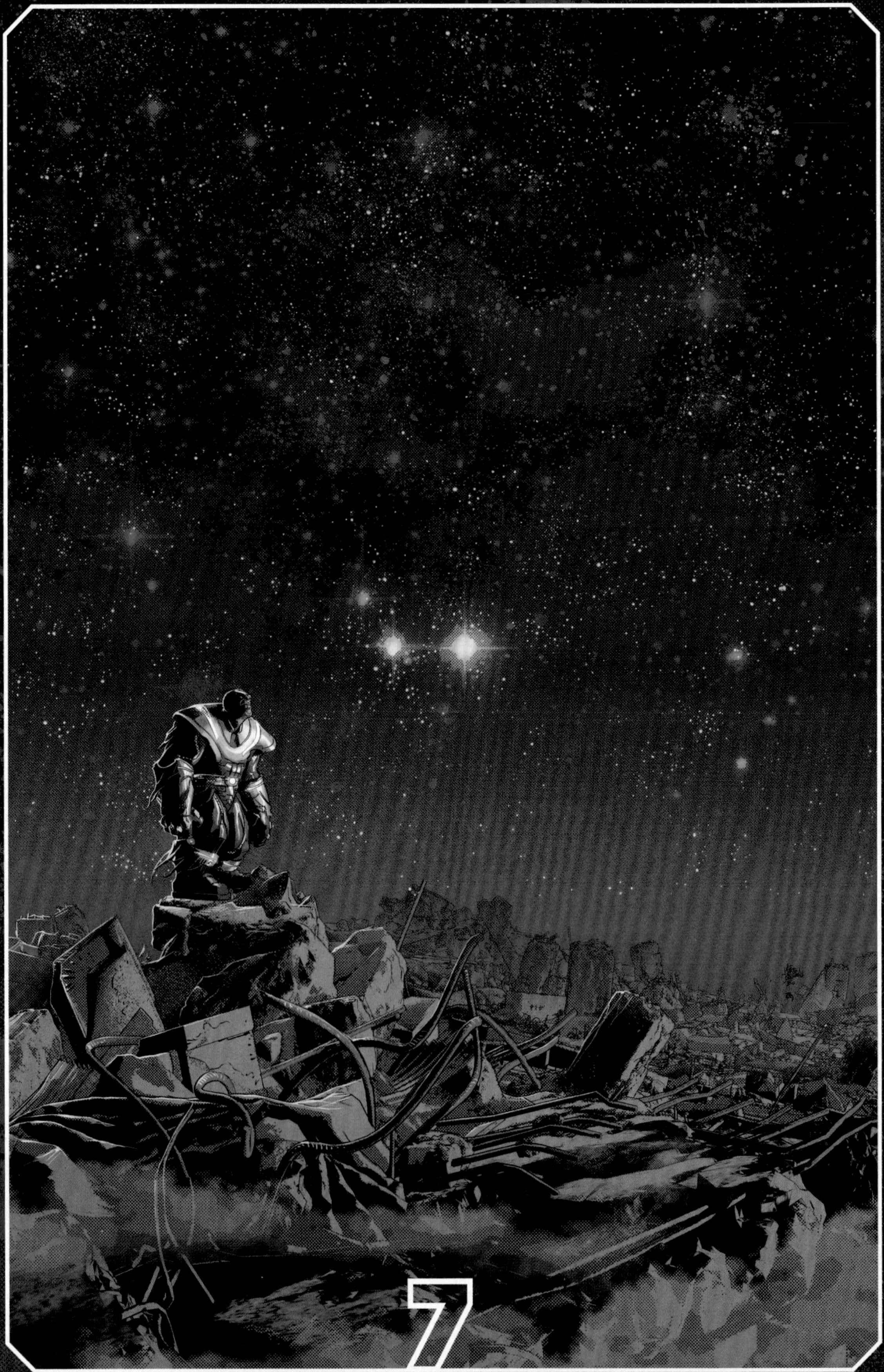
7

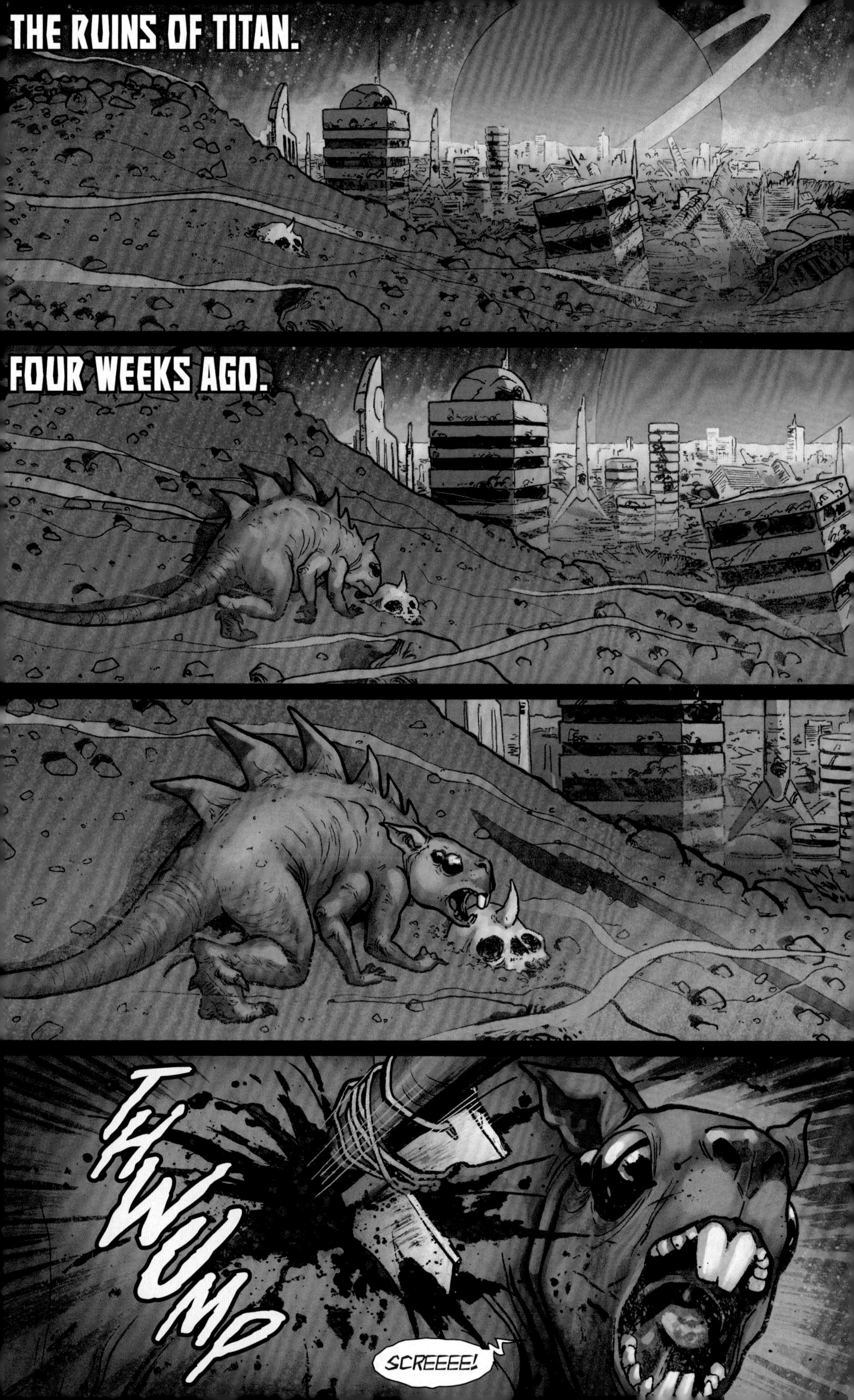
THE RUINS OF TITAN.
FOUR WEEKS AGO.
THWUMP
SCREEEEE!

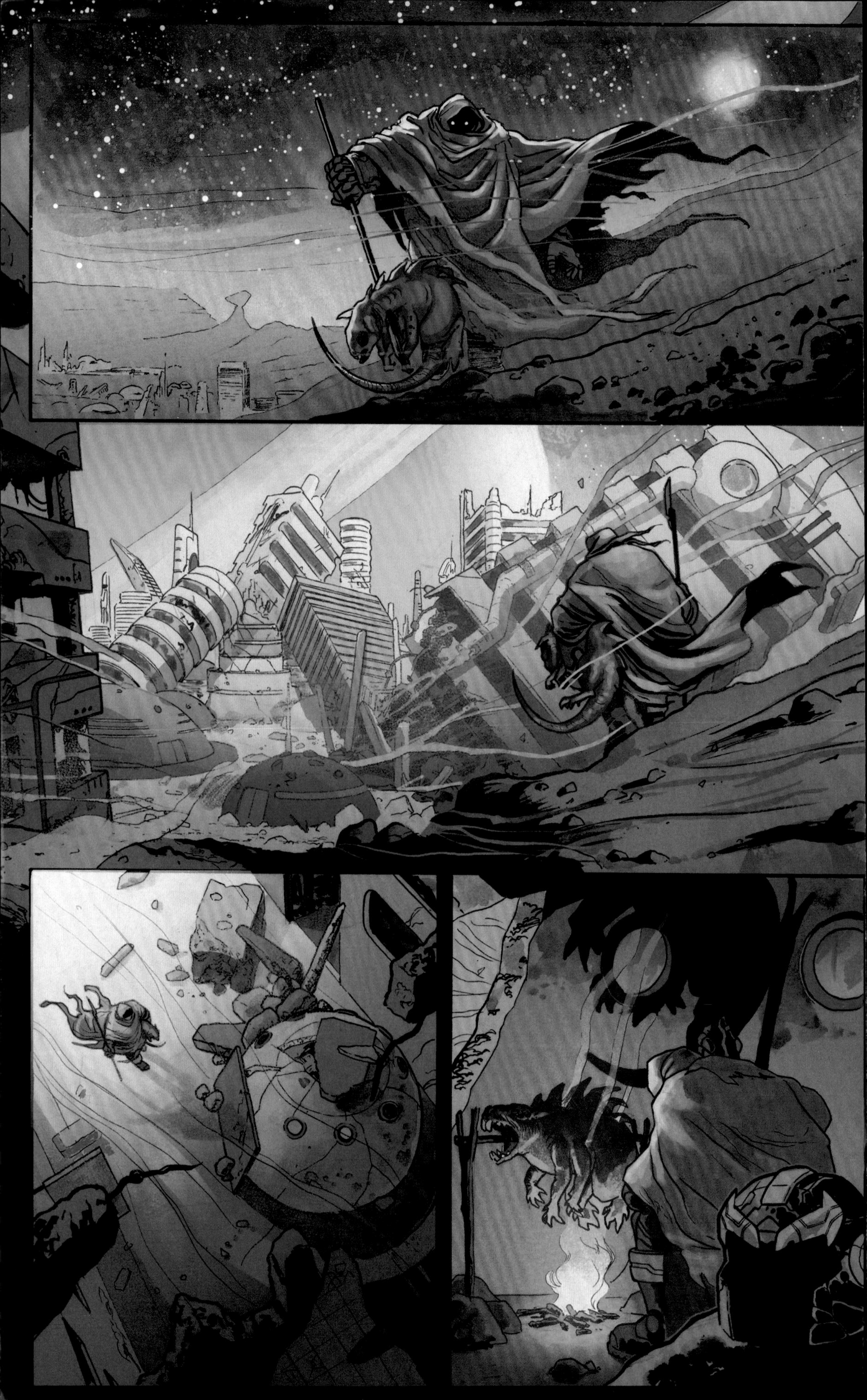

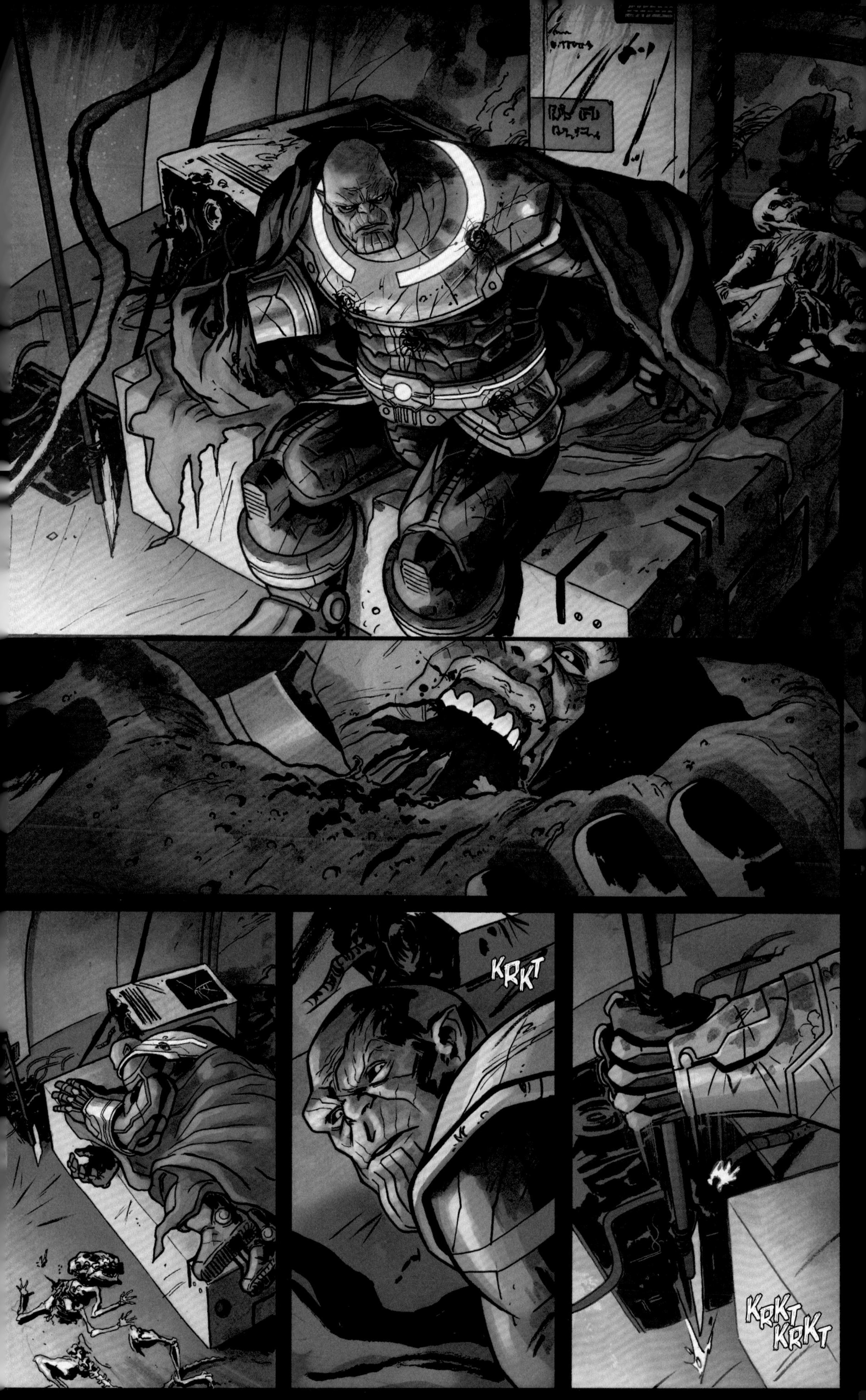

KRKT
KRKT
KRKT

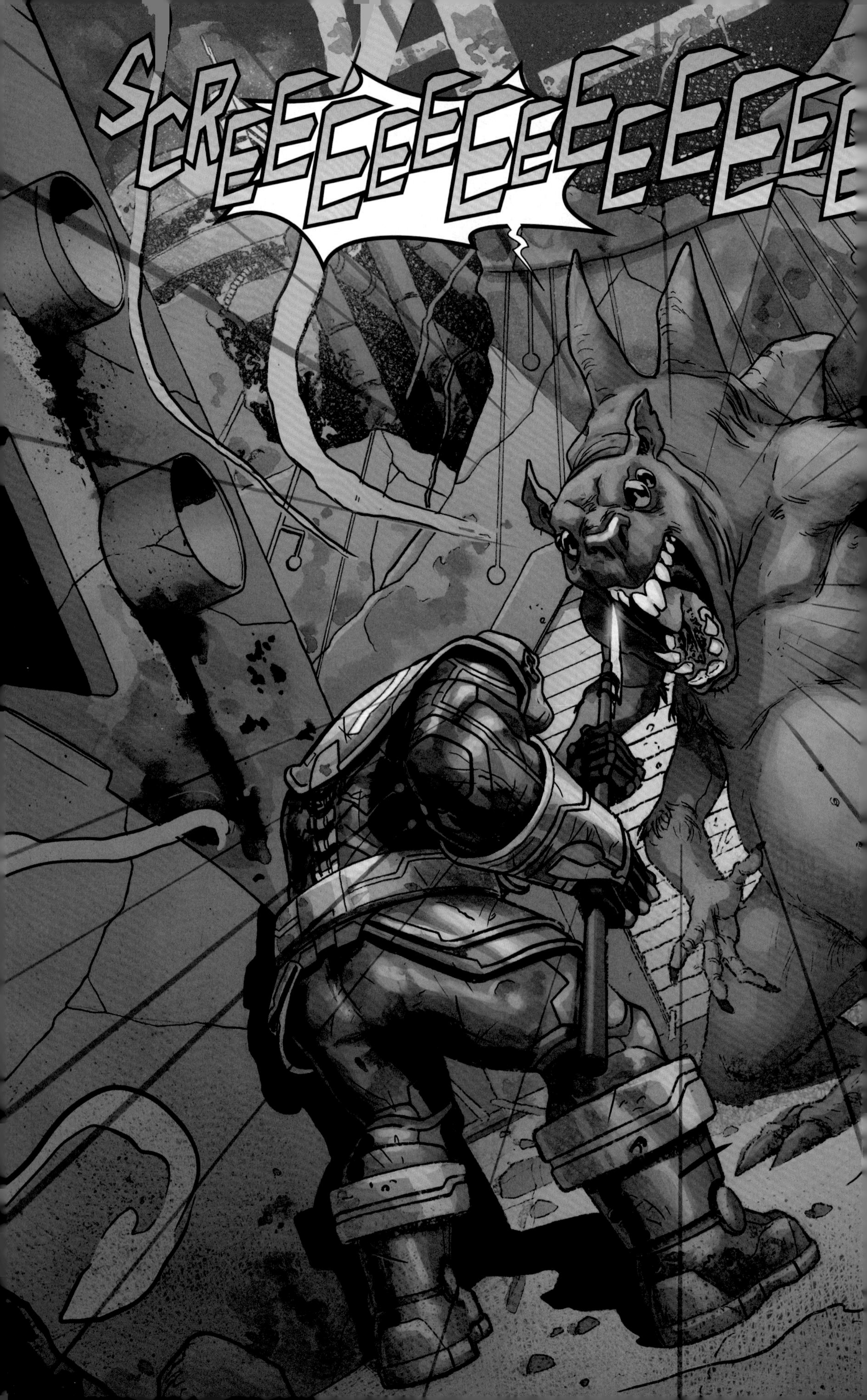
SCREEEEEEEEEEEEEEEE

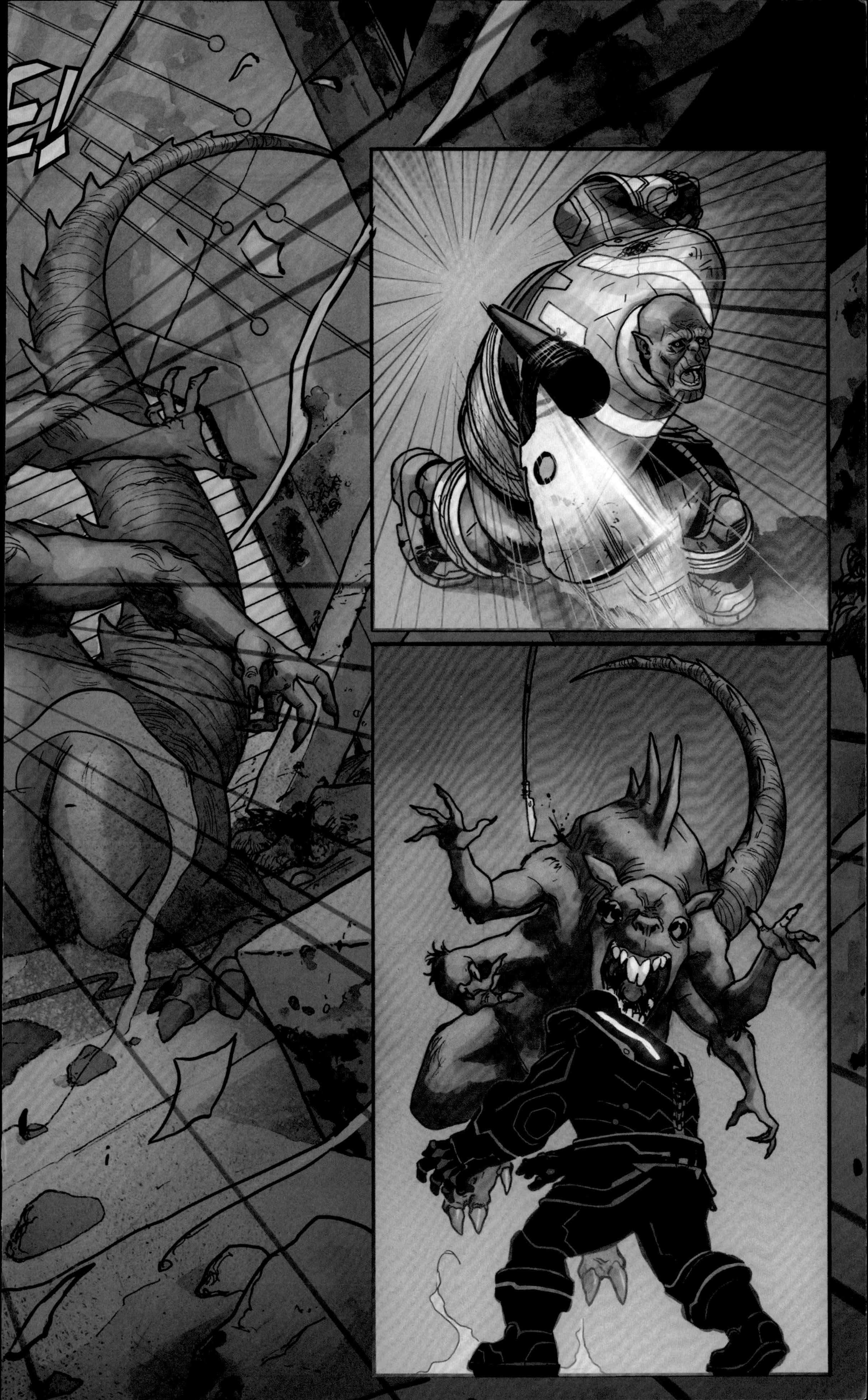

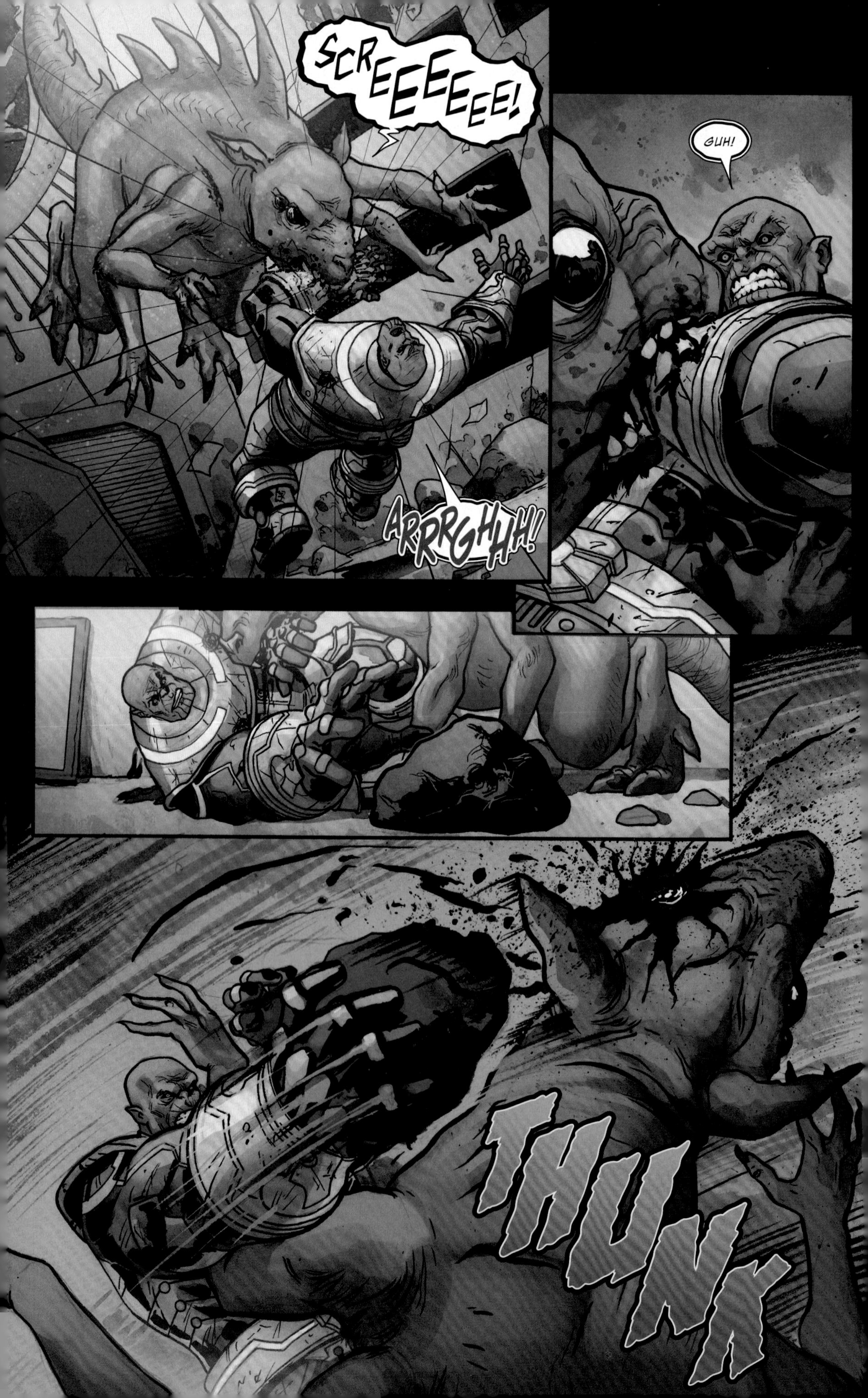
SCREEEEEEE!
ARRRGHHH!
GUH!
THUNK

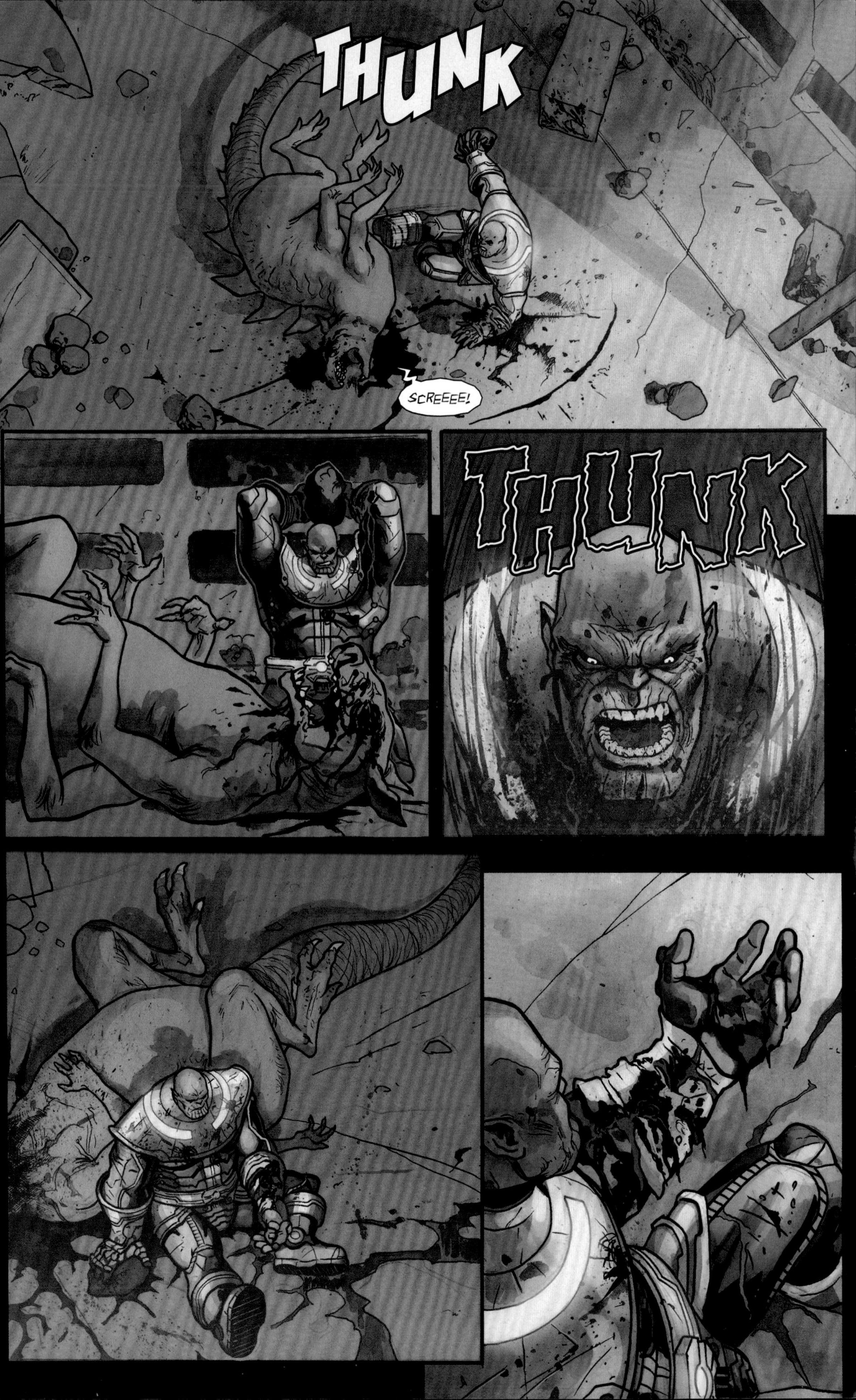
THUNK
SCREEEE!
THUNK

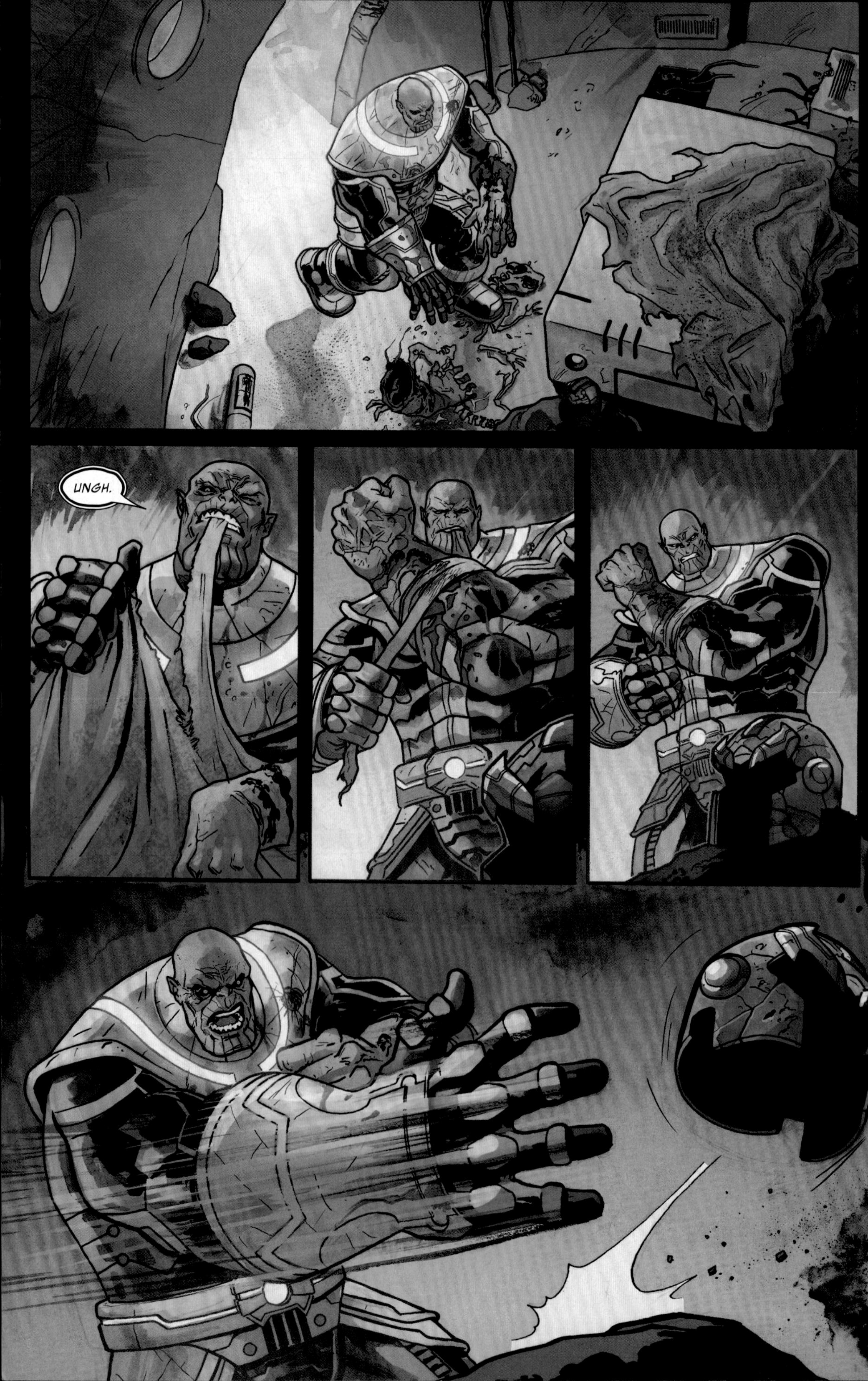
UNGH.

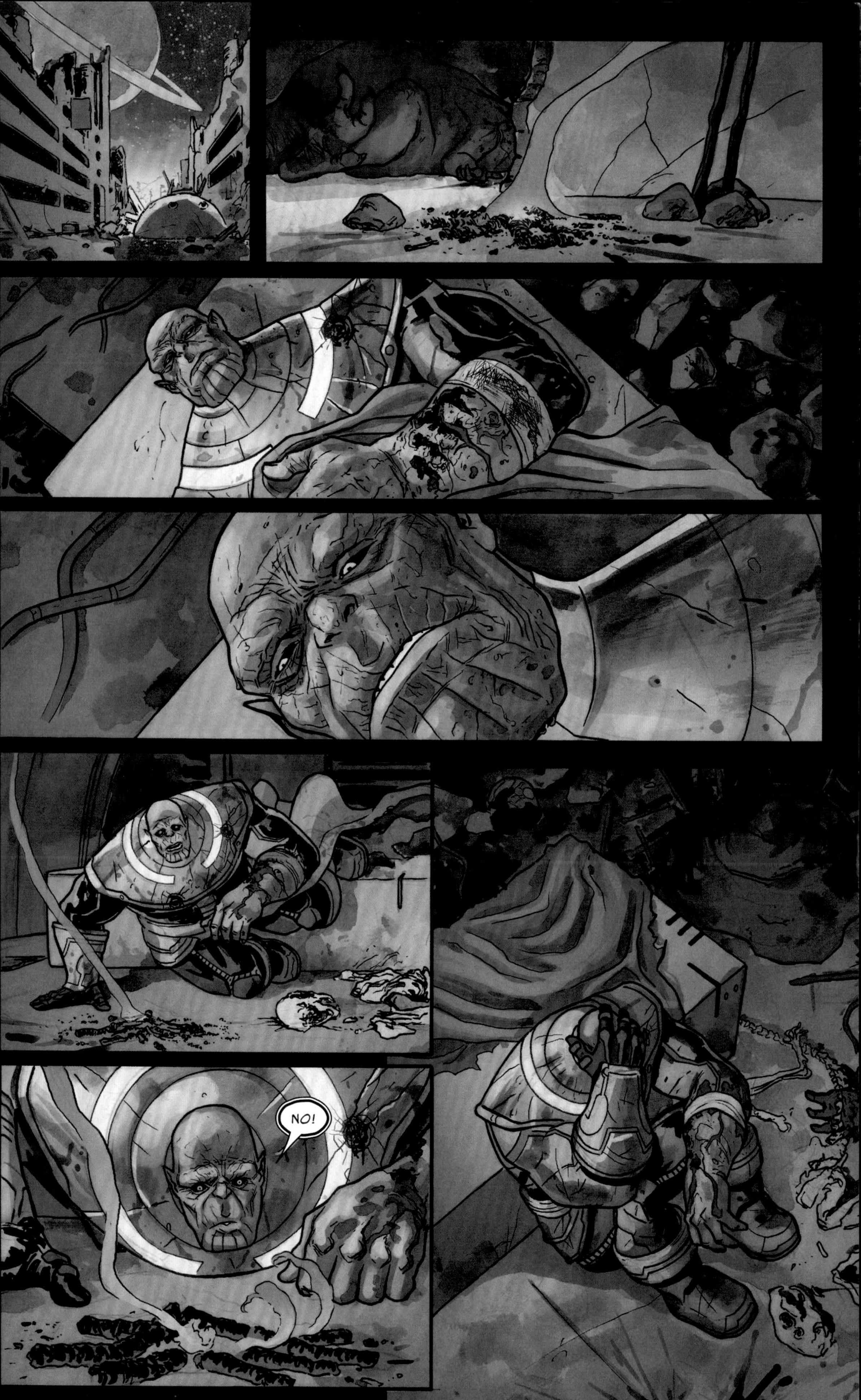
NO!

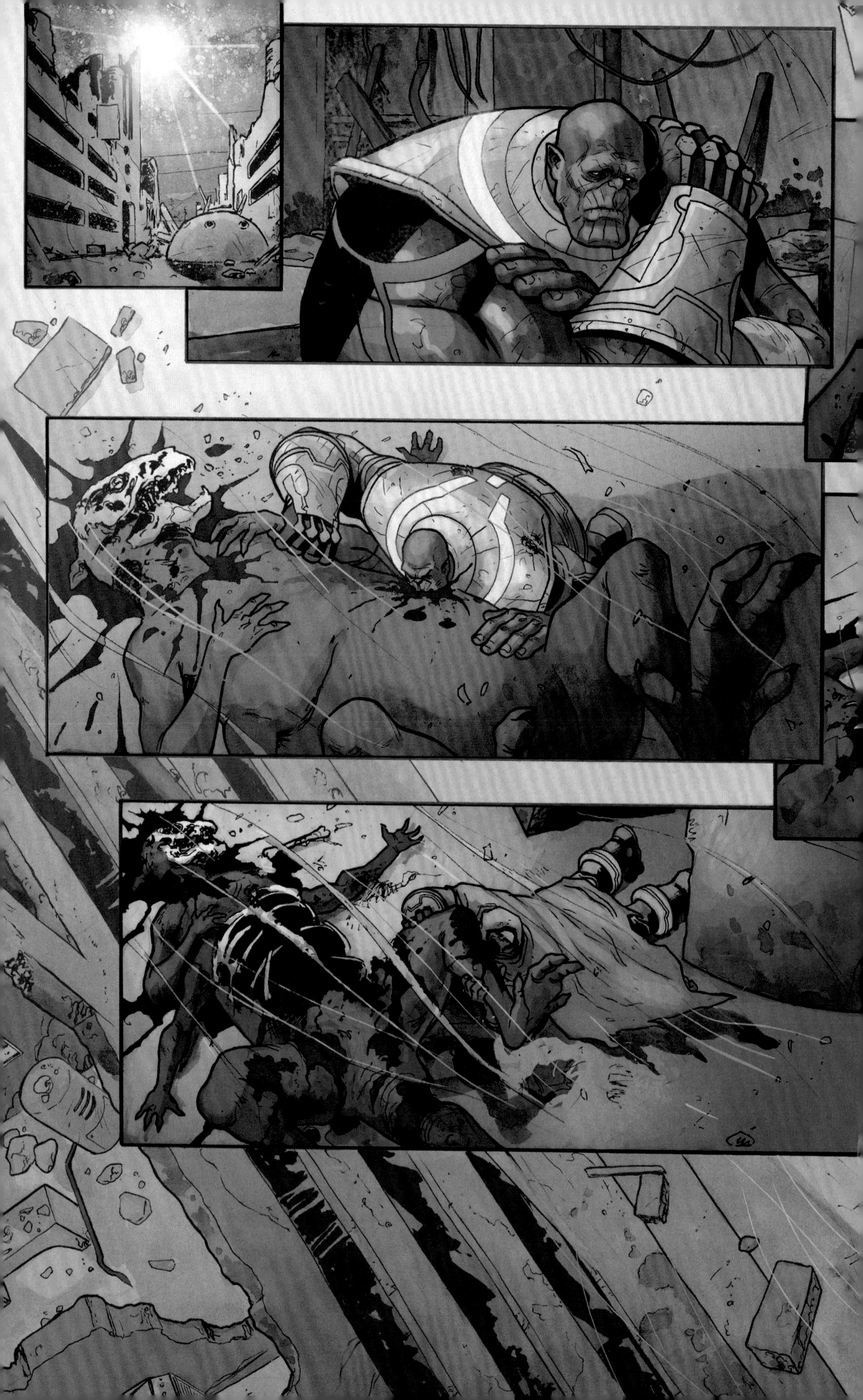

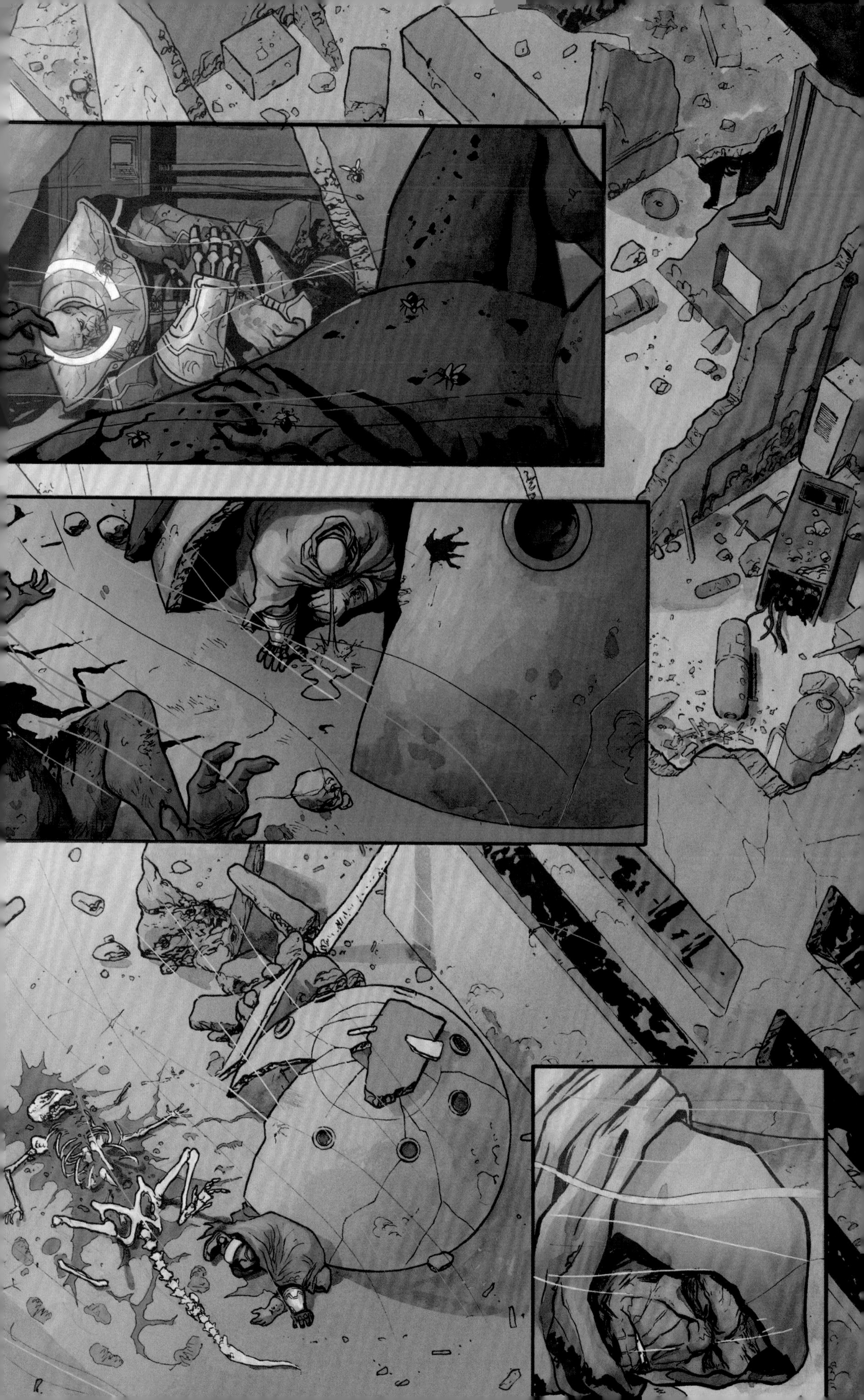

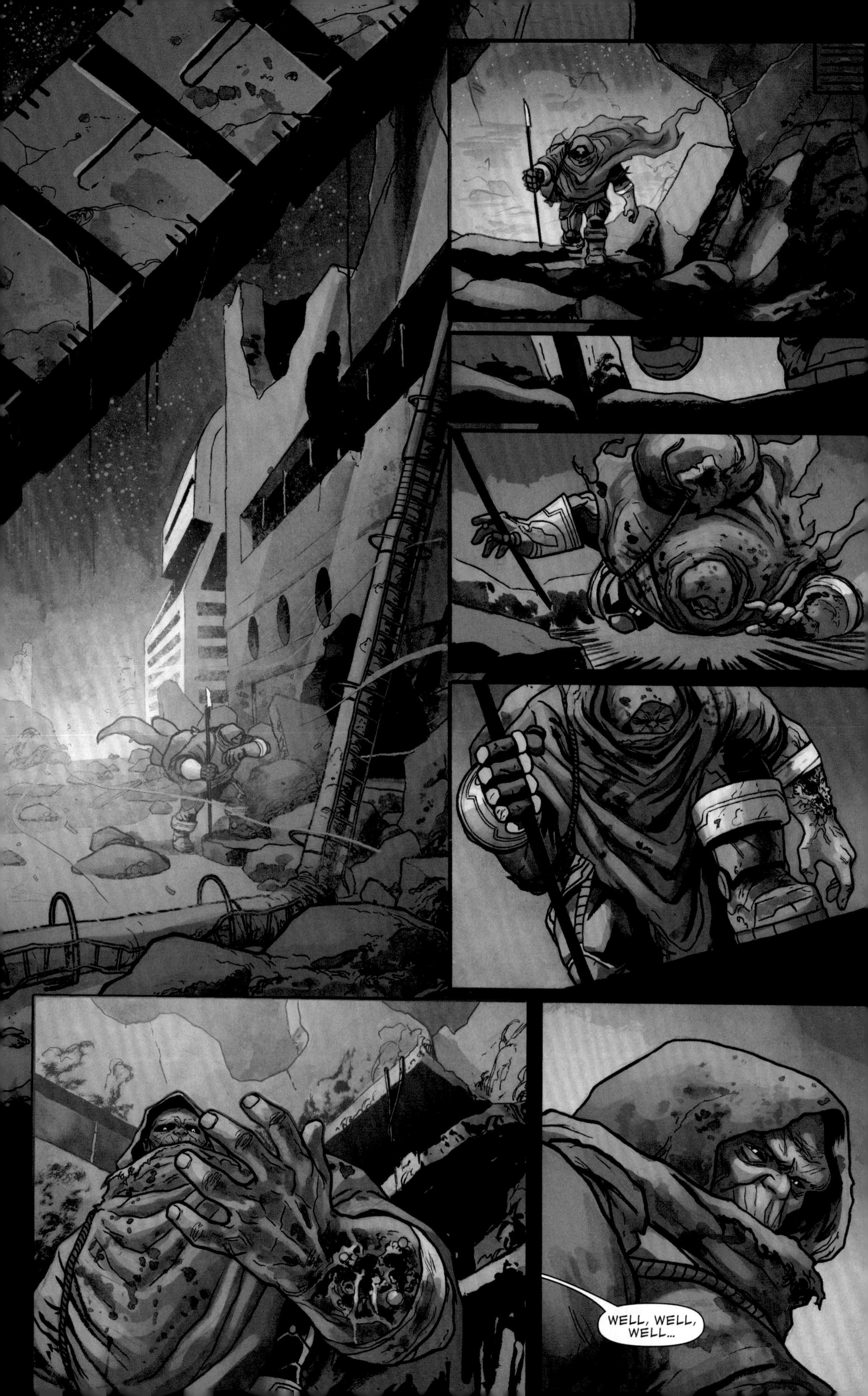
WELL, WELL, WELL...

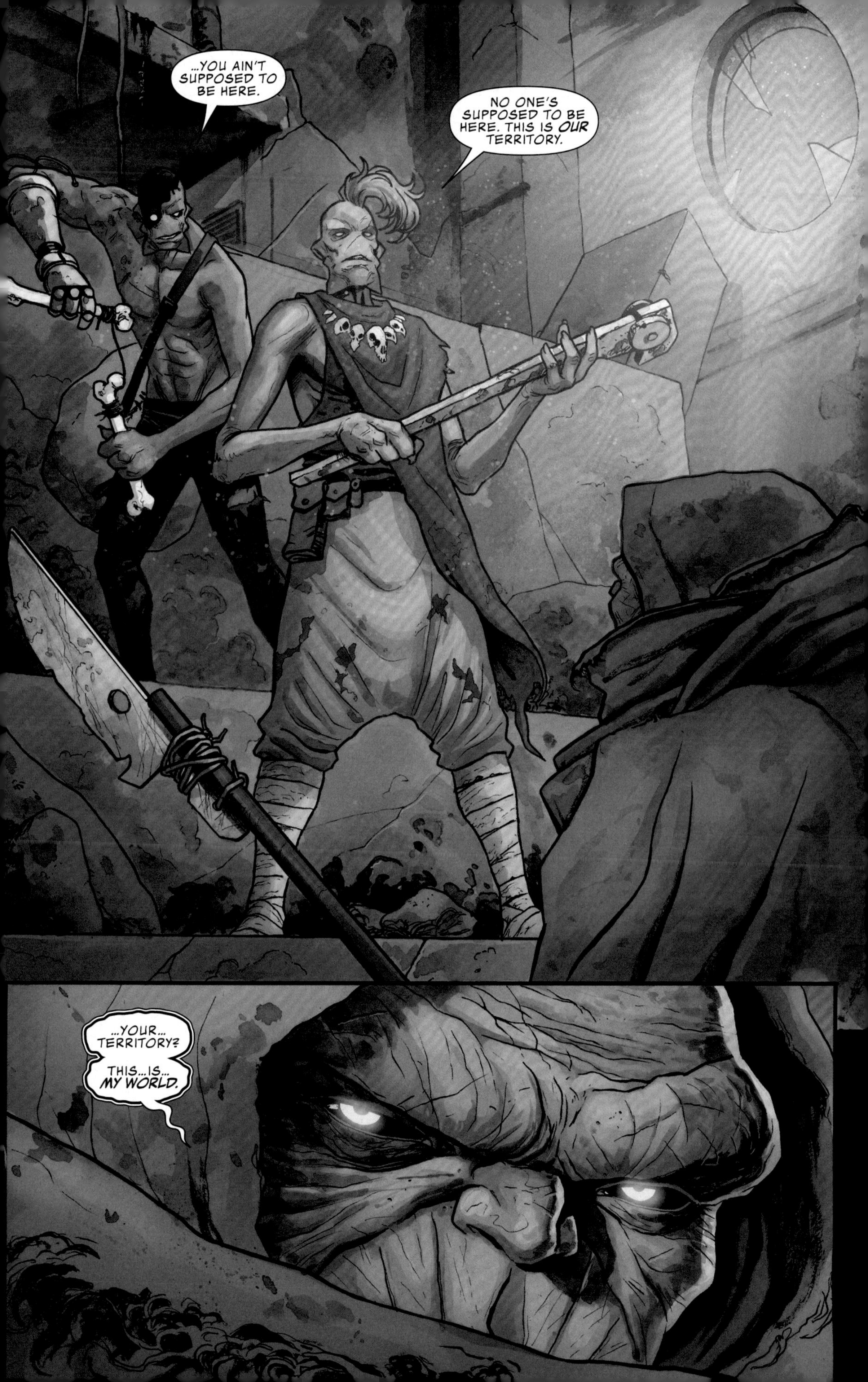
...YOU AIN'T SUPPOSED TO BE HERE.
NO ONE'S SUPPOSED TO BE HERE. THIS IS OUR TERRITORY.
...YOUR... TERRITORY?
THIS...IS... MY WORLD.

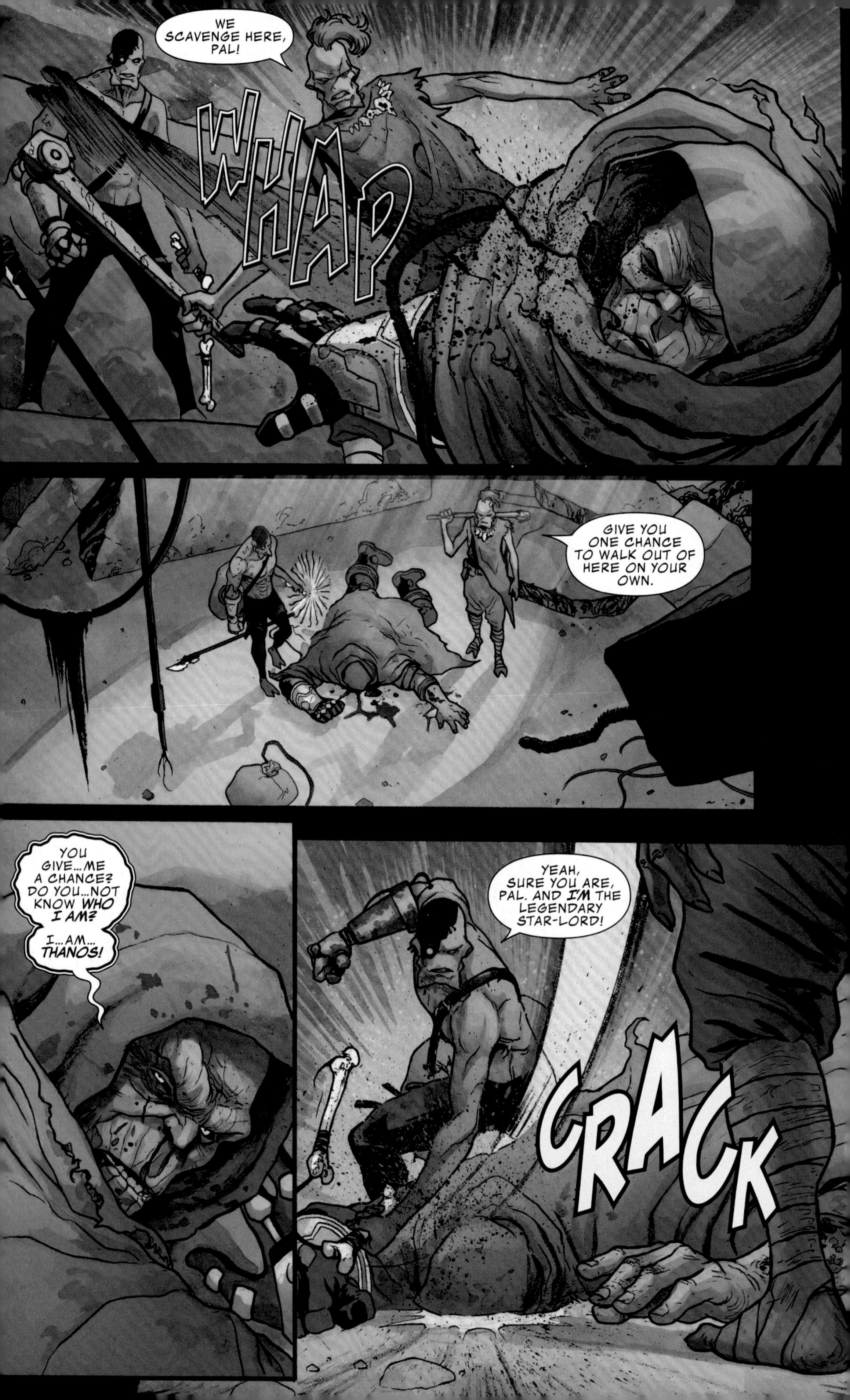
WE SCAVENGE HERE, PAL!
WHAP
GIVE YOU ONE CHANCE TO WALK OUT OF HERE ON YOUR OWN.
YOU GIVE...ME A CHANCE? DO YOU...NOT KNOW WHO I AM?
I...AM... THANOS!
YEAH, SURE YOU ARE, PAL. AND I'M THE LEGENDARY STAR-LORD!
CRACK

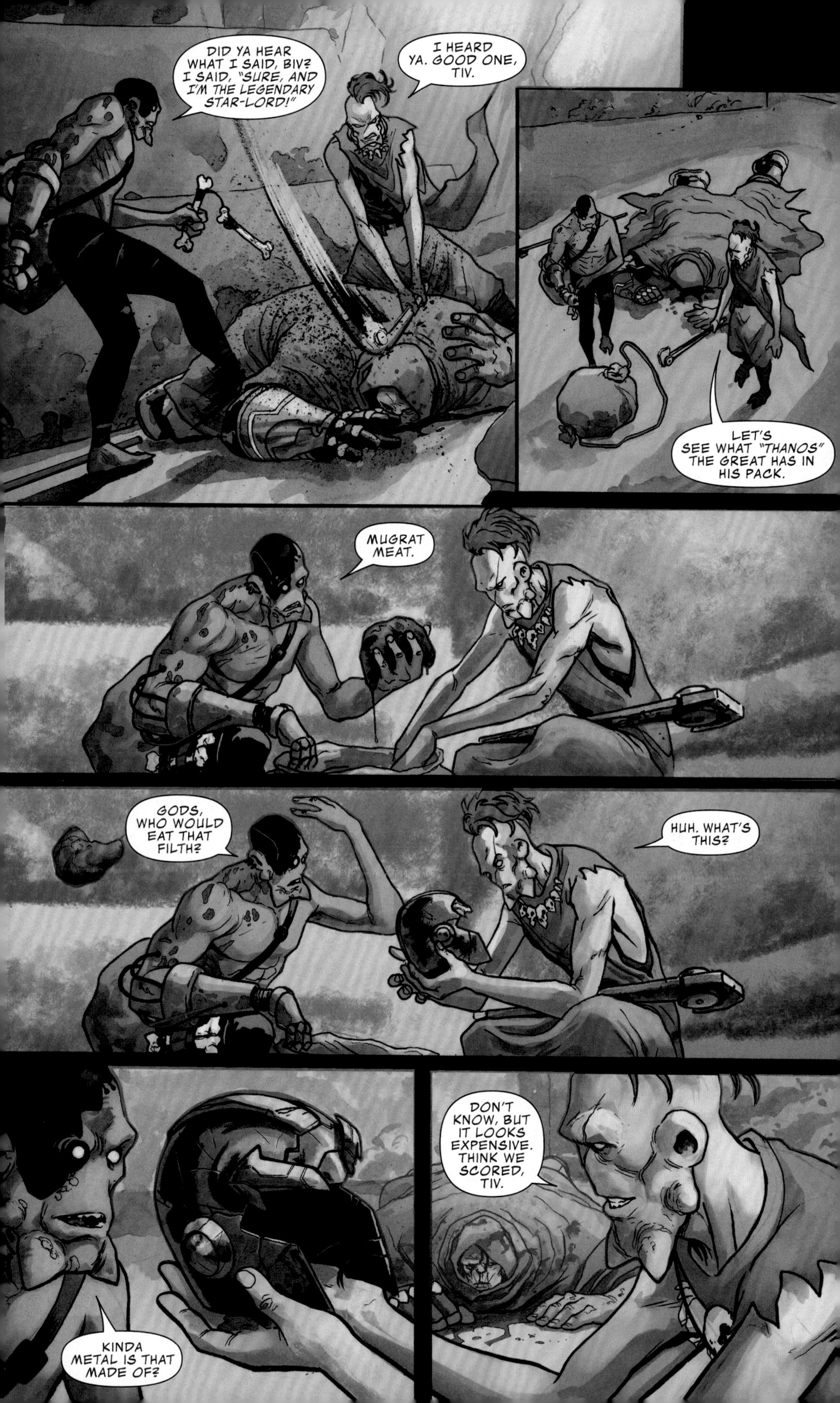
DID YA HEAR WHAT I SAID, BIV? I SAID, "SURE, AND I'M THE LEGENDARY STAR-LORD!"
I HEARD YA. GOOD ONE, TIV.
LET'S SEE WHAT "THANOS" THE GREAT HAS IN HIS PACK.
MUGRAT MEAT.
GODS, WHO WOULD EAT THAT FILTH?
HUH. WHAT'S THIS?
KINDA METAL IS THAT MADE OF?
DON'T KNOW, BUT IT LOOKS EXPENSIVE. THINK WE SCORED, TIV.

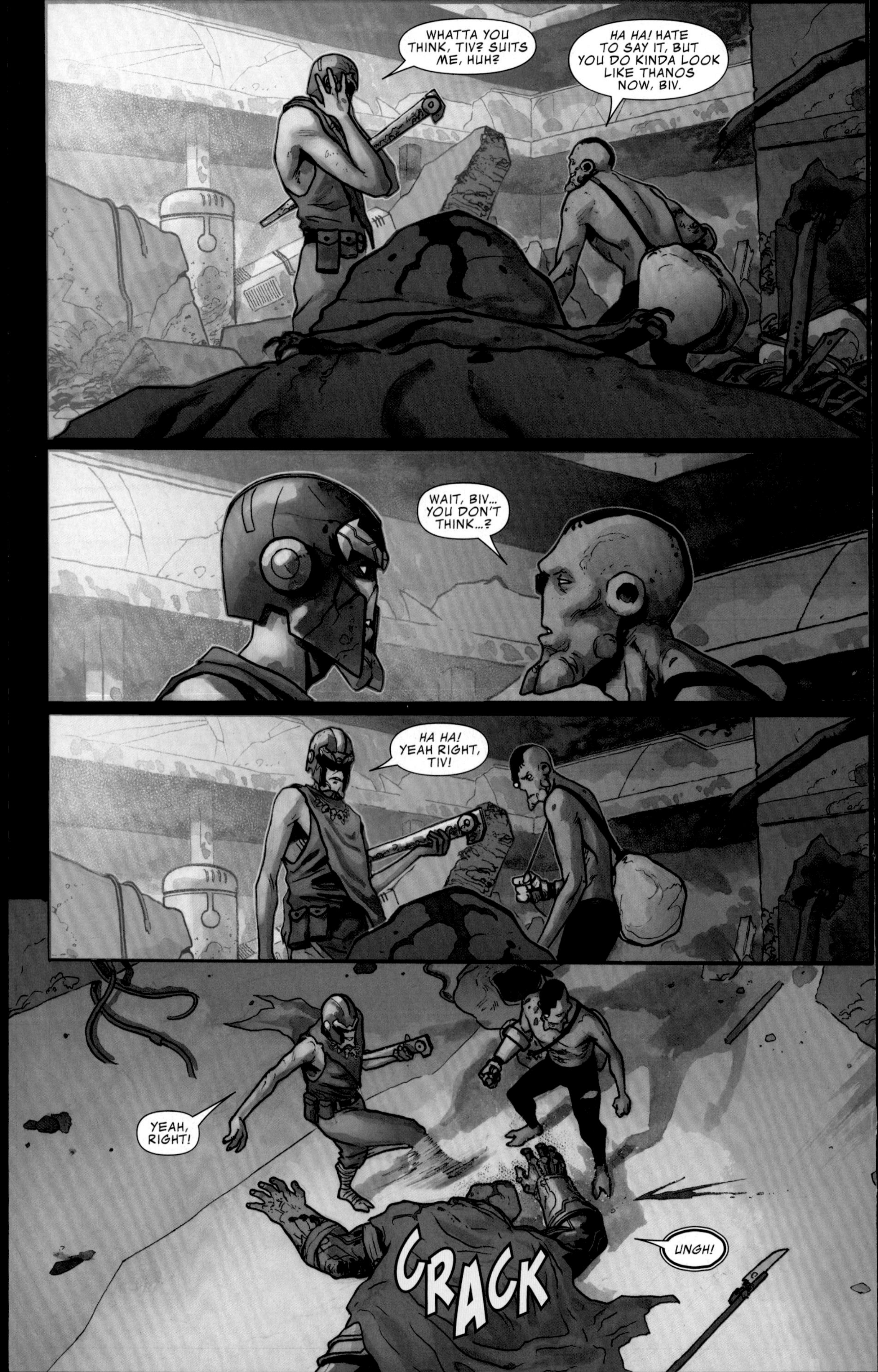
WHATTA YOU THINK, TIV? SUITS ME, HUH?
HA HA! HATE TO SAY IT, BUT YOU DO KINDA LOOK LIKE THANOS NOW, BIV.
WAIT, BIV... YOU DON'T THINK...?
HA HA! YEAH RIGHT, TIV!
YEAH, RIGHT!
CRACK
UNGH!

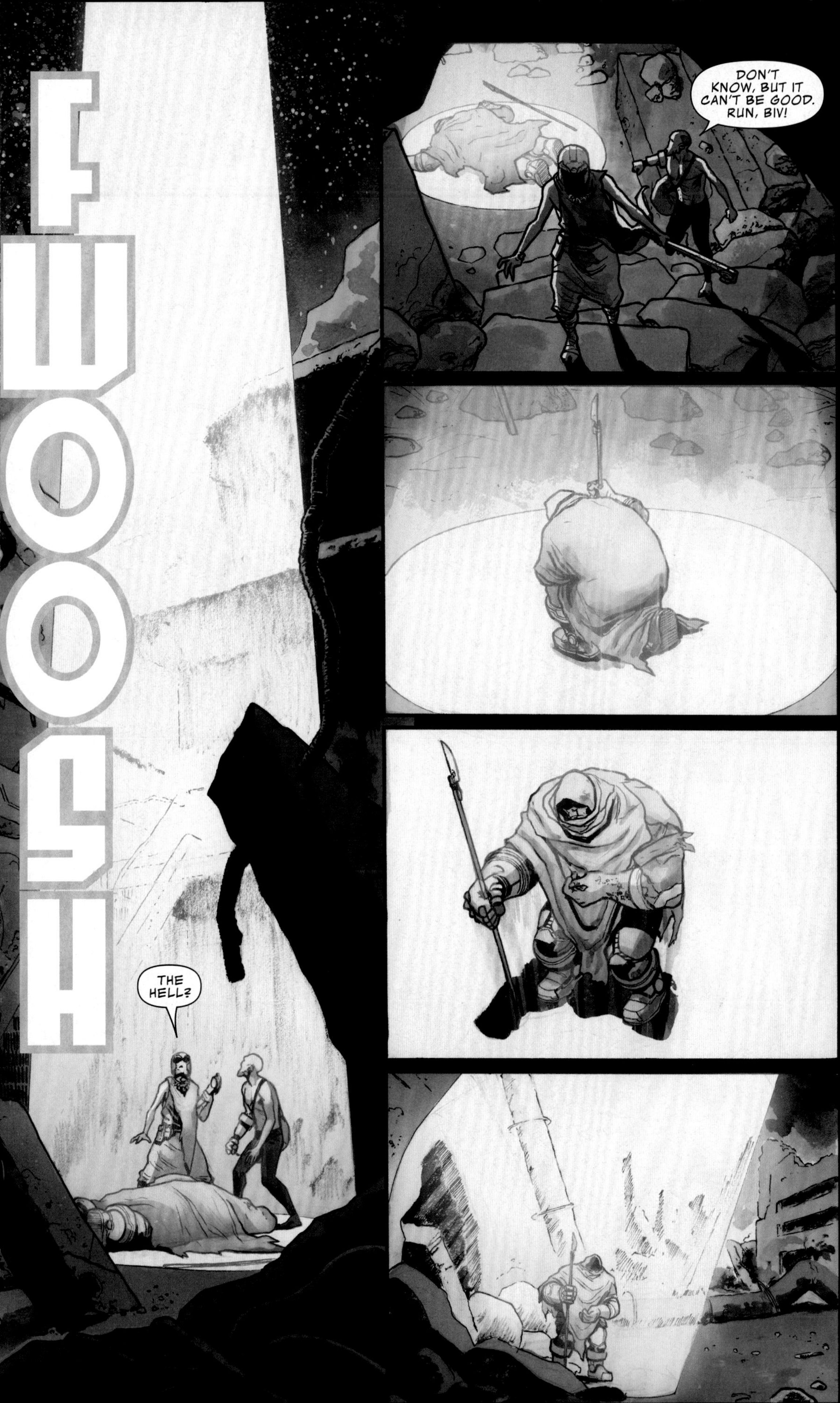
FWOOSH
THE HELL?
DON'T KNOW, BUT IT CAN'T BE GOOD. RUN, BIV!

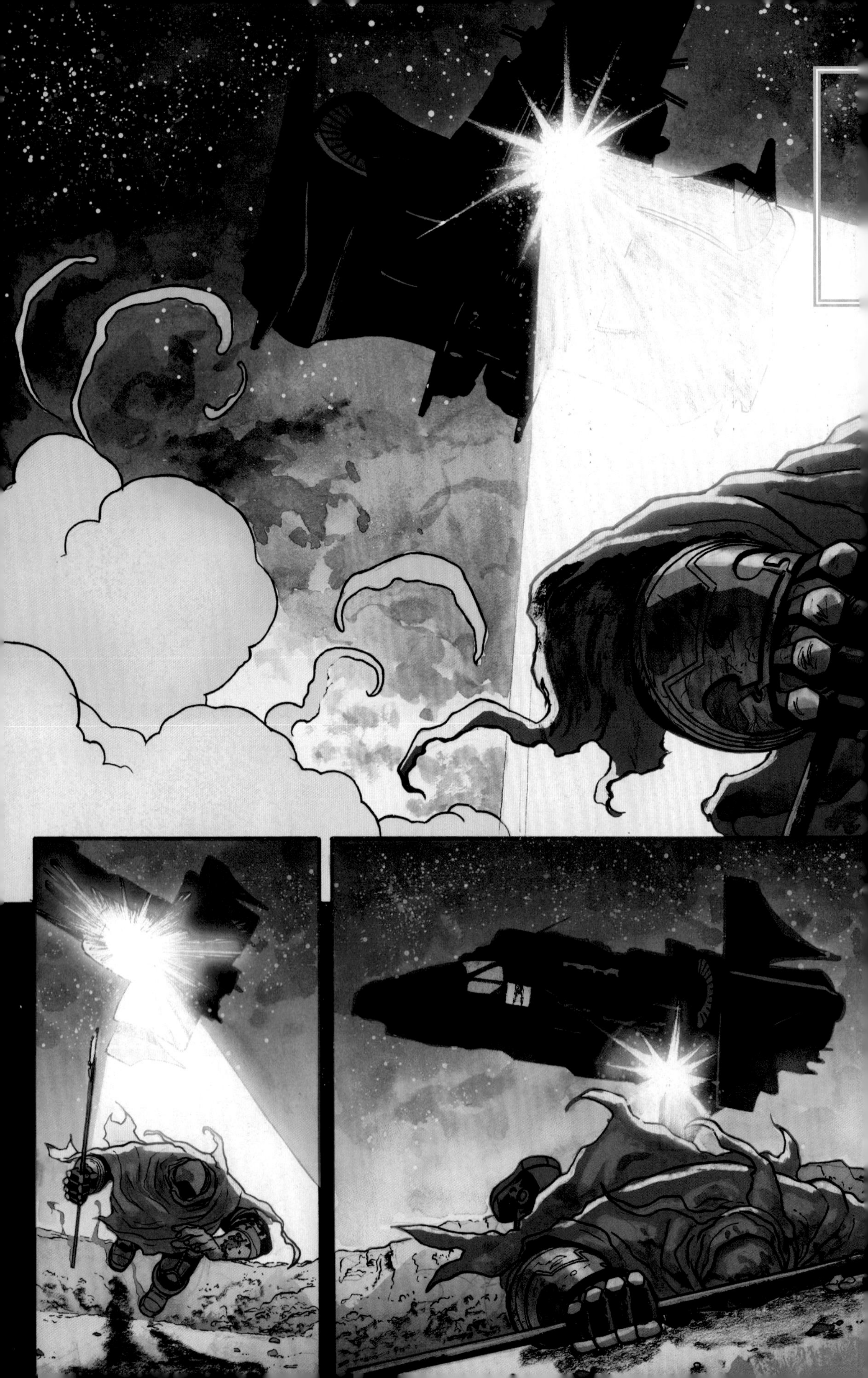

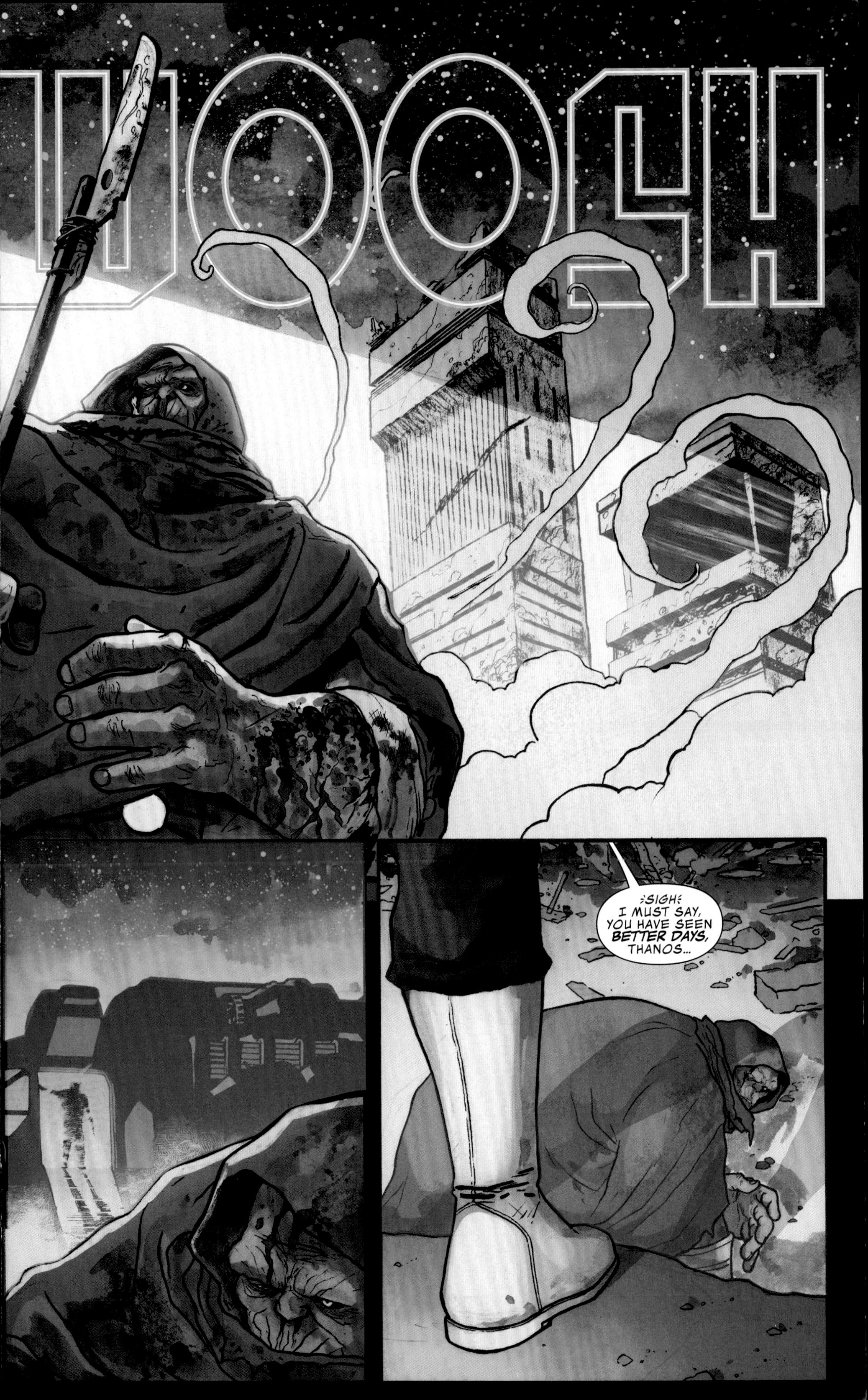
SIGH I MUST SAY, YOU HAVE SEEN BETTER DAYS, THANOS...

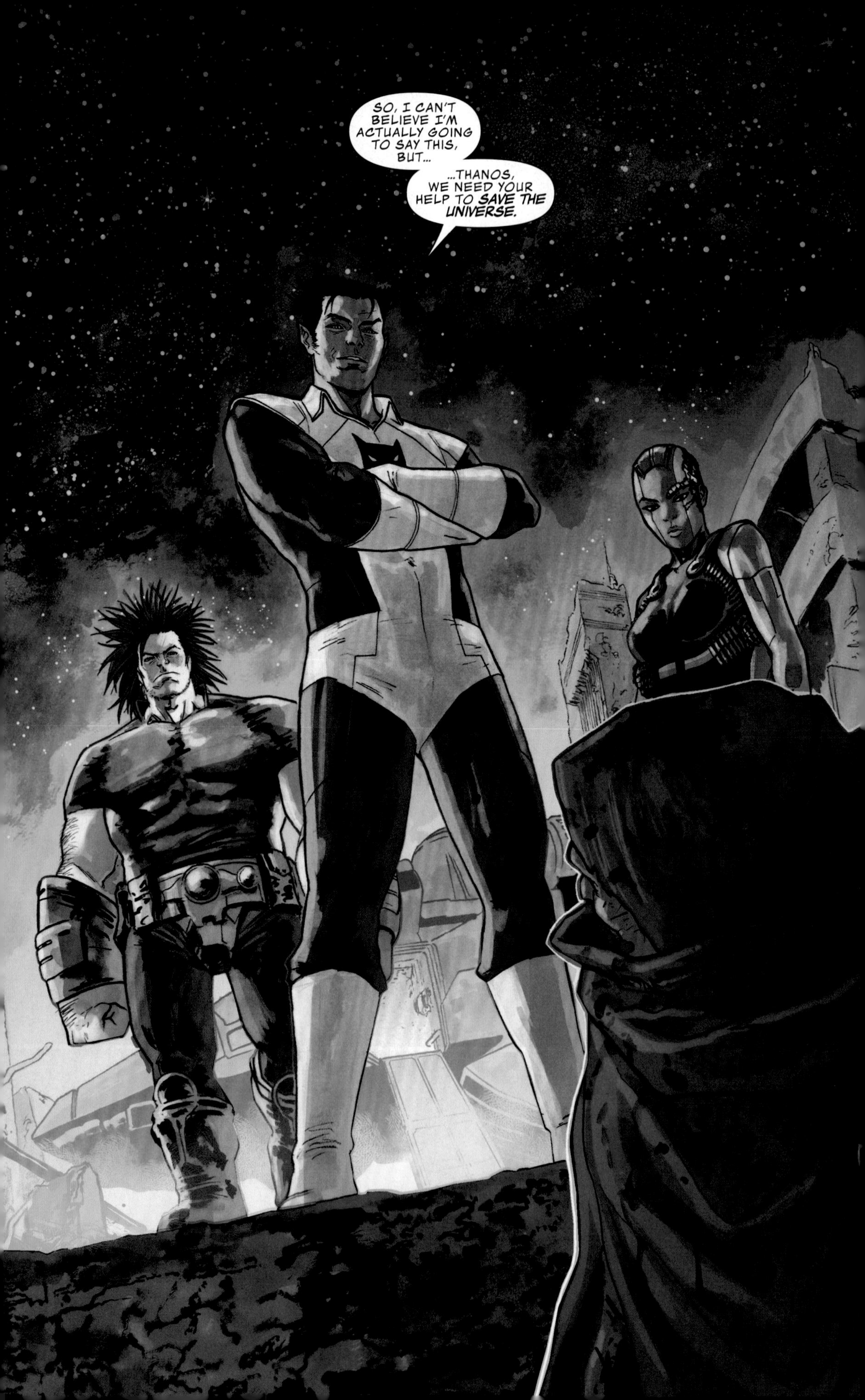
SO, I CAN'T BELIEVE I'M ACTUALLY GOING TO SAY THIS, BUT...
...THANOS, WE NEED YOUR HELP TO SAVE THE UNIVERSE.

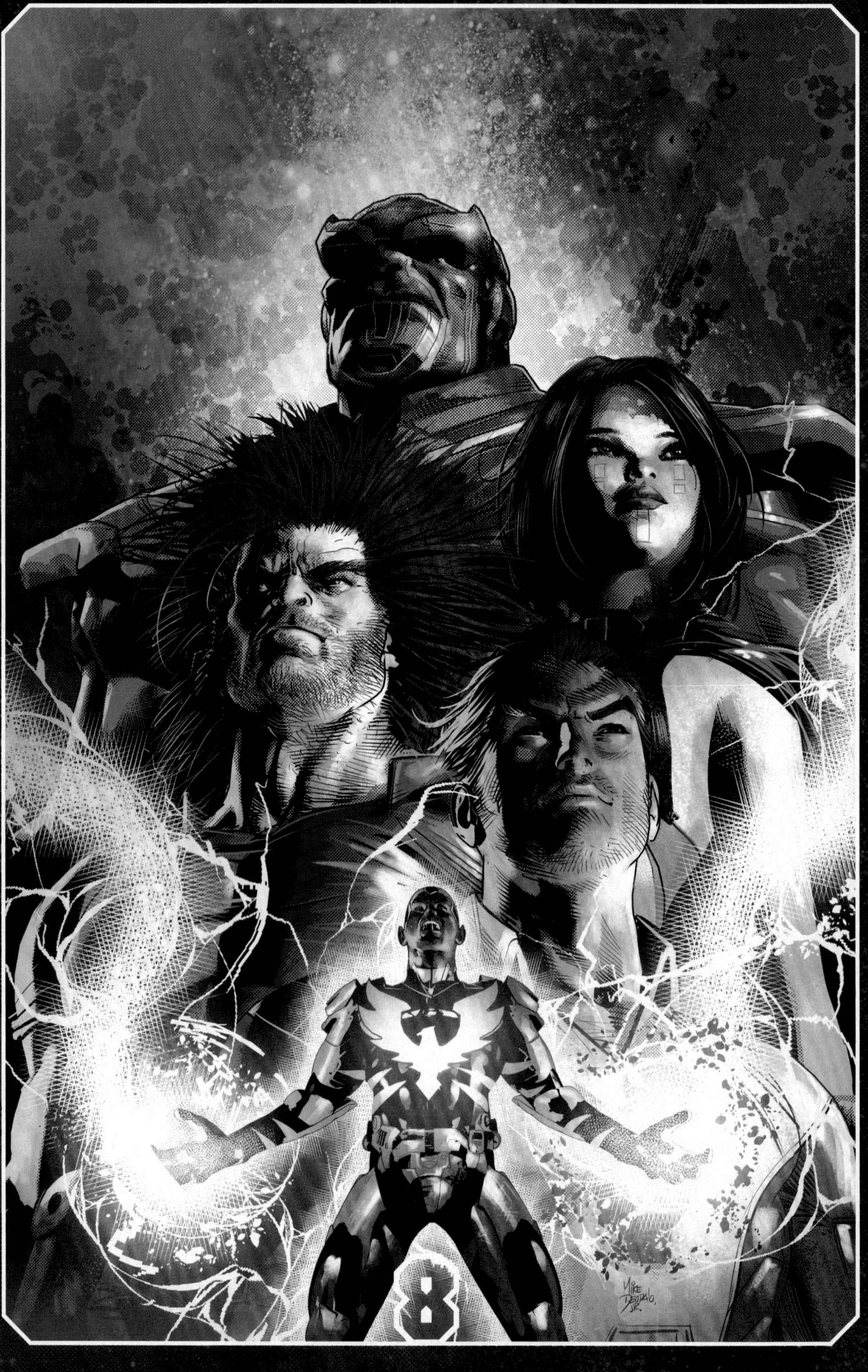
8

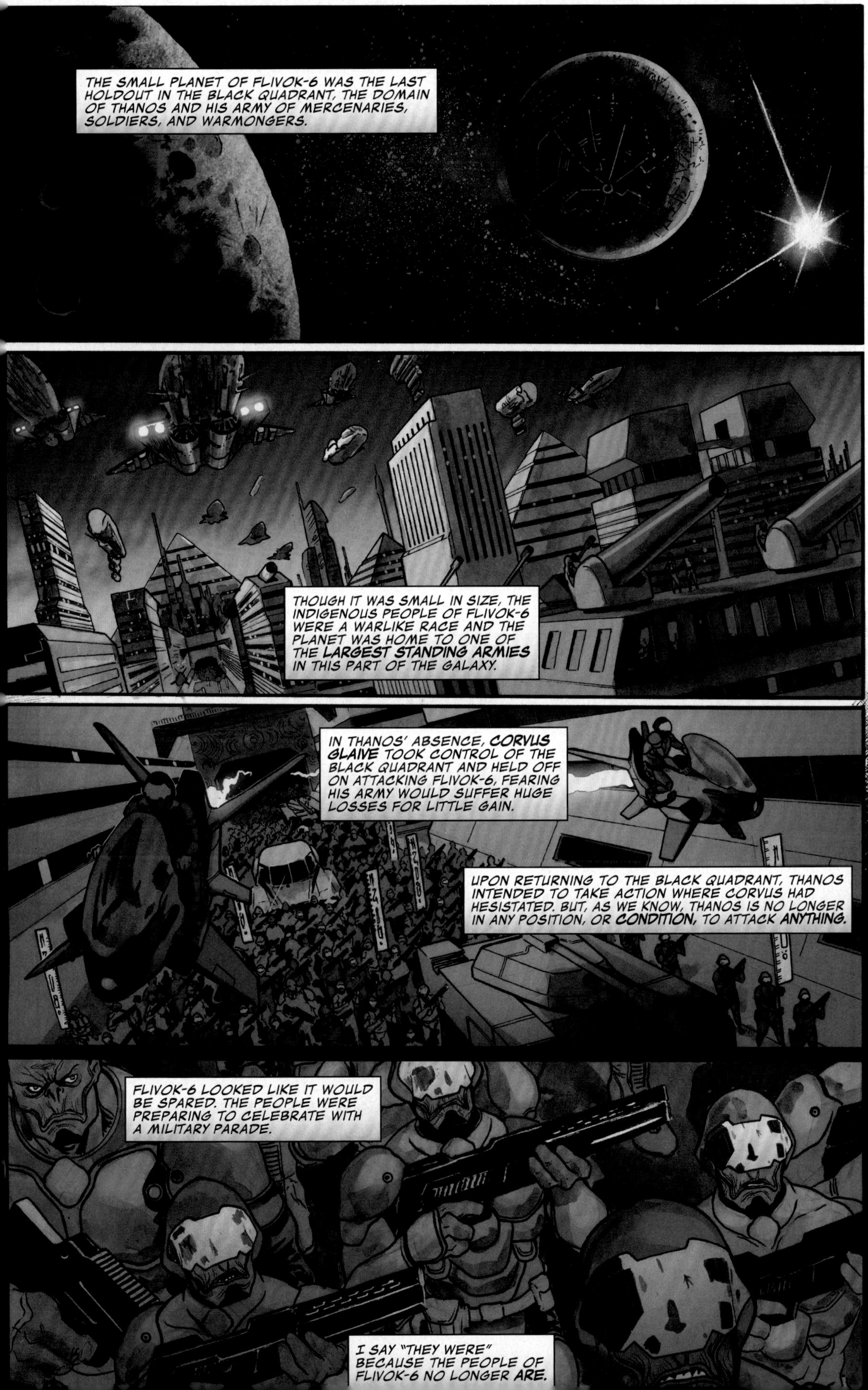
THE SMALL PLANET OF FLIVOK-6 WAS THE LAST HOLDOUT IN THE BLACK QUADRANT, THE DOMAIN OF THANOS AND HIS ARMY OF MERCENARIES, SOLDIERS, AND WARMONGERS.
THOUGH IT WAS SMALL IN SIZE, THE INDIGENOUS PEOPLE OF FLIVOK-6 WERE A WARLIKE RACE AND THE PLANET WAS HOME TO ONE OF THE **LARGEST STANDING ARMIES** IN THIS PART OF THE GALAXY.
IN THANOS' ABSENCE, **CORVUS GLAIVE** TOOK CONTROL OF THE BLACK QUADRANT AND HELD OFF ON ATTACKING FLIVOK-6, FEARING HIS ARMY WOULD SUFFER HUGE LOSSES FOR LITTLE GAIN.
UPON RETURNING TO THE BLACK QUADRANT, THANOS INTENDED TO TAKE ACTION WHERE CORVUS HAD HESITATED. BUT, AS WE KNOW, THANOS IS NO LONGER IN ANY POSITION, OR **CONDITION,** TO ATTACK **ANYTHING.**
FLIVOK-6 LOOKED LIKE IT WOULD BE SPARED. THE PEOPLE WERE PREPARING TO CELEBRATE WITH A MILITARY PARADE.
I SAY "THEY WERE" BECAUSE THE PEOPLE OF FLIVOK-6 NO LONGER **ARE.**

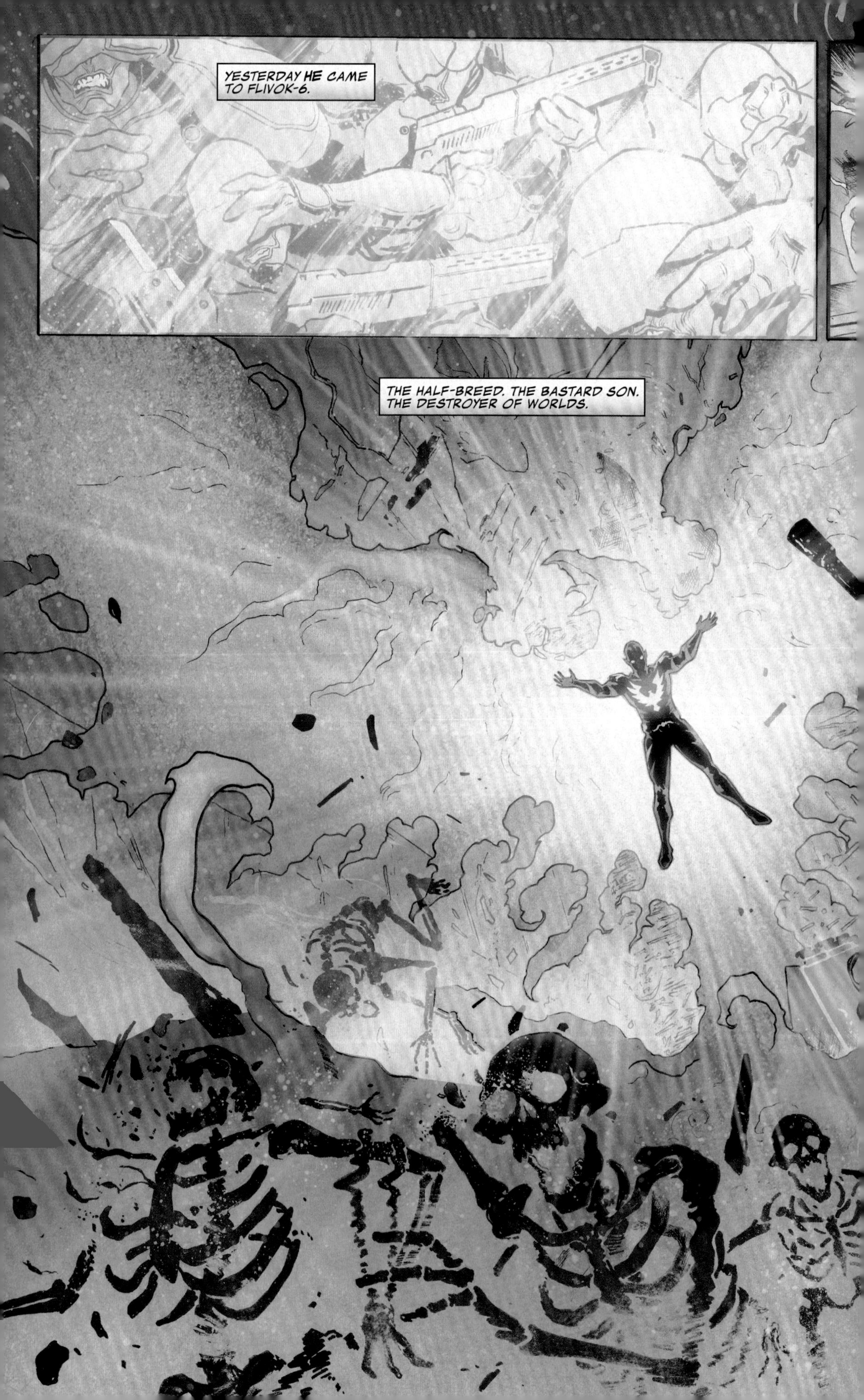
YESTERDAY HE CAME TO FLIVOK-6.
THE HALF-BREED. THE BASTARD SON. THE DESTROYER OF WORLDS.

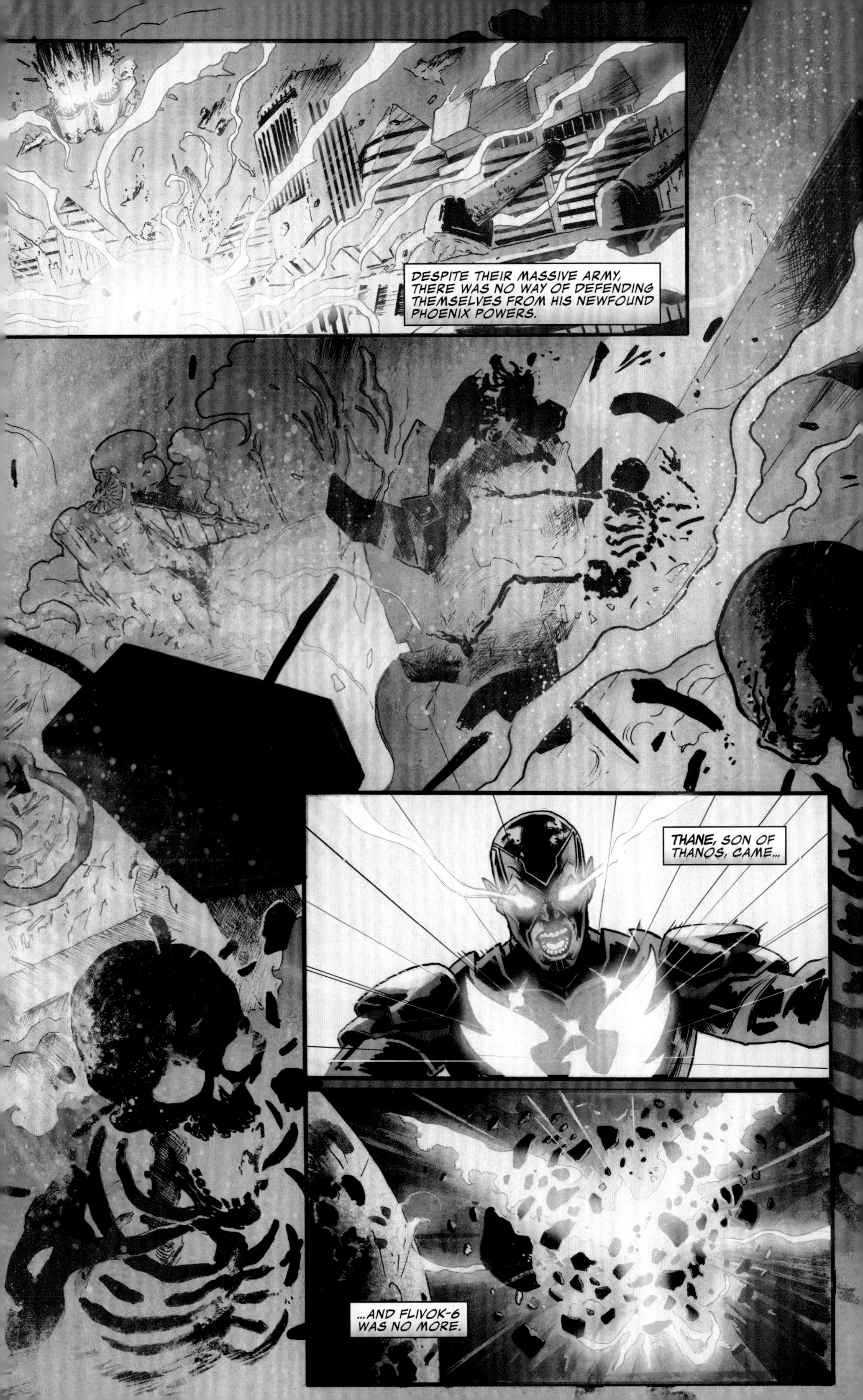
DESPITE THEIR MASSIVE ARMY, THERE WAS NO WAY OF DEFENDING THEMSELVES FROM HIS NEWFOUND PHOENIX POWERS.
THANE, SON OF THANOS, CAME...
...AND FLIVOK-6 WAS NO MORE.

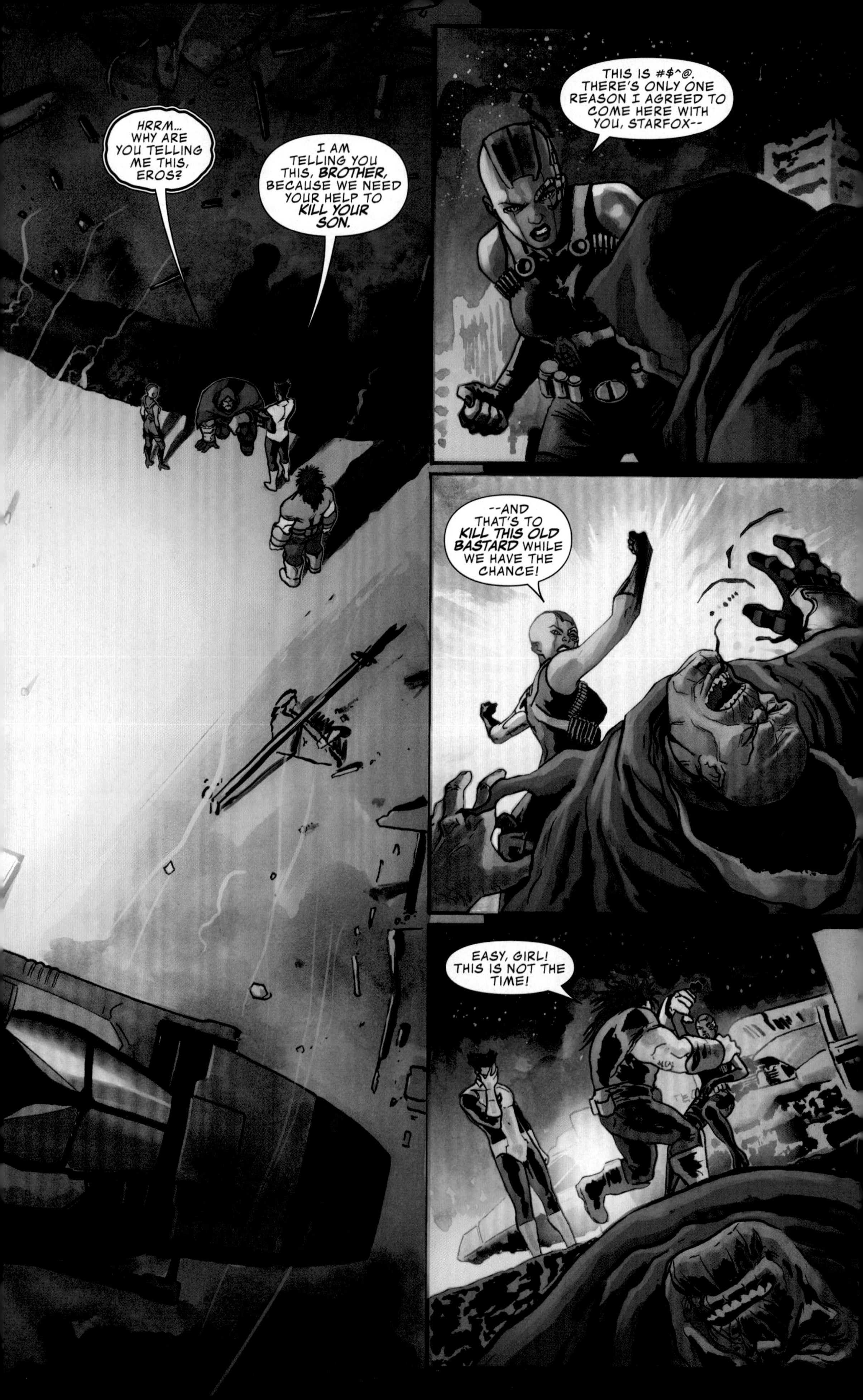
HRRM... WHY ARE YOU TELLING ME THIS, EROS?
I AM TELLING YOU THIS, **BROTHER,** BECAUSE WE NEED YOUR HELP TO ***KILL YOUR SON.***
THIS IS #$^@. THERE'S ONLY ONE REASON I AGREED TO COME HERE WITH YOU, STARFOX--
--AND THAT'S TO ***KILL THIS OLD BASTARD*** WHILE WE HAVE THE CHANCE!
EASY, GIRL! THIS IS NOT THE TIME!

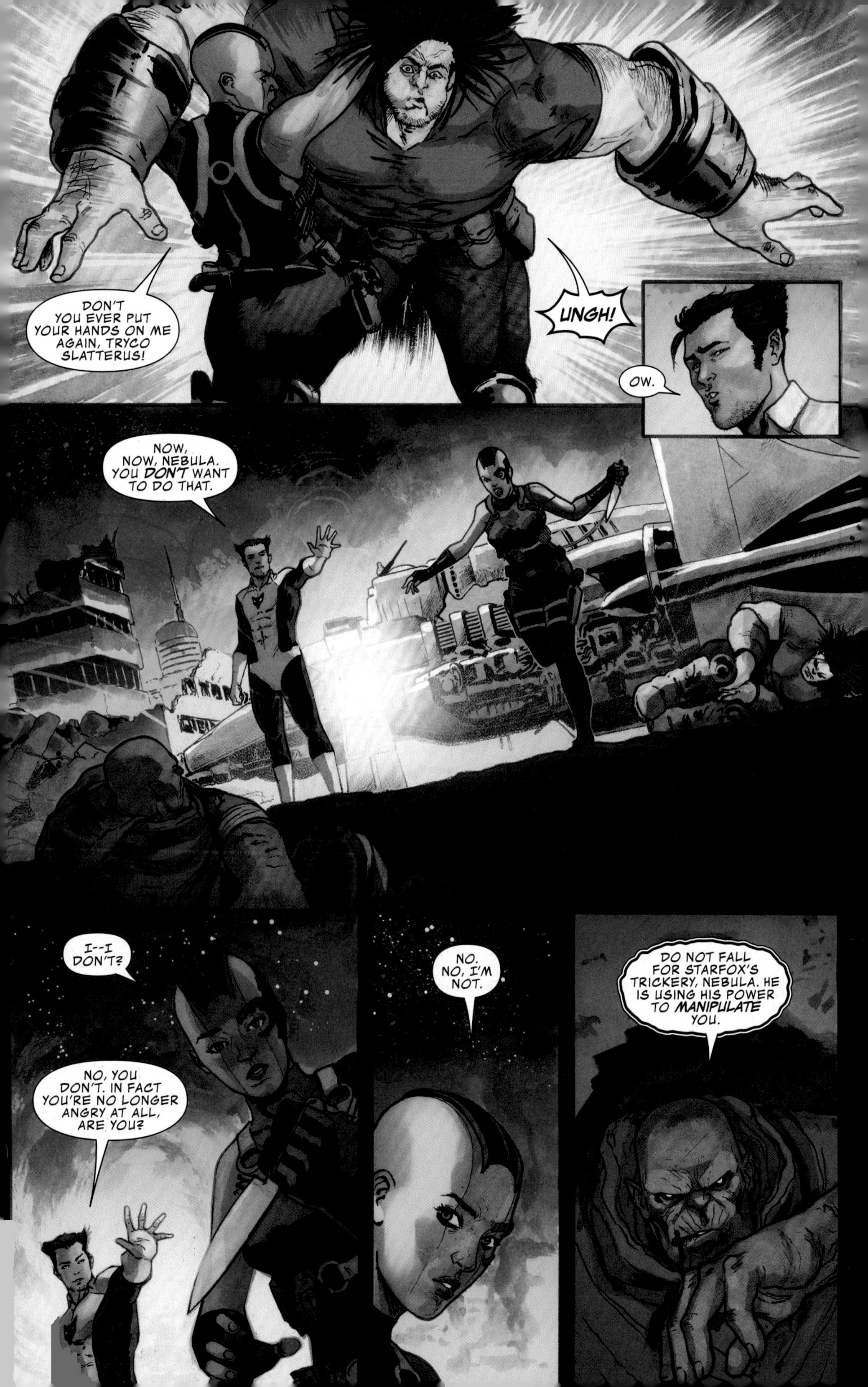
DON'T YOU EVER PUT YOUR HANDS ON ME AGAIN, TRYCO SLATTERUS!
UNGH!
OW.
NOW, NOW, NEBULA. YOU DON'T WANT TO DO THAT.
I--I DON'T?
NO, YOU DON'T. IN FACT YOU'RE NO LONGER ANGRY AT ALL, ARE YOU?
NO. NO, I'M NOT.
DO NOT FALL FOR STARFOX'S TRICKERY, NEBULA. HE IS USING HIS POWER TO MANIPULATE YOU.

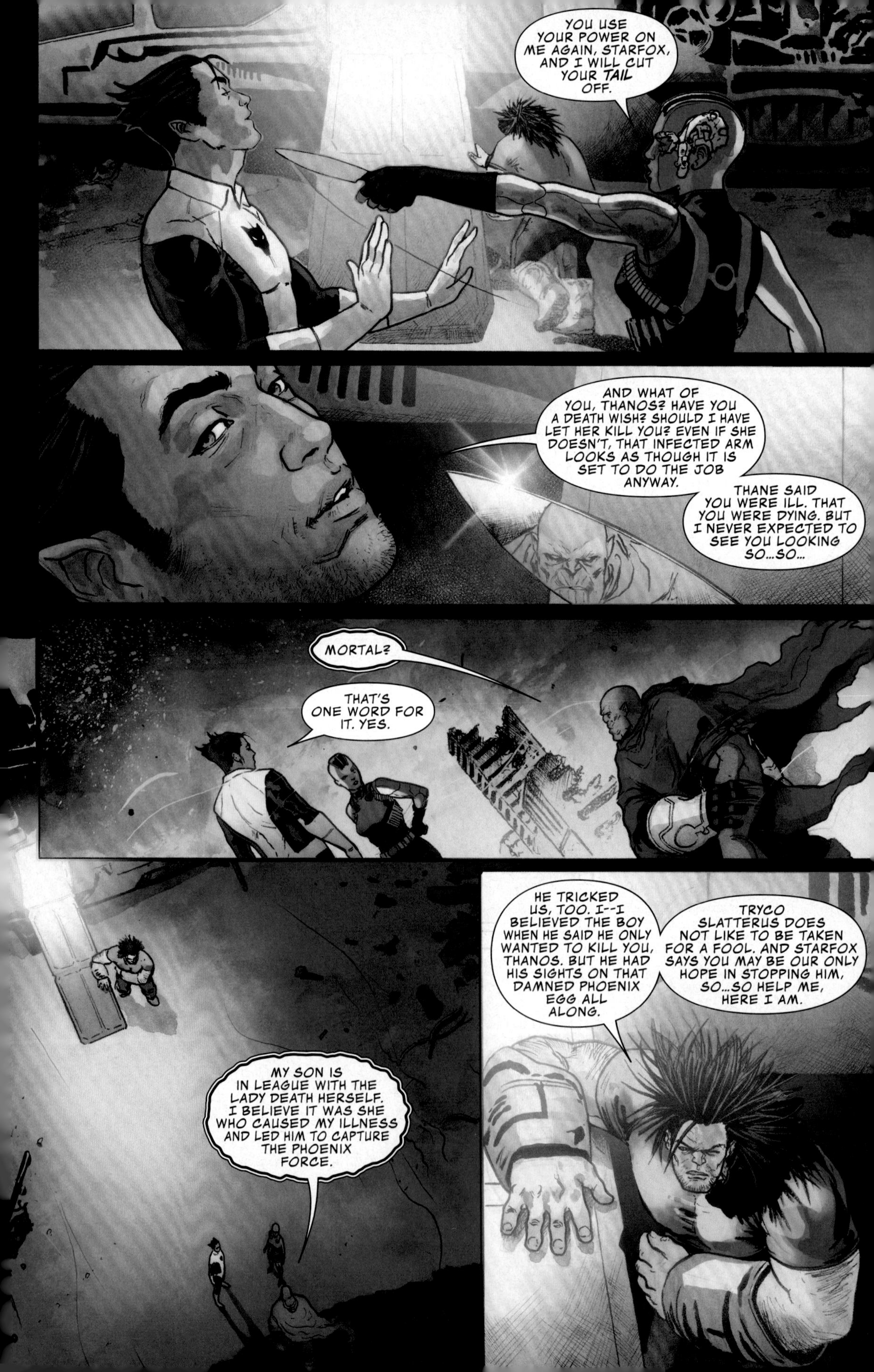
YOU USE YOUR POWER ON ME AGAIN, STARFOX, AND I WILL CUT YOUR TAIL OFF.
AND WHAT OF YOU, THANOS? HAVE YOU A DEATH WISH? SHOULD I HAVE LET HER KILL YOU? EVEN IF SHE DOESN'T, THAT INFECTED ARM LOOKS AS THOUGH IT IS SET TO DO THE JOB ANYWAY.
THANE SAID YOU WERE ILL. THAT YOU WERE DYING. BUT I NEVER EXPECTED TO SEE YOU LOOKING SO...SO...
MORTAL?
THAT'S ONE WORD FOR IT. YES.
MY SON IS IN LEAGUE WITH THE LADY DEATH HERSELF. I BELIEVE IT WAS SHE WHO CAUSED MY ILLNESS AND LED HIM TO CAPTURE THE PHOENIX FORCE.
HE TRICKED US, TOO. I--I BELIEVED THE BOY WHEN HE SAID HE ONLY WANTED TO KILL YOU, THANOS. BUT HE HAD HIS SIGHTS ON THAT DAMNED PHOENIX EGG ALL ALONG.
TRYCO SLATTERUS DOES NOT LIKE TO BE TAKEN FOR A FOOL. AND STARFOX SAYS YOU MAY BE OUR ONLY HOPE IN STOPPING HIM, SO...SO HELP ME, HERE I AM.

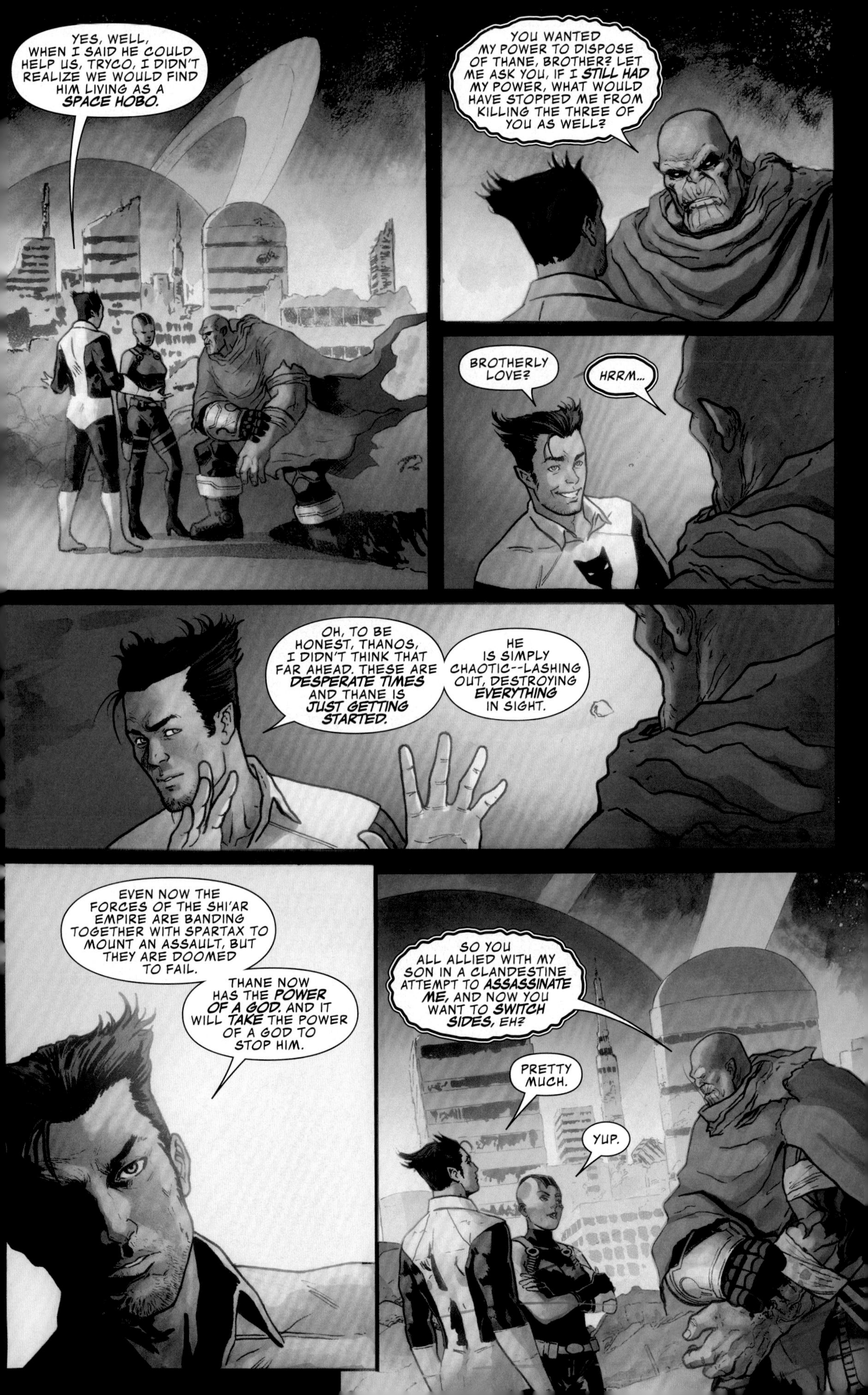
YES, WELL, WHEN I SAID HE COULD HELP US, TRYCO, I DIDN'T REALIZE WE WOULD FIND HIM LIVING AS A SPACE HOBO.
YOU WANTED MY POWER TO DISPOSE OF THANE, BROTHER? LET ME ASK YOU, IF I STILL HAD MY POWER, WHAT WOULD HAVE STOPPED ME FROM KILLING THE THREE OF YOU AS WELL?
BROTHERLY LOVE?
HRRM...
OH, TO BE HONEST, THANOS, I DIDN'T THINK THAT FAR AHEAD. THESE ARE DESPERATE TIMES AND THANE IS JUST GETTING STARTED.
HE IS SIMPLY CHAOTIC--LASHING OUT, DESTROYING EVERYTHING IN SIGHT.
EVEN NOW THE FORCES OF THE SHI'AR EMPIRE ARE BANDING TOGETHER WITH SPARTAX TO MOUNT AN ASSAULT, BUT THEY ARE DOOMED TO FAIL.
THANE NOW HAS THE POWER OF A GOD. AND IT WILL TAKE THE POWER OF A GOD TO STOP HIM.
SO YOU ALL ALLIED WITH MY SON IN A CLANDESTINE ATTEMPT TO ASSASSINATE ME, AND NOW YOU WANT TO SWITCH SIDES, EH?
PRETTY MUCH.
YUP.

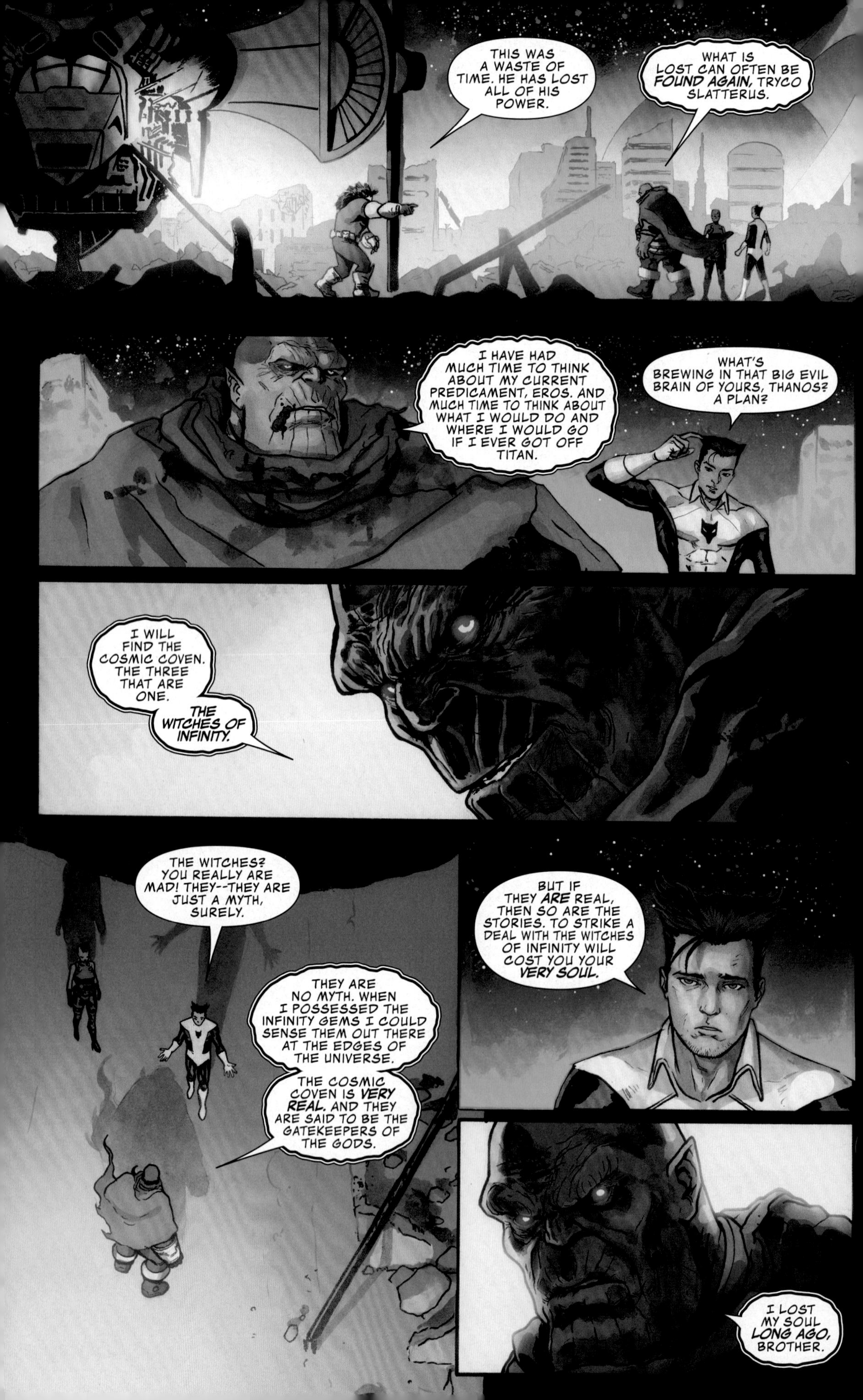
THIS WAS A WASTE OF TIME. HE HAS LOST ALL OF HIS POWER.
WHAT IS LOST CAN OFTEN BE FOUND AGAIN, TRYCO SLATTERUS.
I HAVE HAD MUCH TIME TO THINK ABOUT MY CURRENT PREDICAMENT, EROS. AND MUCH TIME TO THINK ABOUT WHAT I WOULD DO AND WHERE I WOULD GO IF I EVER GOT OFF TITAN.
WHAT'S BREWING IN THAT BIG EVIL BRAIN OF YOURS, THANOS? A PLAN?
I WILL FIND THE COSMIC COVEN. THE THREE THAT ARE ONE.
THE WITCHES OF INFINITY.
THE WITCHES? YOU REALLY ARE MAD! THEY--THEY ARE JUST A MYTH, SURELY.
THEY ARE NO MYTH. WHEN I POSSESSED THE INFINITY GEMS I COULD SENSE THEM OUT THERE AT THE EDGES OF THE UNIVERSE.
THE COSMIC COVEN IS VERY REAL. AND THEY ARE SAID TO BE THE GATEKEEPERS OF THE GODS.
BUT IF THEY ARE REAL, THEN SO ARE THE STORIES. TO STRIKE A DEAL WITH THE WITCHES OF INFINITY WILL COST YOU YOUR VERY SOUL.
I LOST MY SOUL LONG AGO, BROTHER.

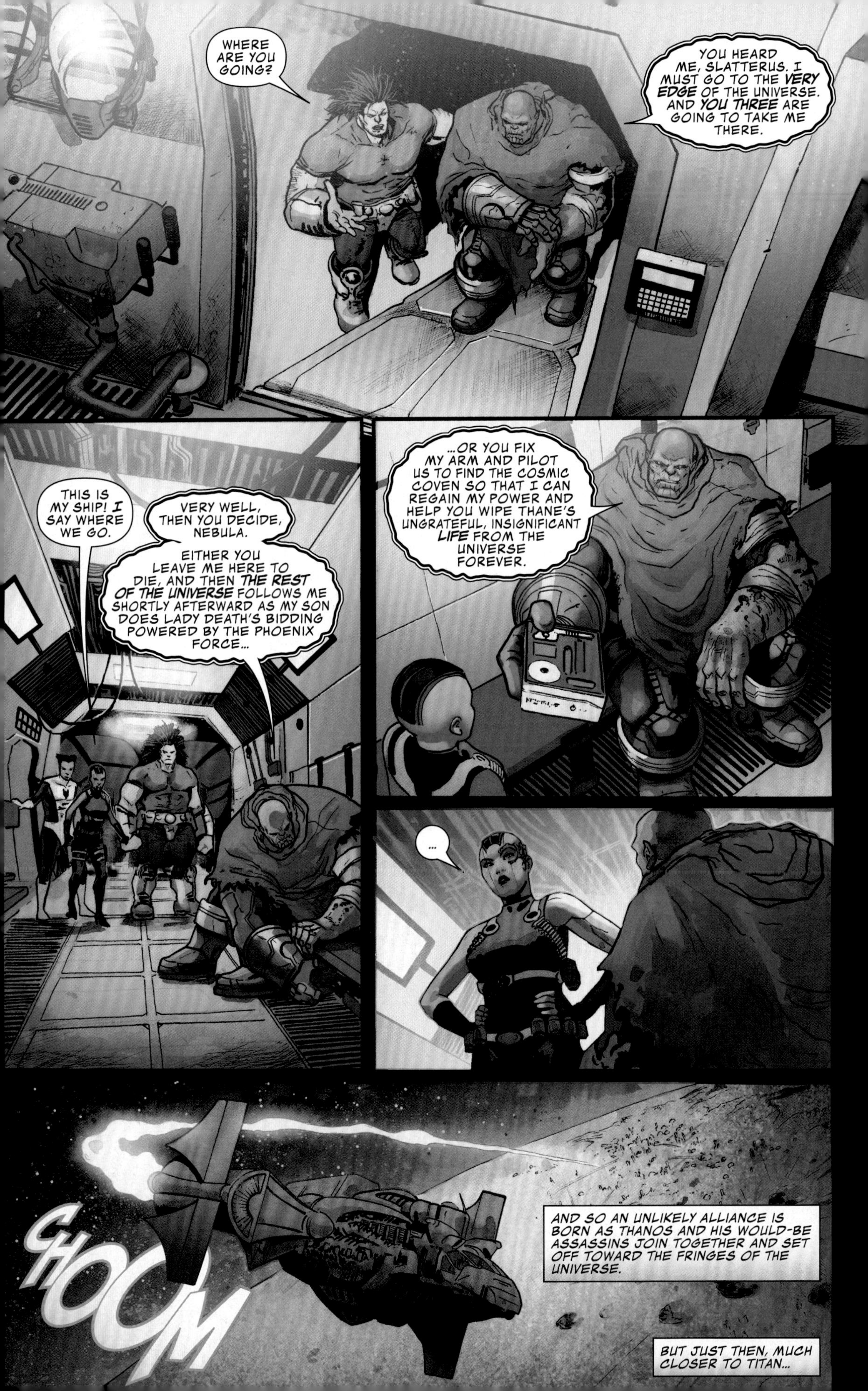
WHERE ARE YOU GOING?
YOU HEARD ME, SLATTERUS. I MUST GO TO THE VERY EDGE OF THE UNIVERSE. AND YOU THREE ARE GOING TO TAKE ME THERE.
THIS IS MY SHIP! I SAY WHERE WE GO.
VERY WELL, THEN YOU DECIDE, NEBULA.
EITHER YOU LEAVE ME HERE TO DIE, AND THEN THE REST OF THE UNIVERSE FOLLOWS ME SHORTLY AFTERWARD AS MY SON DOES LADY DEATH'S BIDDING POWERED BY THE PHOENIX FORCE...
...OR YOU FIX MY ARM AND PILOT US TO FIND THE COSMIC COVEN SO THAT I CAN REGAIN MY POWER AND HELP YOU WIPE THANE'S UNGRATEFUL, INSIGNIFICANT LIFE FROM THE UNIVERSE FOREVER.
...
CHOOM
AND SO AN UNLIKELY ALLIANCE IS BORN AS THANOS AND HIS WOULD-BE ASSASSINS JOIN TOGETHER AND SET OFF TOWARD THE FRINGES OF THE UNIVERSE.
BUT JUST THEN, MUCH CLOSER TO TITAN...

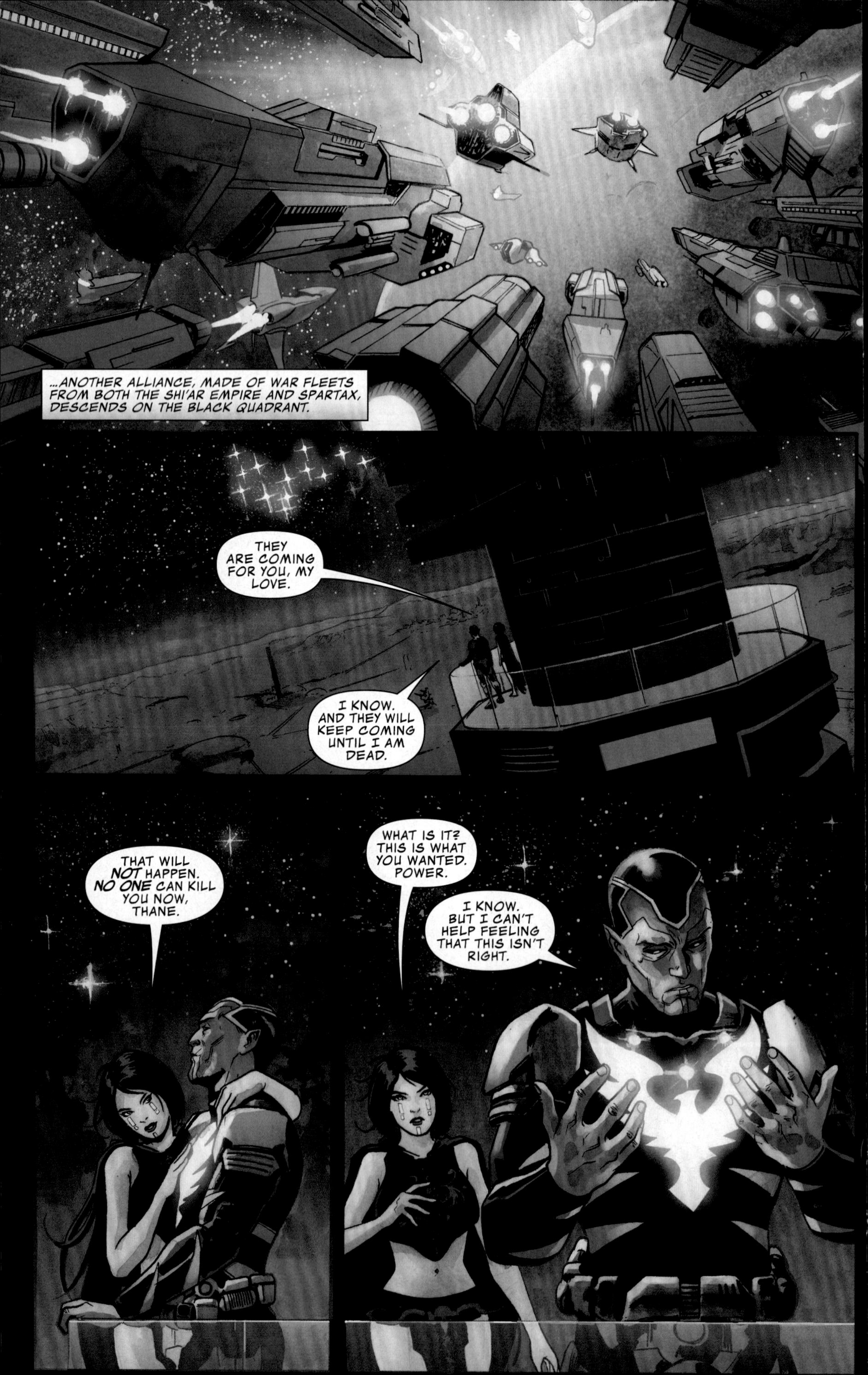
...ANOTHER ALLIANCE, MADE OF WAR FLEETS FROM BOTH THE SHI'AR EMPIRE AND SPARTAX, DESCENDS ON THE BLACK QUADRANT.
THEY ARE COMING FOR YOU, MY LOVE.
I KNOW. AND THEY WILL KEEP COMING UNTIL I AM DEAD.
THAT WILL NOT HAPPEN. NO ONE CAN KILL YOU NOW, THANE.
WHAT IS IT? THIS IS WHAT YOU WANTED. POWER.
I KNOW. BUT I CAN'T HELP FEELING THAT THIS ISN'T RIGHT.

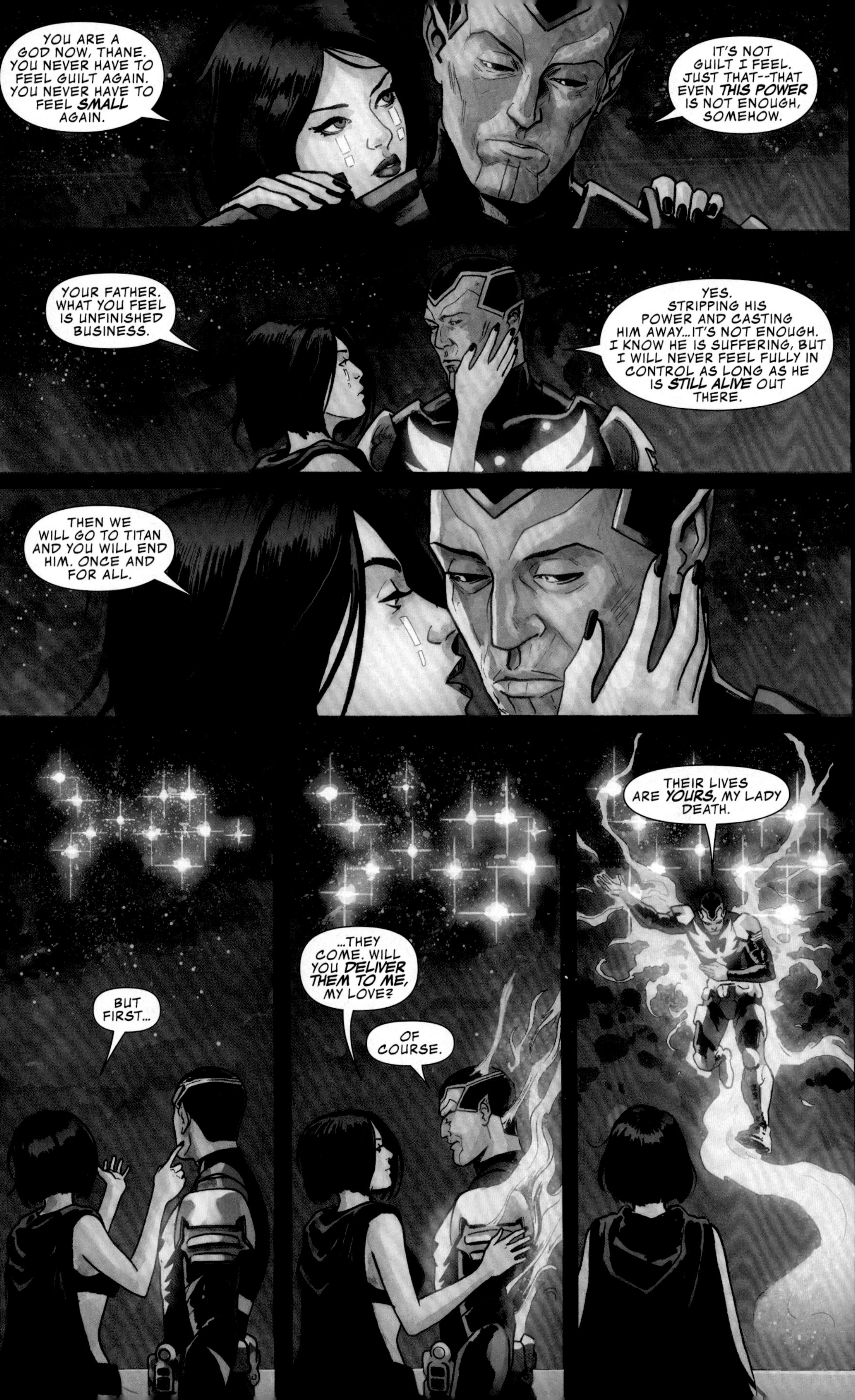
YOU ARE A GOD NOW, THANE. YOU NEVER HAVE TO FEEL GUILT AGAIN. YOU NEVER HAVE TO FEEL SMALL AGAIN.
IT'S NOT GUILT I FEEL. JUST THAT--THAT EVEN THIS POWER IS NOT ENOUGH, SOMEHOW.
YOUR FATHER. WHAT YOU FEEL IS UNFINISHED BUSINESS.
YES. STRIPPING HIS POWER AND CASTING HIM AWAY...IT'S NOT ENOUGH. I KNOW HE IS SUFFERING, BUT I WILL NEVER FEEL FULLY IN CONTROL AS LONG AS HE IS STILL ALIVE OUT THERE.
THEN WE WILL GO TO TITAN AND YOU WILL END HIM. ONCE AND FOR ALL.
BUT FIRST...
...THEY COME. WILL YOU DELIVER THEM TO ME, MY LOVE?
OF COURSE.
THEIR LIVES ARE YOURS, MY LADY DEATH.

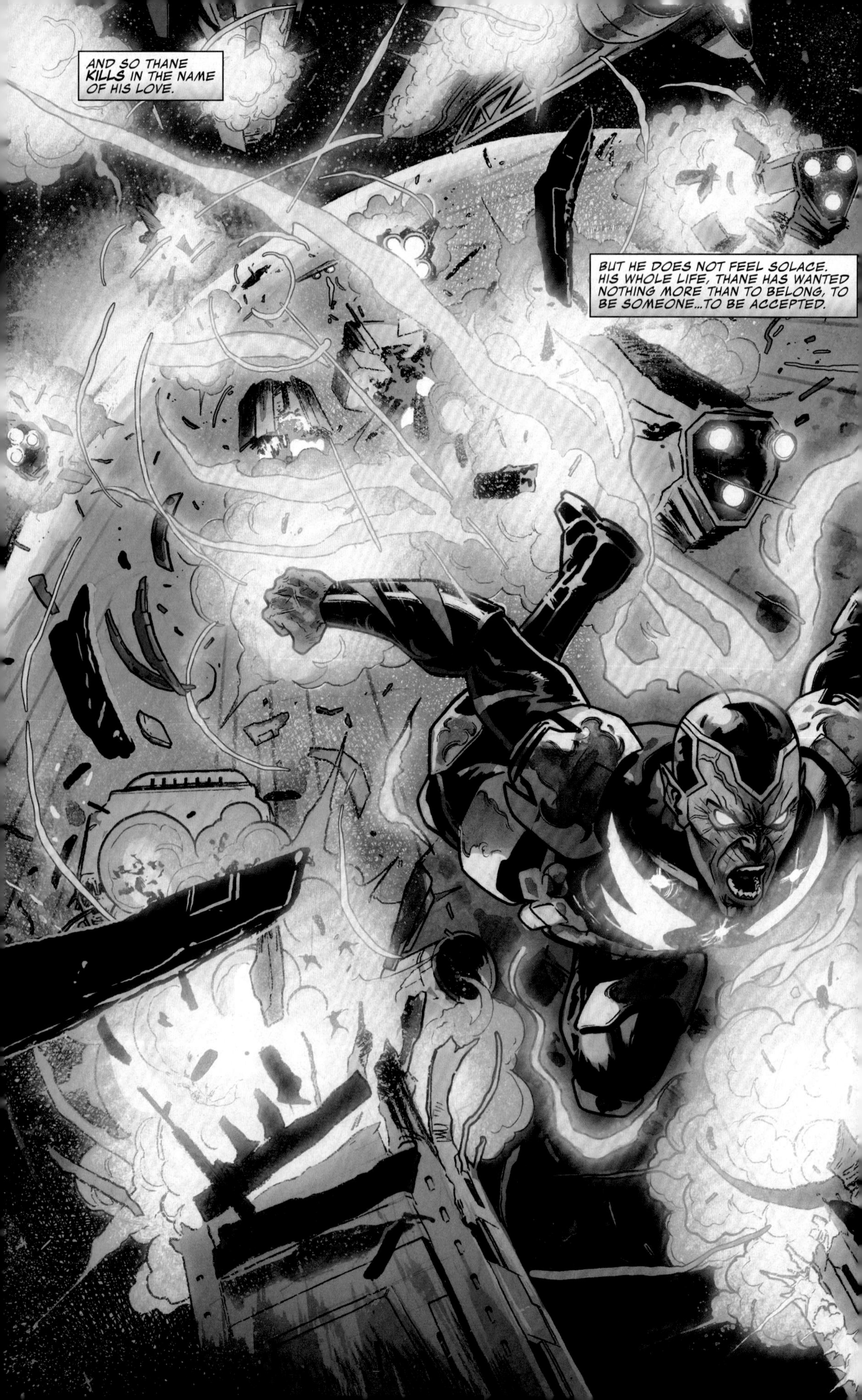
AND SO THANE KILLS IN THE NAME OF HIS LOVE.
BUT HE DOES NOT FEEL SOLACE. HIS WHOLE LIFE, THANE HAS WANTED NOTHING MORE THAN TO BELONG, TO BE SOMEONE...TO BE ACCEPTED.

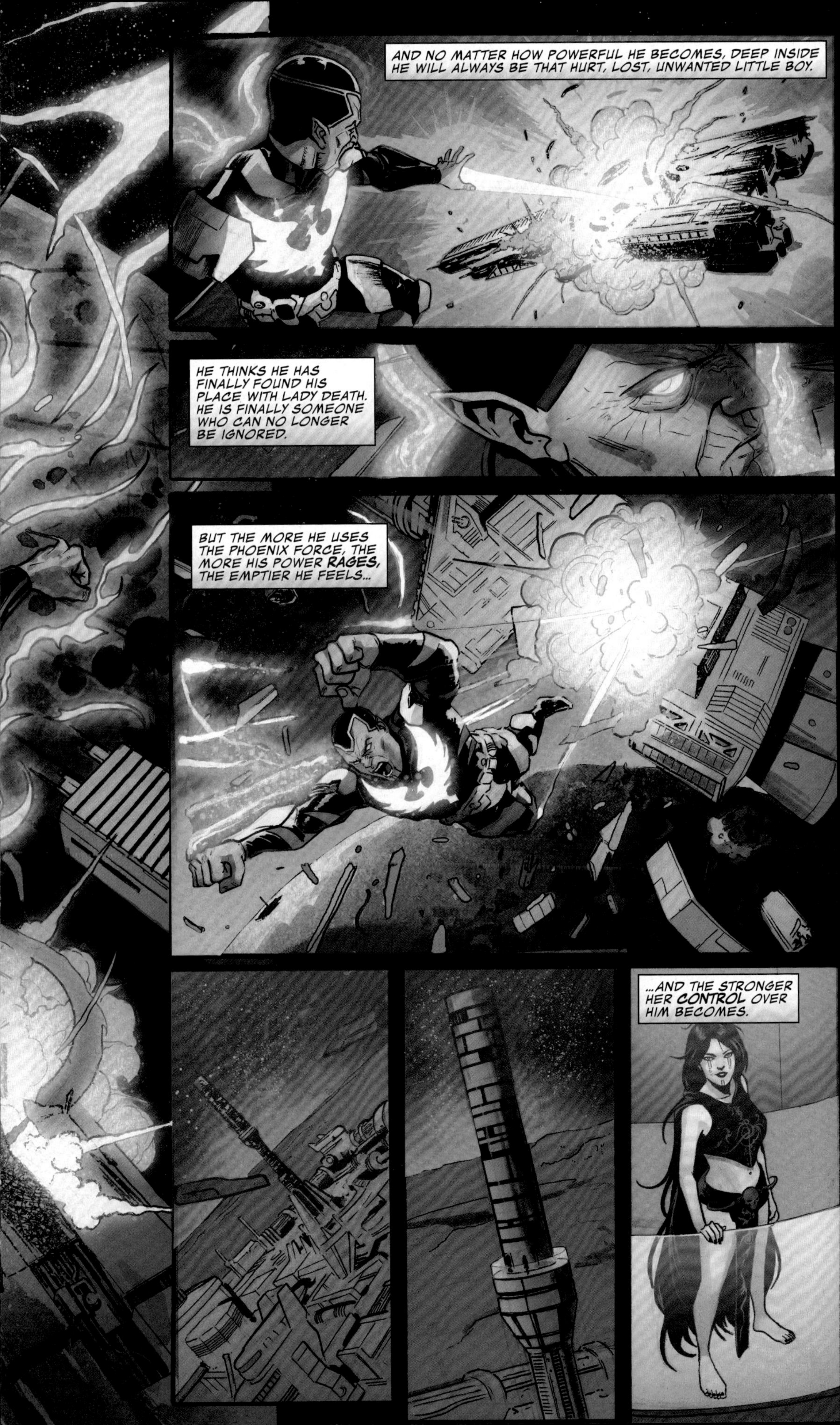
AND NO MATTER HOW POWERFUL HE BECOMES, DEEP INSIDE HE WILL ALWAYS BE THAT HURT, LOST, UNWANTED LITTLE BOY.
HE THINKS HE HAS FINALLY FOUND HIS PLACE WITH LADY DEATH. HE IS FINALLY SOMEONE WHO CAN NO LONGER BE IGNORED.
BUT THE MORE HE USES THE PHOENIX FORCE, THE MORE HIS POWER **RAGES**, THE EMPTIER HE FEELS...
...AND THE STRONGER HER **CONTROL** OVER HIM BECOMES.

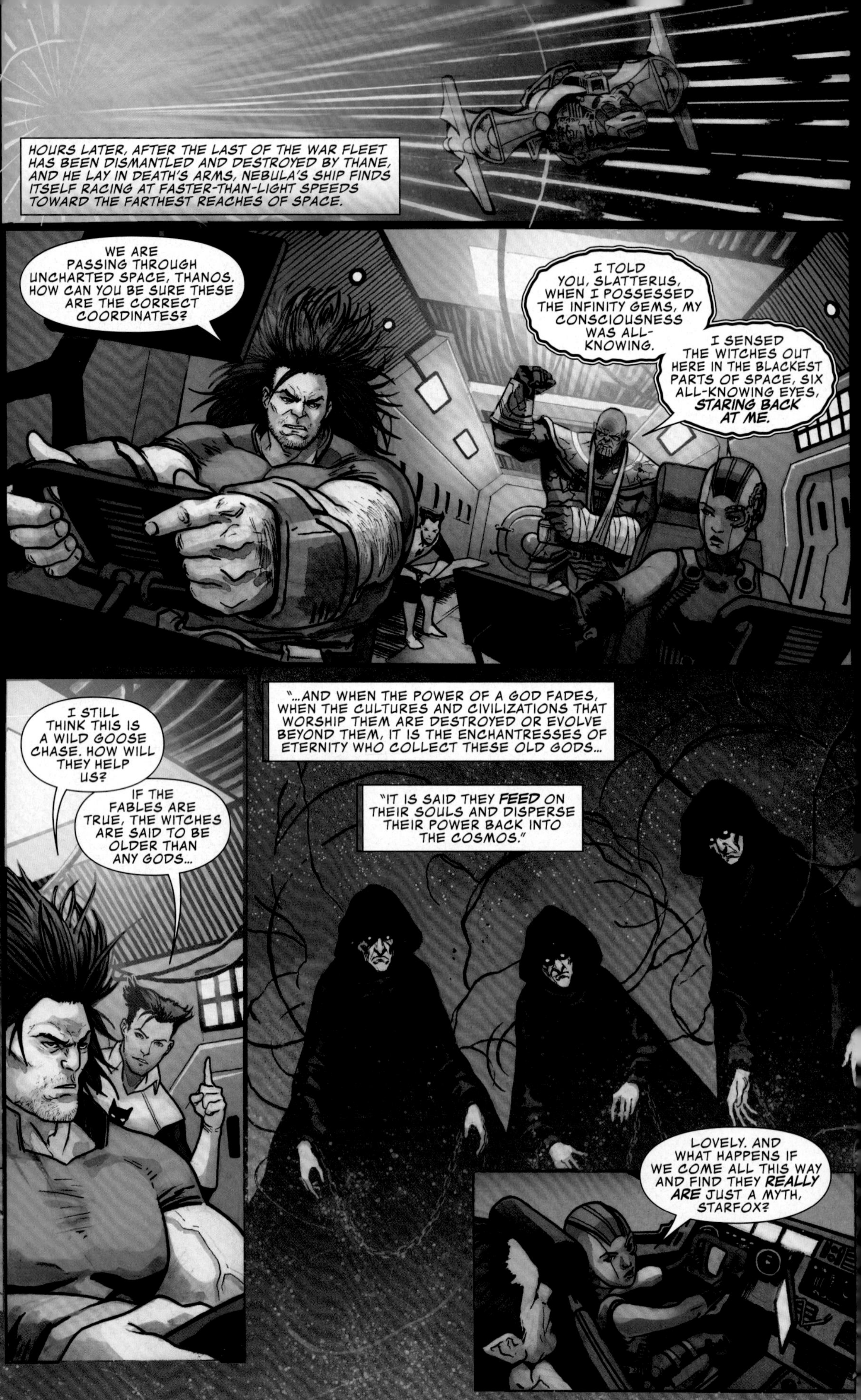
HOURS LATER, AFTER THE LAST OF THE WAR FLEET HAS BEEN DISMANTLED AND DESTROYED BY THANE, AND HE LAY IN DEATH'S ARMS, NEBULA'S SHIP FINDS ITSELF RACING AT FASTER-THAN-LIGHT SPEEDS TOWARD THE FARTHEST REACHES OF SPACE.
WE ARE PASSING THROUGH UNCHARTED SPACE, THANOS. HOW CAN YOU BE SURE THESE ARE THE CORRECT COORDINATES?
I TOLD YOU, SLATTERUS, WHEN I POSSESSED THE INFINITY GEMS, MY CONSCIOUSNESS WAS ALL-KNOWING.
I SENSED THE WITCHES OUT HERE IN THE BLACKEST PARTS OF SPACE, SIX ALL-KNOWING EYES, STARING BACK AT ME.
I STILL THINK THIS IS A WILD GOOSE CHASE. HOW WILL THEY HELP US?
IF THE FABLES ARE TRUE, THE WITCHES ARE SAID TO BE OLDER THAN ANY GODS...
"...AND WHEN THE POWER OF A GOD FADES, WHEN THE CULTURES AND CIVILIZATIONS THAT WORSHIP THEM ARE DESTROYED OR EVOLVE BEYOND THEM, IT IS THE ENCHANTRESSES OF ETERNITY WHO COLLECT THESE OLD GODS...
"IT IS SAID THEY FEED ON THEIR SOULS AND DISPERSE THEIR POWER BACK INTO THE COSMOS."
LOVELY. AND WHAT HAPPENS IF WE COME ALL THIS WAY AND FIND THEY REALLY ARE JUST A MYTH, STARFOX?

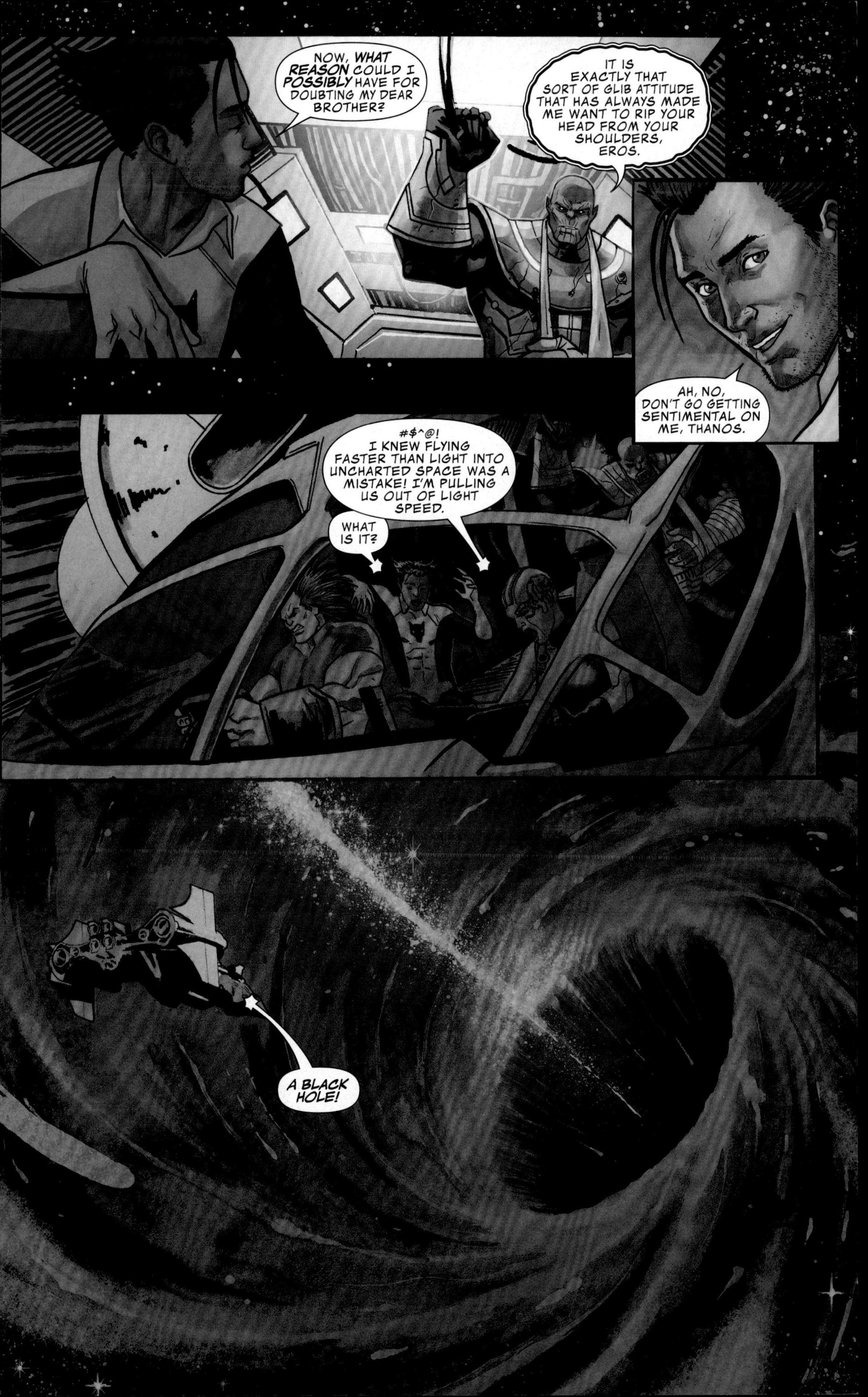
NOW, WHAT REASON COULD I POSSIBLY HAVE FOR DOUBTING MY DEAR BROTHER?
IT IS EXACTLY THAT SORT OF GLIB ATTITUDE THAT HAS ALWAYS MADE ME WANT TO RIP YOUR HEAD FROM YOUR SHOULDERS, EROS.
AH, NO, DON'T GO GETTING SENTIMENTAL ON ME, THANOS.
#$^@! I KNEW FLYING FASTER THAN LIGHT INTO UNCHARTED SPACE WAS A MISTAKE! I'M PULLING US OUT OF LIGHT SPEED.
WHAT IS IT?
A BLACK HOLE!

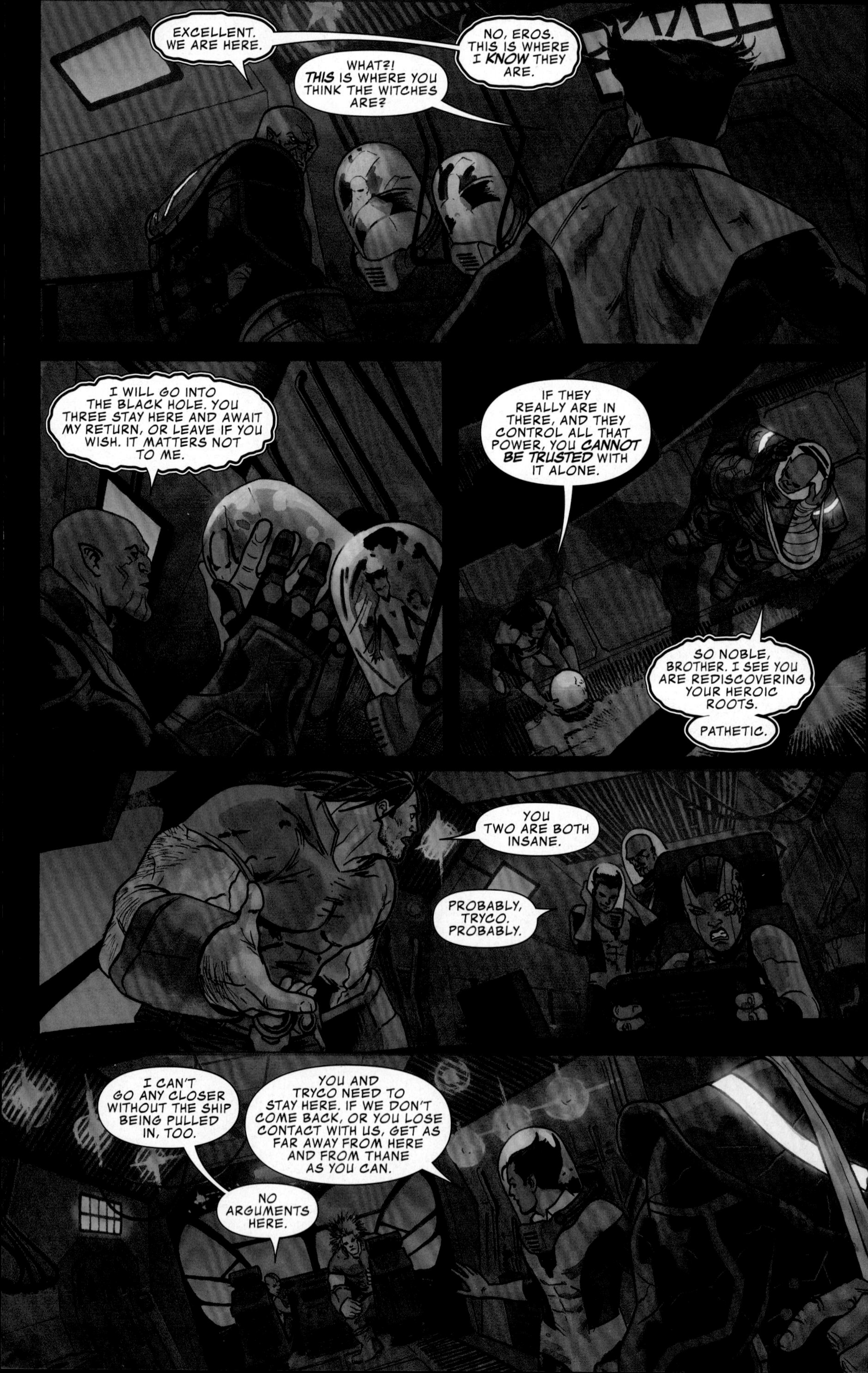
EXCELLENT. WE ARE HERE.
NO, EROS. THIS IS WHERE I KNOW THEY ARE.
WHAT?! THIS IS WHERE YOU THINK THE WITCHES ARE?
I WILL GO INTO THE BLACK HOLE. YOU THREE STAY HERE AND AWAIT MY RETURN, OR LEAVE IF YOU WISH. IT MATTERS NOT TO ME.
IF THEY REALLY ARE IN THERE, AND THEY CONTROL ALL THAT POWER, YOU CANNOT BE TRUSTED WITH IT ALONE.
SO NOBLE, BROTHER. I SEE YOU ARE REDISCOVERING YOUR HEROIC ROOTS.
PATHETIC.
YOU TWO ARE BOTH INSANE.
PROBABLY, TRYCO. PROBABLY.
I CAN'T GO ANY CLOSER WITHOUT THE SHIP BEING PULLED IN, TOO.
YOU AND TRYCO NEED TO STAY HERE. IF WE DON'T COME BACK, OR YOU LOSE CONTACT WITH US, GET AS FAR AWAY FROM HERE AND FROM THANE AS YOU CAN.
NO ARGUMENTS HERE.

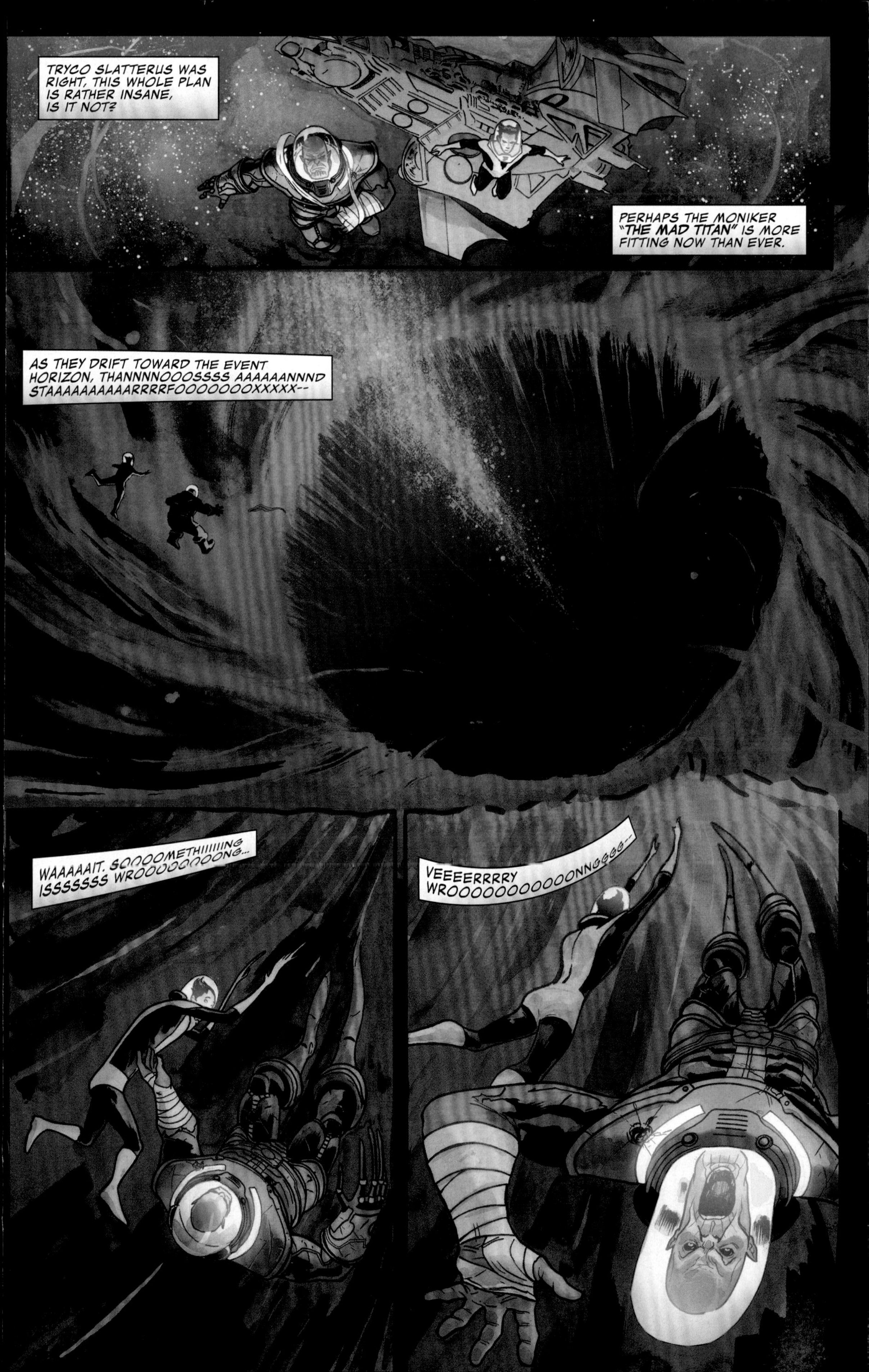
TRYCO SLATTERUS WAS RIGHT, THIS WHOLE PLAN IS RATHER INSANE, IS IT NOT?
PERHAPS THE MONIKER "THE MAD TITAN" IS MORE FITTING NOW THAN EVER.
AS THEY DRIFT TOWARD THE EVENT HORIZON, THANNNNOOOSSSS AAAAAANNND STAAAAAAAAAARRRRFOOOOOOOXXXXX--
WAAAAAIT. SOOOOMETHIIIIIING ISSSSSSS WROOOOOOOOONG...
VEEEERRRRY WROOOOOOOOOOONNGGGG--

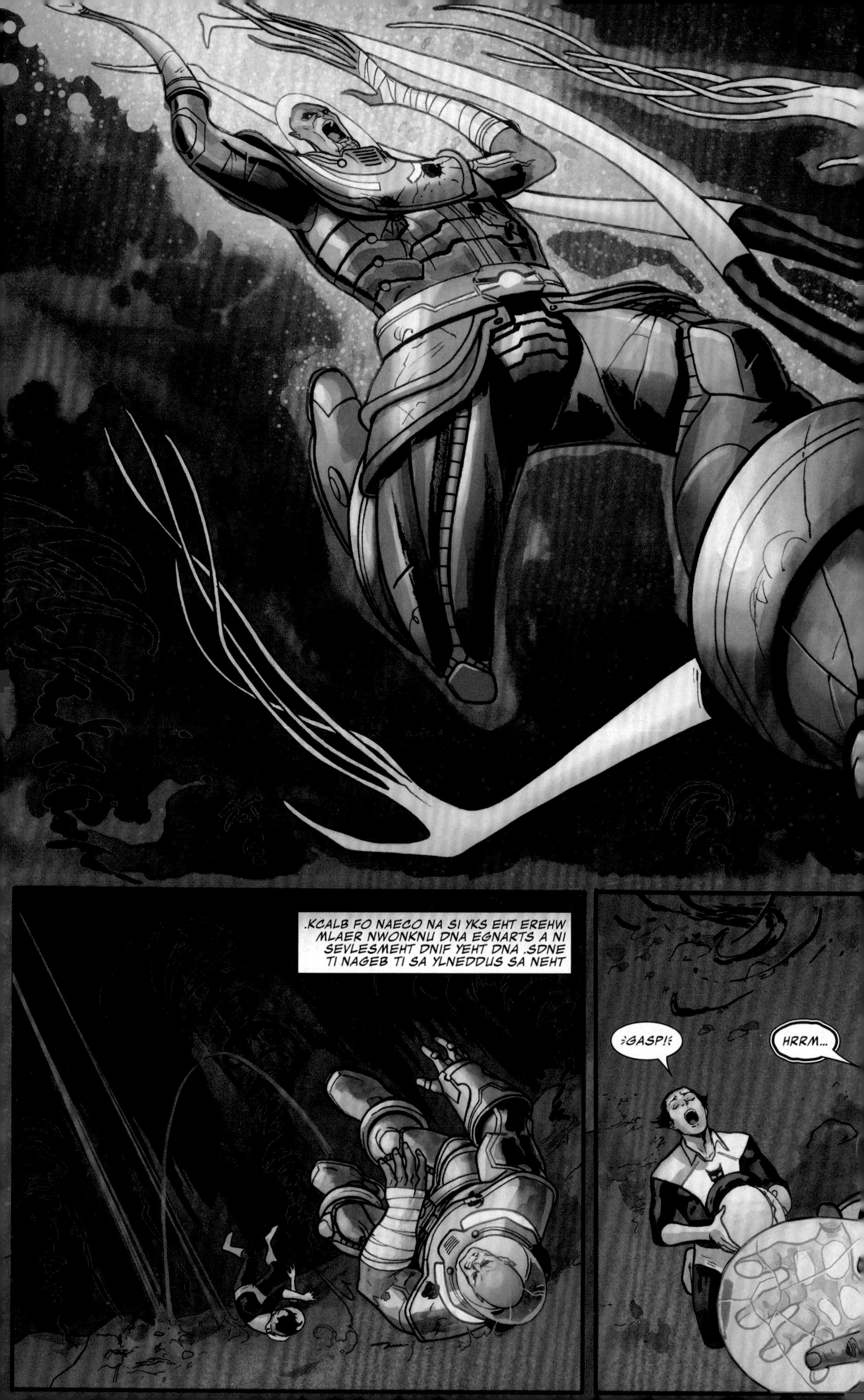
.KCALB FO NAECO NA SI YKS EHT EREHW
MLAER NWONKNU DNA EGNARTS A NI
SEVLESMEHT DNIF YEHT DNA .SDNE
TI NAGEB TI SA YLNEDDUS SA NEHT
¡GASP!¡
HRRM...

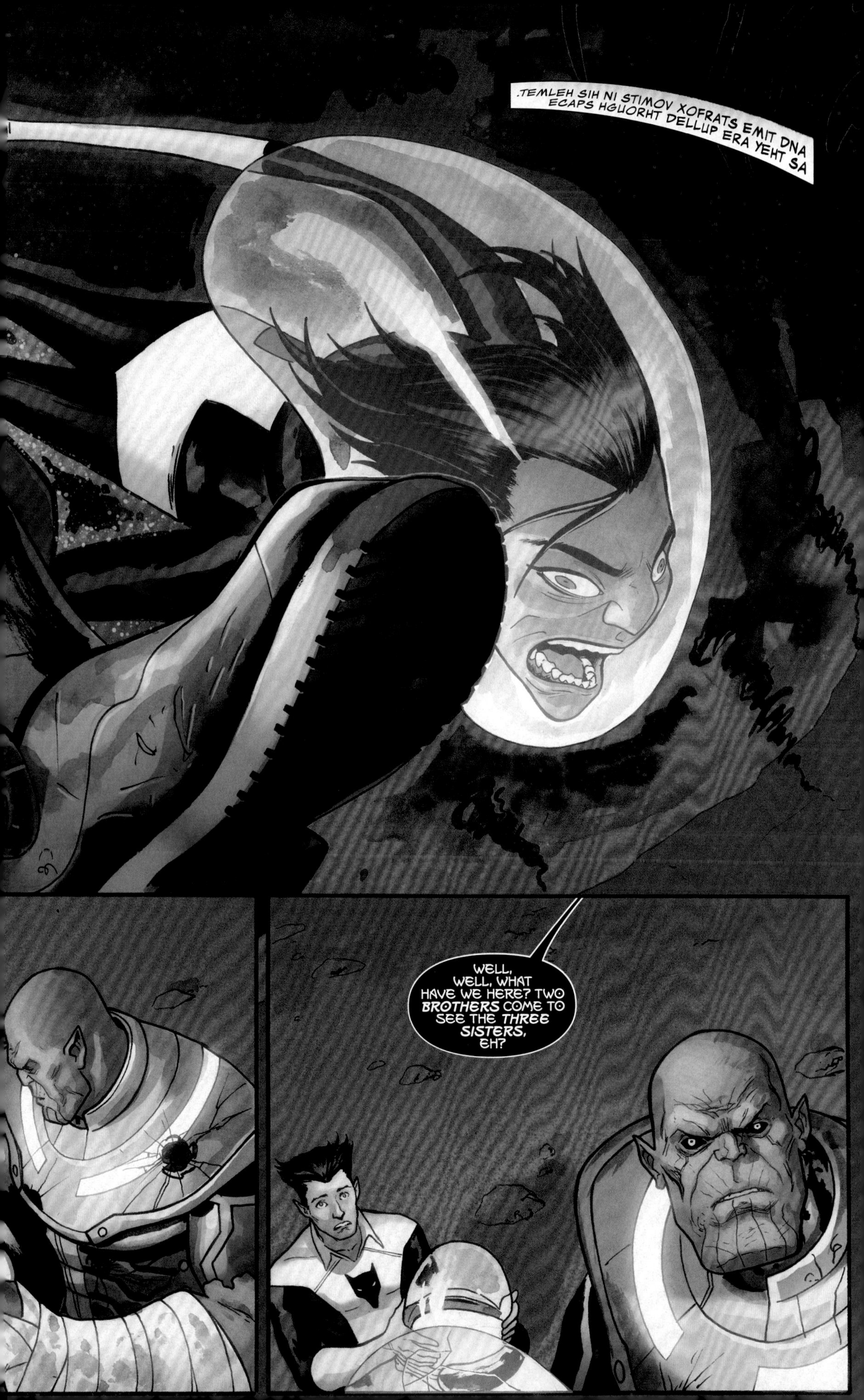
.TEMLEH SIH NI STIMOV XOFRATS EMIT DNA
ECAPS HGUORHT DELLUP ERA YEHT SA
WELL, WELL, WHAT HAVE WE HERE? TWO *BROTHERS* COME TO SEE THE *THREE SISTERS,* EH?

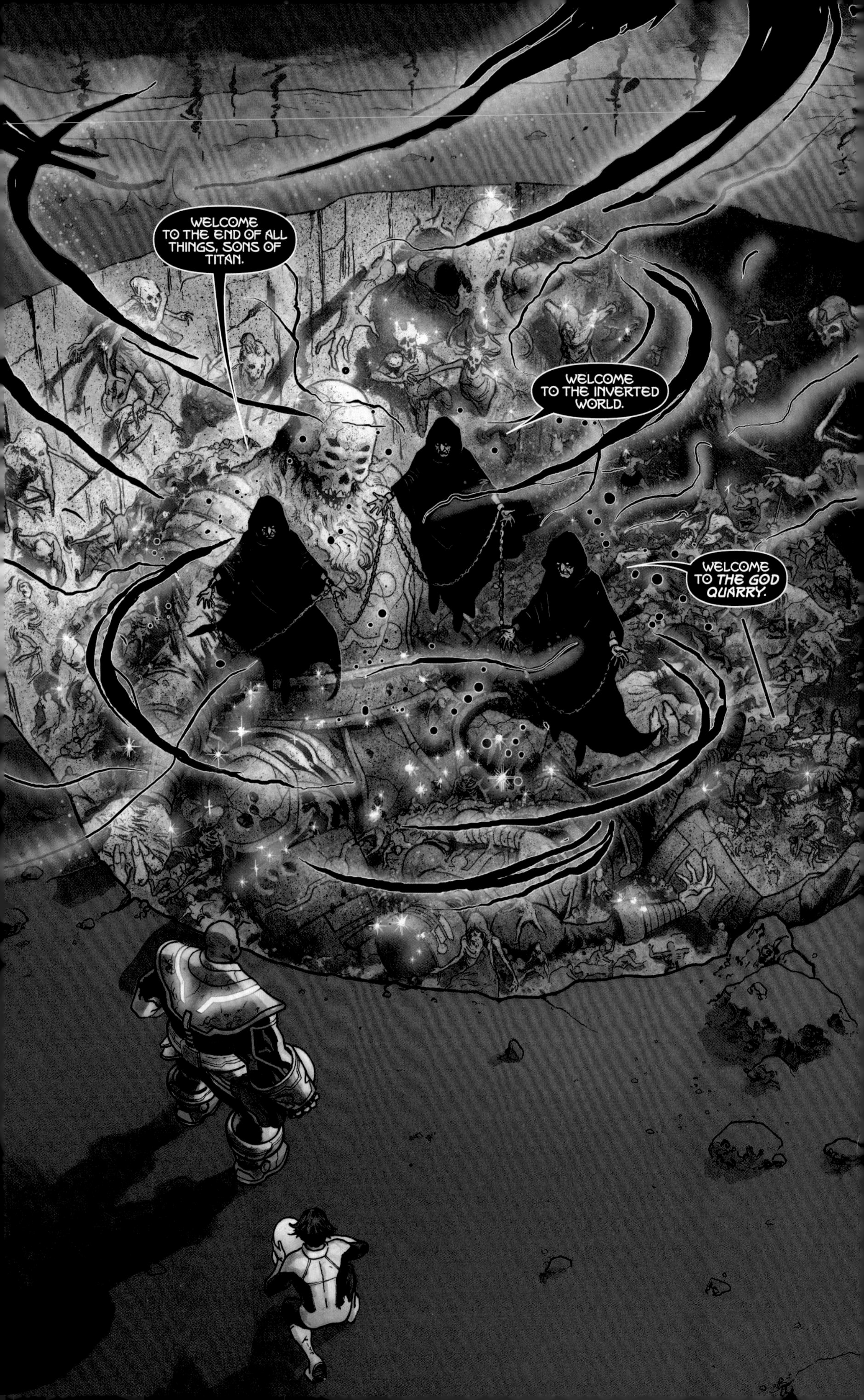
WELCOME TO THE END OF ALL THINGS, SONS OF TITAN.
WELCOME TO THE INVERTED WORLD.
WELCOME TO THE GOD QUARRY.

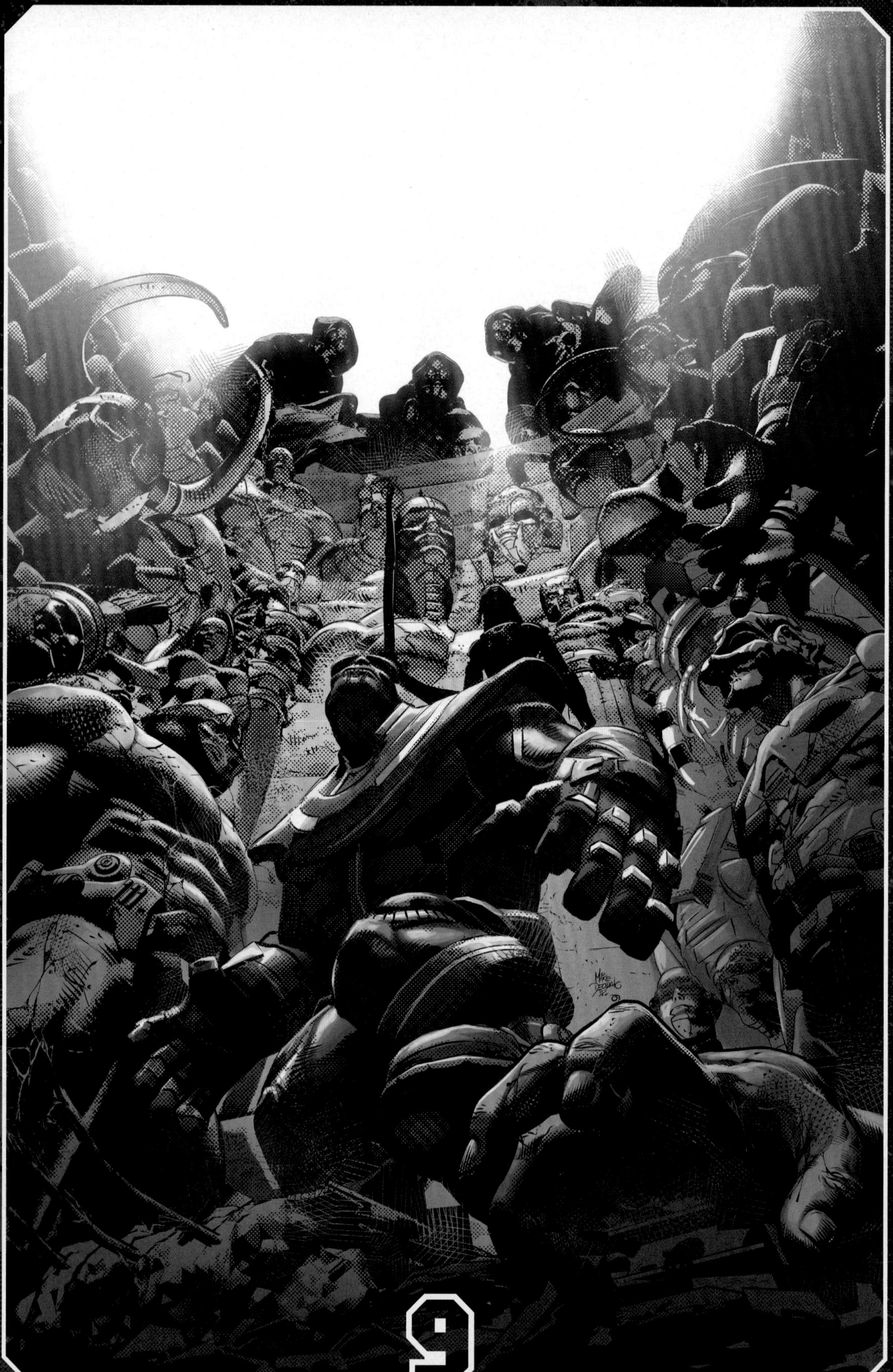
9

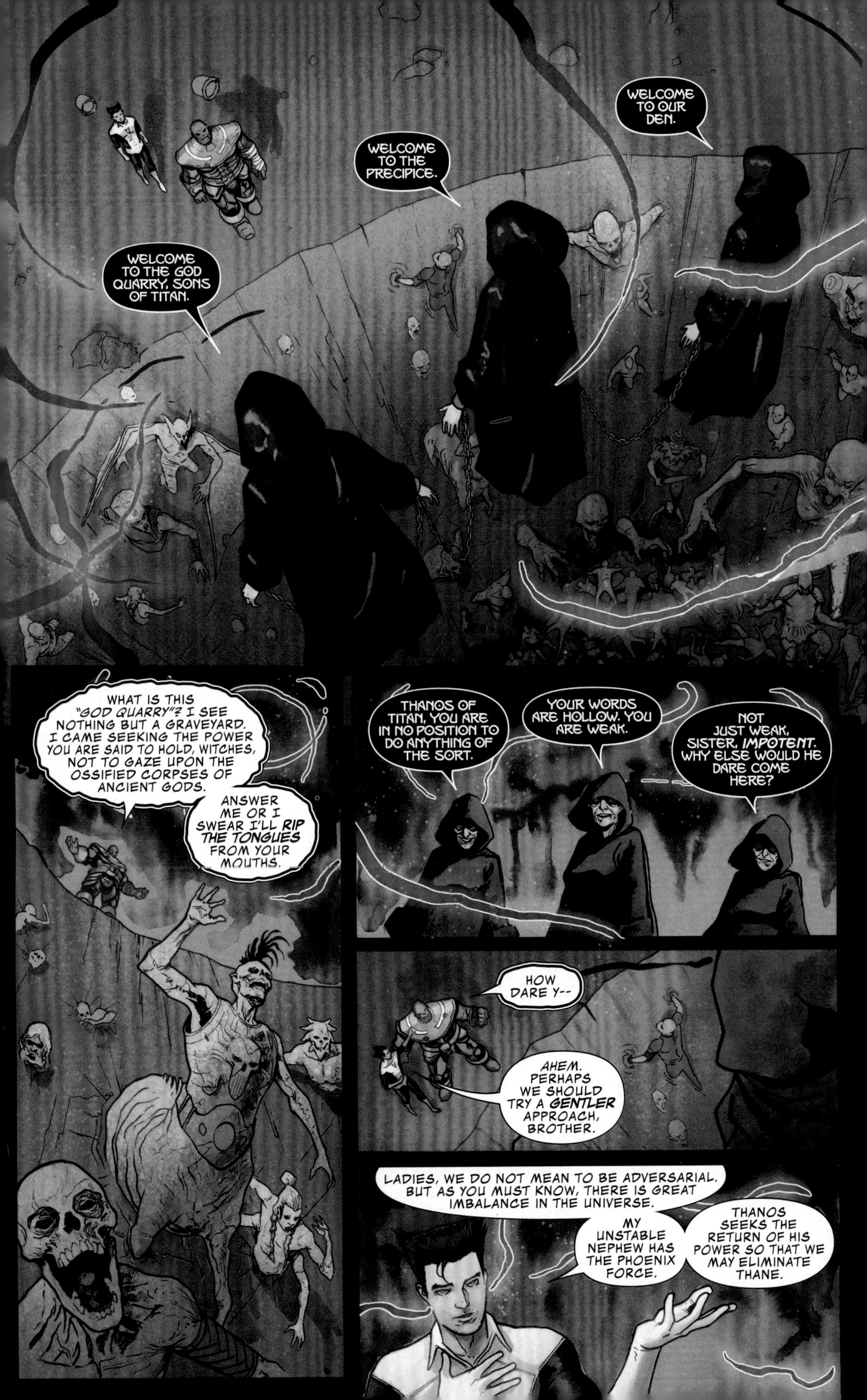

WELCOME TO THE GOD QUARRY, SONS OF TITAN.
WELCOME TO THE PRECIPICE.
WELCOME TO OUR DEN.
WHAT IS THIS "GOD QUARRY"? I SEE NOTHING BUT A GRAVEYARD. I CAME SEEKING THE POWER YOU ARE SAID TO HOLD, WITCHES, NOT TO GAZE UPON THE OSSIFIED CORPSES OF ANCIENT GODS.
ANSWER ME OR I SWEAR I'LL RIP THE TONGUES FROM YOUR MOUTHS.
THANOS OF TITAN, YOU ARE IN NO POSITION TO DO ANYTHING OF THE SORT.
YOUR WORDS ARE HOLLOW. YOU ARE WEAK.
NOT JUST WEAK, SISTER, IMPOTENT. WHY ELSE WOULD HE DARE COME HERE?
HOW DARE Y--
AHEM. PERHAPS WE SHOULD TRY A GENTLER APPROACH, BROTHER.
LADIES, WE DO NOT MEAN TO BE ADVERSARIAL. BUT AS YOU MUST KNOW, THERE IS GREAT IMBALANCE IN THE UNIVERSE.
MY UNSTABLE NEPHEW HAS THE PHOENIX FORCE.
THANOS SEEKS THE RETURN OF HIS POWER SO THAT WE MAY ELIMINATE THANE.

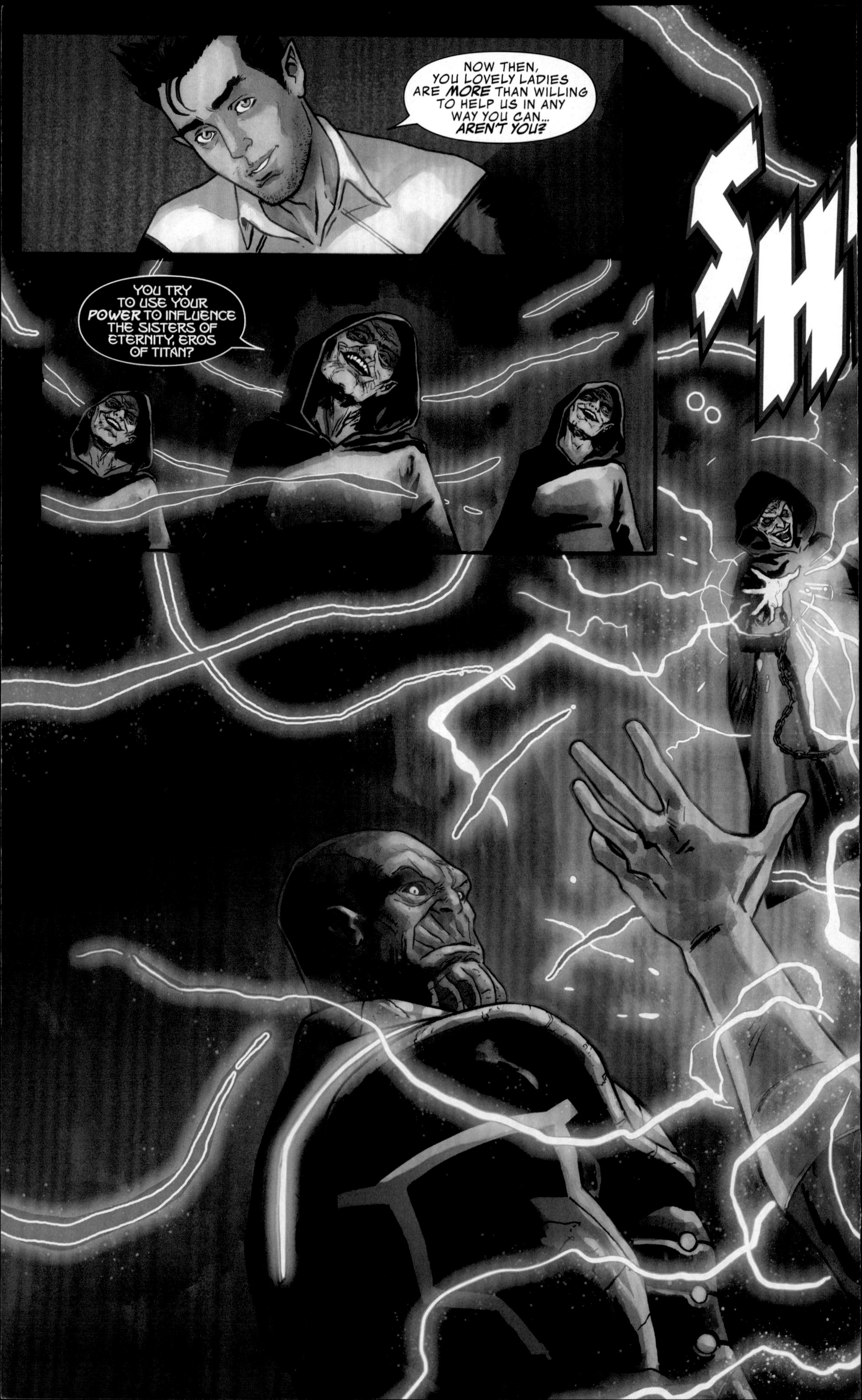
NOW THEN, YOU LOVELY LADIES ARE MORE THAN WILLING TO HELP US IN ANY WAY YOU CAN... AREN'T YOU?
YOU TRY TO USE YOUR POWER TO INFLUENCE THE SISTERS OF ETERNITY, EROS OF TITAN?

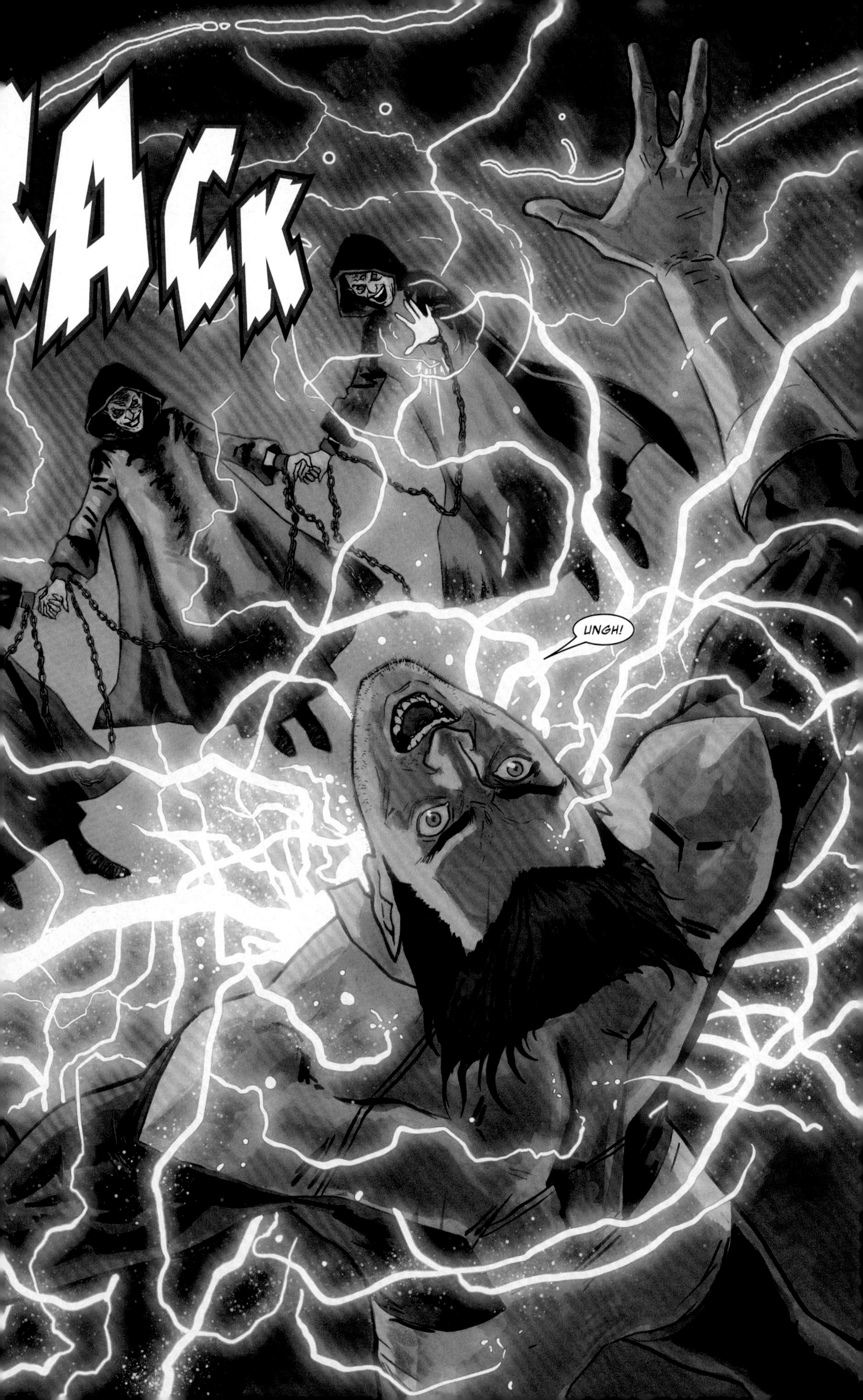

ACK
UNGH!

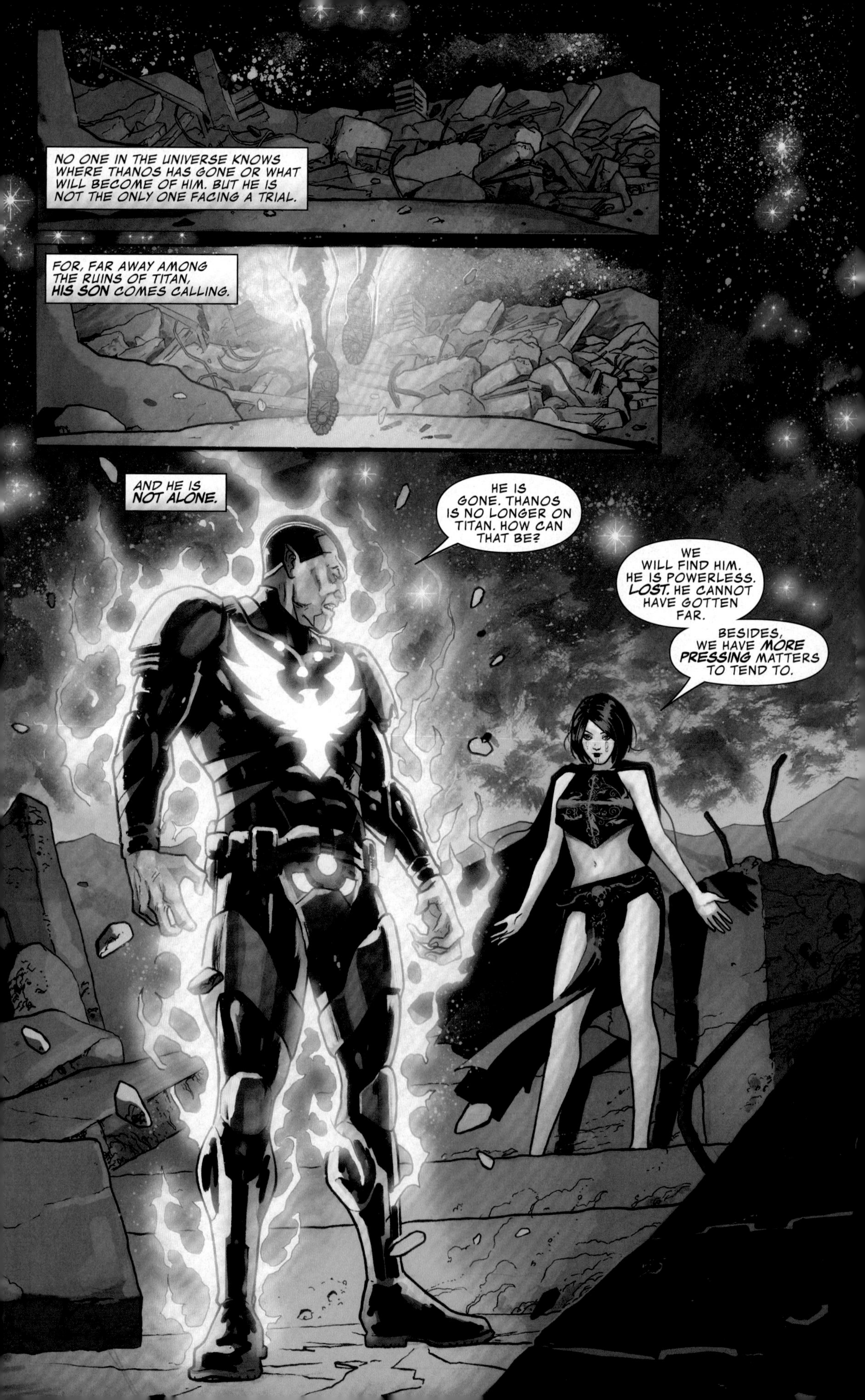
NO ONE IN THE UNIVERSE KNOWS WHERE THANOS HAS GONE OR WHAT WILL BECOME OF HIM. BUT HE IS NOT THE ONLY ONE FACING A TRIAL.
FOR, FAR AWAY AMONG THE RUINS OF TITAN, **HIS SON** COMES CALLING.
AND HE IS ***NOT ALONE.***
HE IS GONE. THANOS IS NO LONGER ON TITAN. HOW CAN THAT BE?
WE WILL FIND HIM. HE IS POWERLESS. ***LOST.*** HE CANNOT HAVE GOTTEN FAR.
BESIDES, WE HAVE ***MORE PRESSING*** MATTERS TO TEND TO.

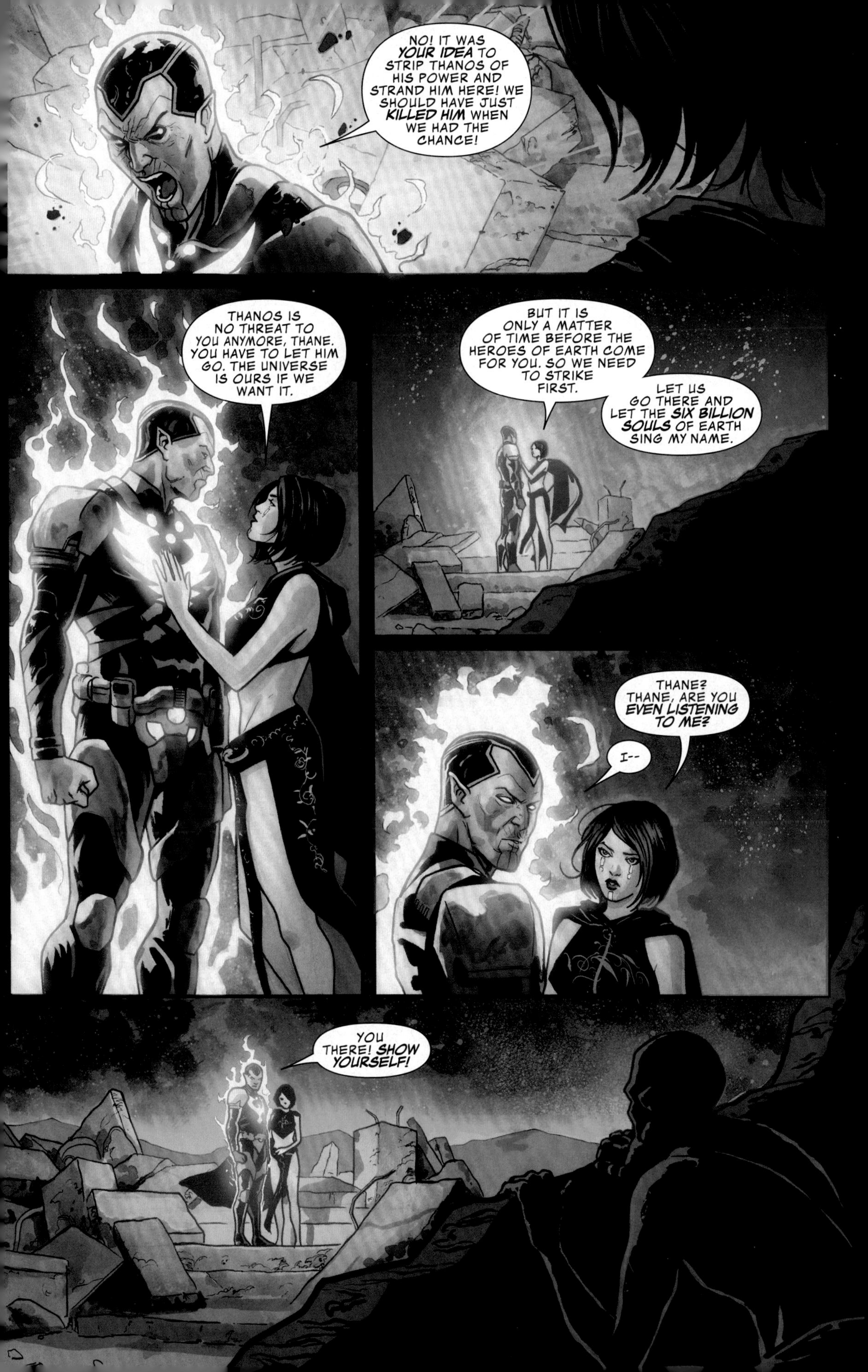
NO! IT WAS YOUR IDEA TO STRIP THANOS OF HIS POWER AND STRAND HIM HERE! WE SHOULD HAVE JUST KILLED HIM WHEN WE HAD THE CHANCE!
THANOS IS NO THREAT TO YOU ANYMORE, THANE. YOU HAVE TO LET HIM GO. THE UNIVERSE IS OURS IF WE WANT IT.
BUT IT IS ONLY A MATTER OF TIME BEFORE THE HEROES OF EARTH COME FOR YOU. SO WE NEED TO STRIKE FIRST.
LET US GO THERE AND LET THE SIX BILLION SOULS OF EARTH SING MY NAME.
THANE? THANE, ARE YOU EVEN LISTENING TO ME?
I--
YOU THERE! SHOW YOURSELF!

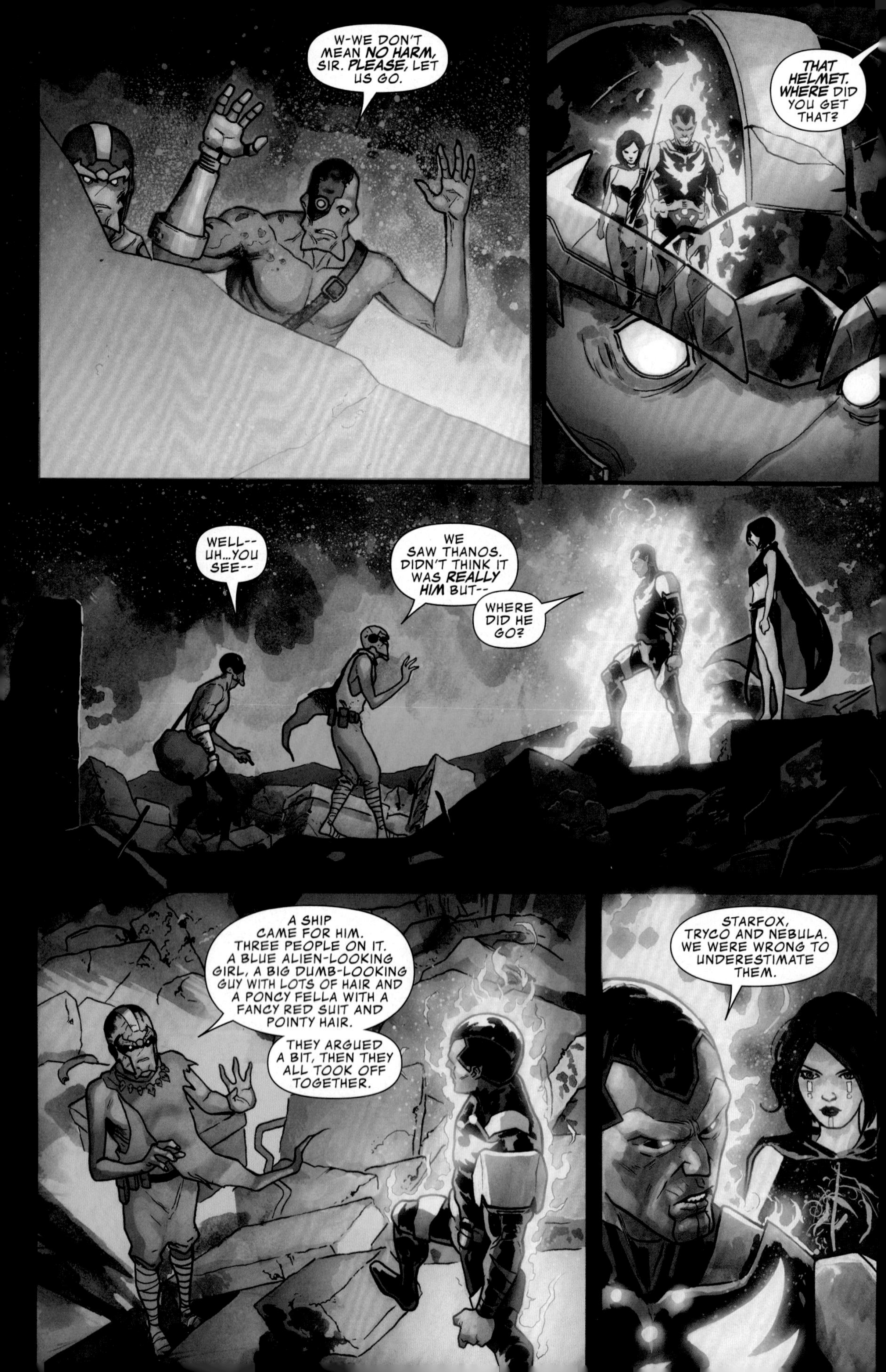
W-WE DON'T MEAN NO HARM, SIR. PLEASE, LET US GO.
THAT HELMET. WHERE DID YOU GET THAT?
WELL-- UH...YOU SEE--
WE SAW THANOS. DIDN'T THINK IT WAS REALLY HIM BUT--
WHERE DID HE GO?
A SHIP CAME FOR HIM. THREE PEOPLE ON IT. A BLUE ALIEN-LOOKING GIRL, A BIG DUMB-LOOKING GUY WITH LOTS OF HAIR AND A PONCY FELLA WITH A FANCY RED SUIT AND POINTY HAIR.
THEY ARGUED A BIT, THEN THEY ALL TOOK OFF TOGETHER.
STARFOX, TRYCO AND NEBULA. WE WERE WRONG TO UNDERESTIMATE THEM.

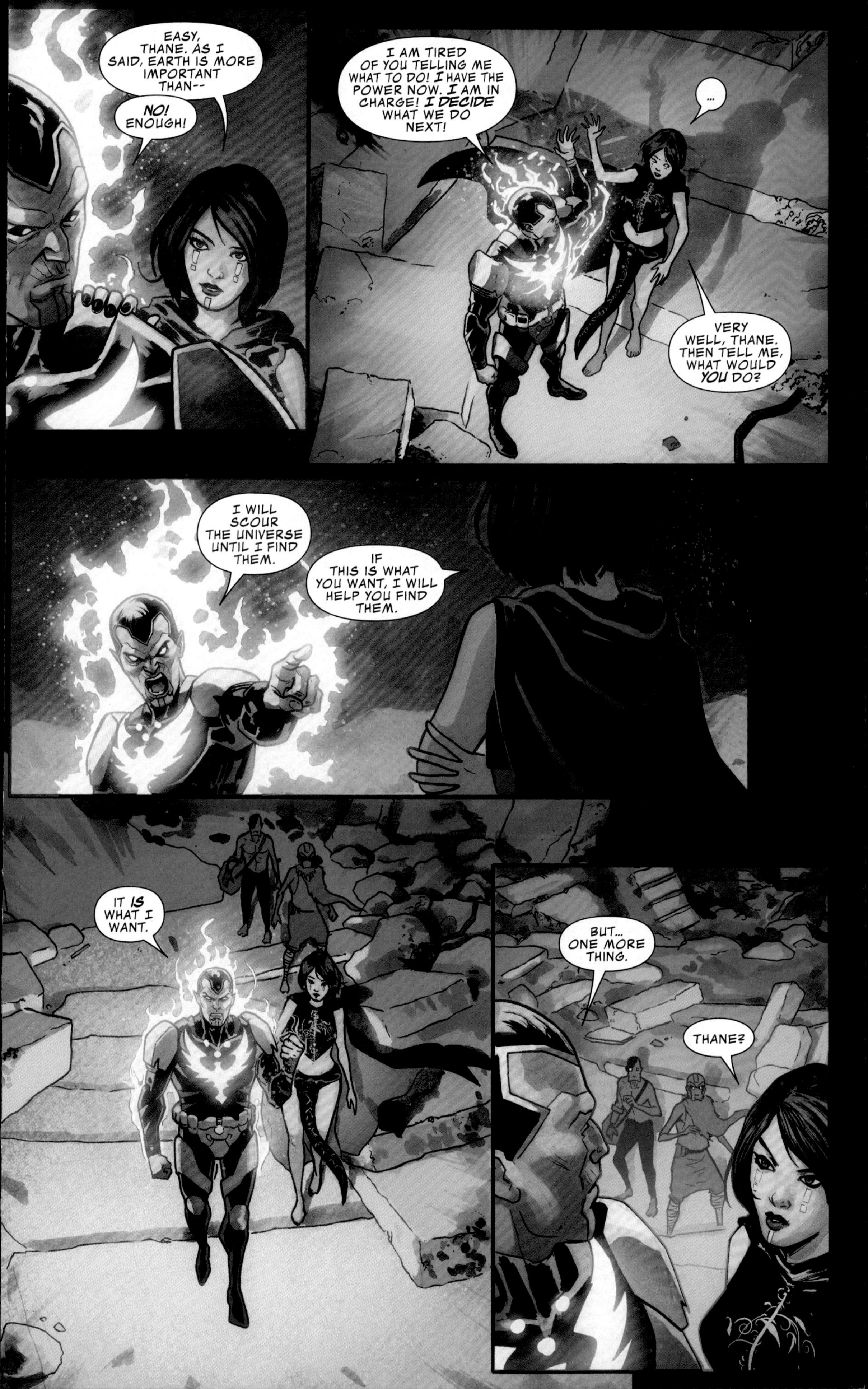
EASY, THANE. AS I SAID, EARTH IS MORE IMPORTANT THAN--
NO! ENOUGH!
I AM TIRED OF YOU TELLING ME WHAT TO DO! I HAVE THE POWER NOW. I AM IN CHARGE! I DECIDE WHAT WE DO NEXT!
...
VERY WELL, THANE. THEN TELL ME, WHAT WOULD YOU DO?
I WILL SCOUR THE UNIVERSE UNTIL I FIND THEM.
IF THIS IS WHAT YOU WANT, I WILL HELP YOU FIND THEM.
IT IS WHAT I WANT.
BUT... ONE MORE THING.
THANE?

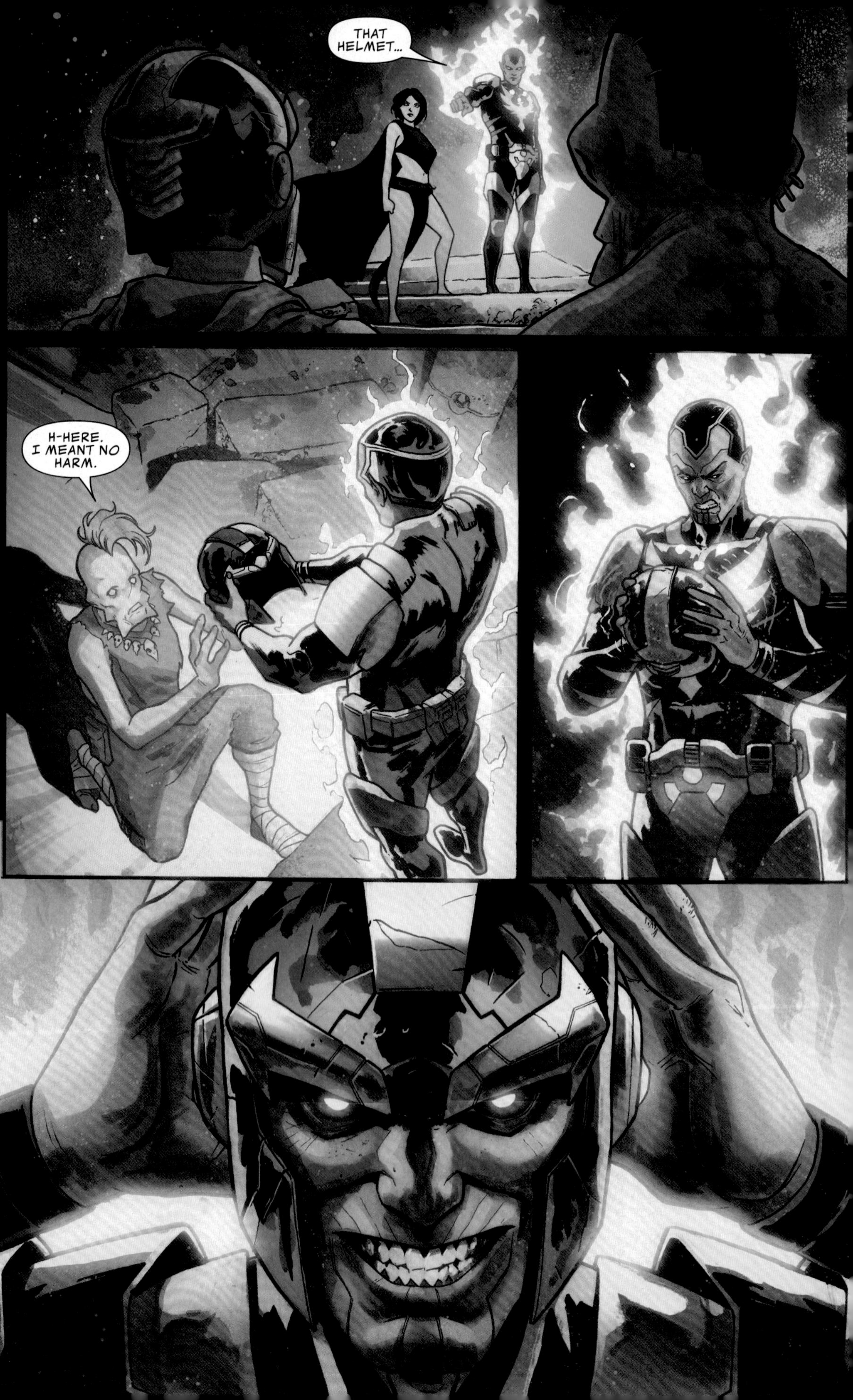
THAT HELMET...
H-HERE. I MEANT NO HARM.

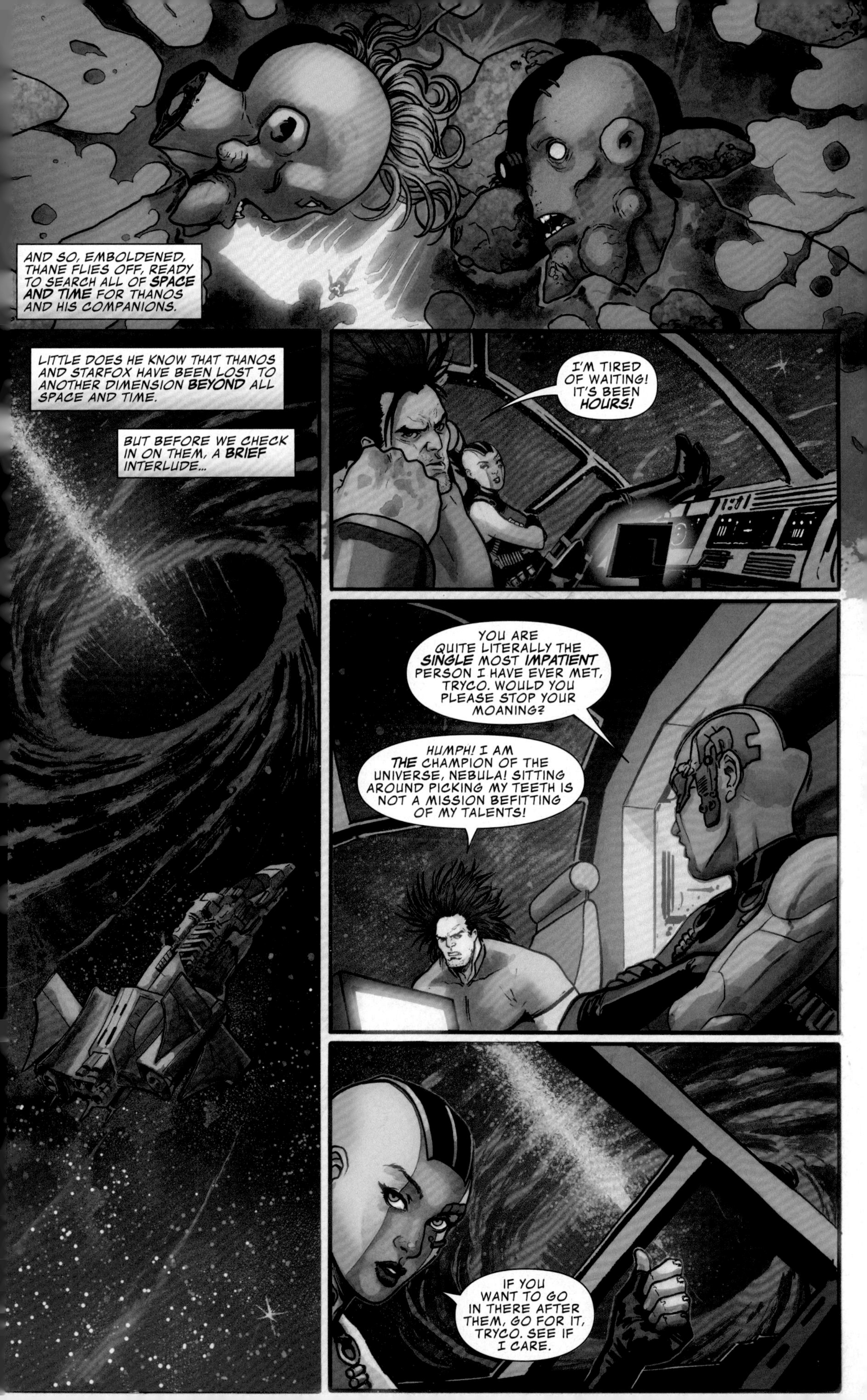
AND SO, EMBOLDENED, THANE FLIES OFF, READY TO SEARCH ALL OF SPACE AND TIME FOR THANOS AND HIS COMPANIONS.
LITTLE DOES HE KNOW THAT THANOS AND STARFOX HAVE BEEN LOST TO ANOTHER DIMENSION BEYOND ALL SPACE AND TIME.
BUT BEFORE WE CHECK IN ON THEM, A BRIEF INTERLUDE...
I'M TIRED OF WAITING! IT'S BEEN HOURS!
YOU ARE QUITE LITERALLY THE SINGLE MOST IMPATIENT PERSON I HAVE EVER MET, TRYCO. WOULD YOU PLEASE STOP YOUR MOANING?
HUMPH! I AM THE CHAMPION OF THE UNIVERSE, NEBULA! SITTING AROUND PICKING MY TEETH IS NOT A MISSION BEFITTING OF MY TALENTS!
IF YOU WANT TO GO IN THERE AFTER THEM, GO FOR IT, TRYCO. SEE IF I CARE.

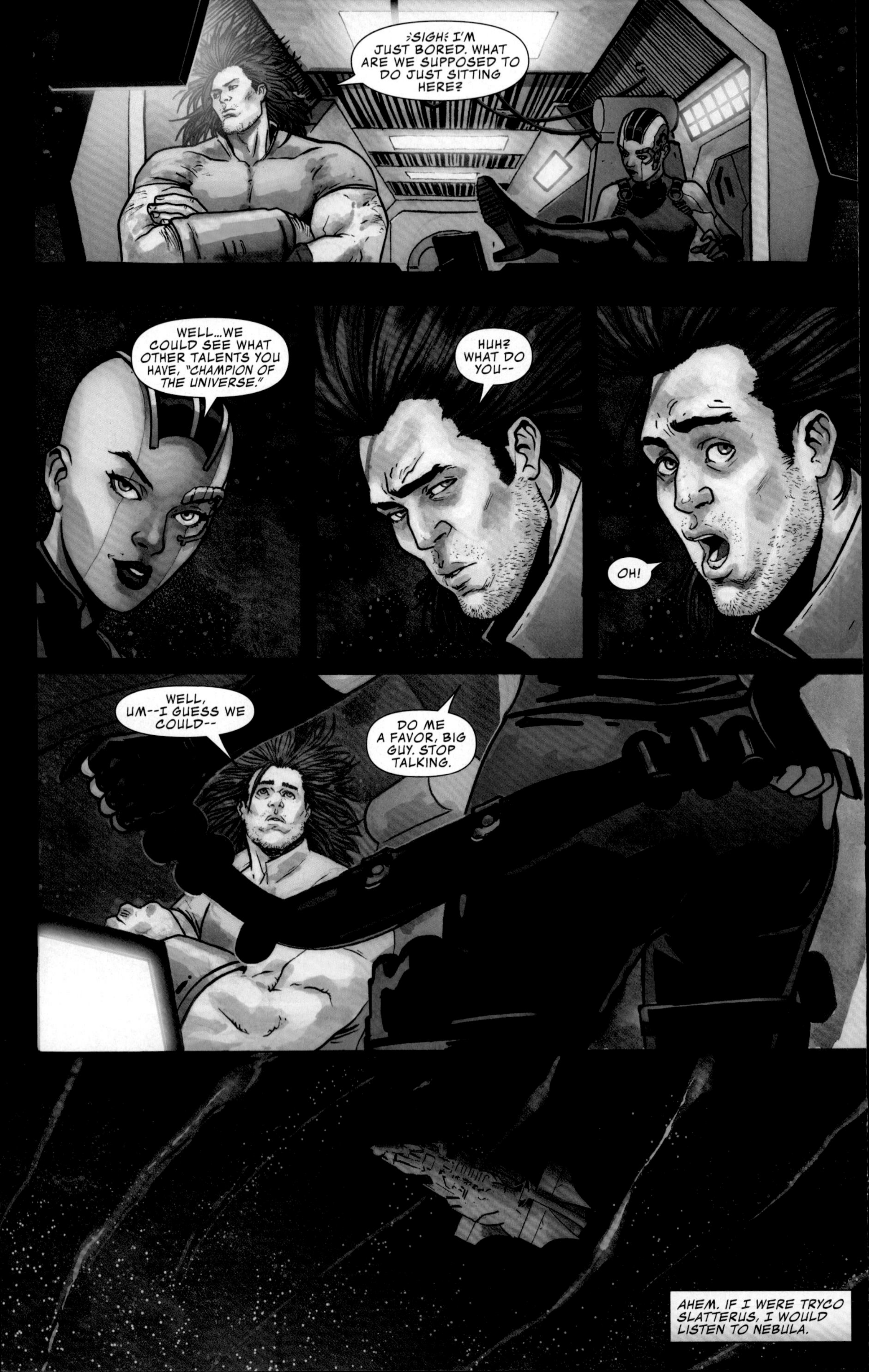

:SIGH: I'M JUST BORED. WHAT ARE WE SUPPOSED TO DO JUST SITTING HERE?
WELL...WE COULD SEE WHAT OTHER TALENTS YOU HAVE, "CHAMPION OF THE UNIVERSE."
HUH? WHAT DO YOU--
OH!
WELL, UM--I GUESS WE COULD--
DO ME A FAVOR, BIG GUY. STOP TALKING.
AHEM. IF I WERE TRYCO SLATTERUS, I WOULD LISTEN TO NEBULA.

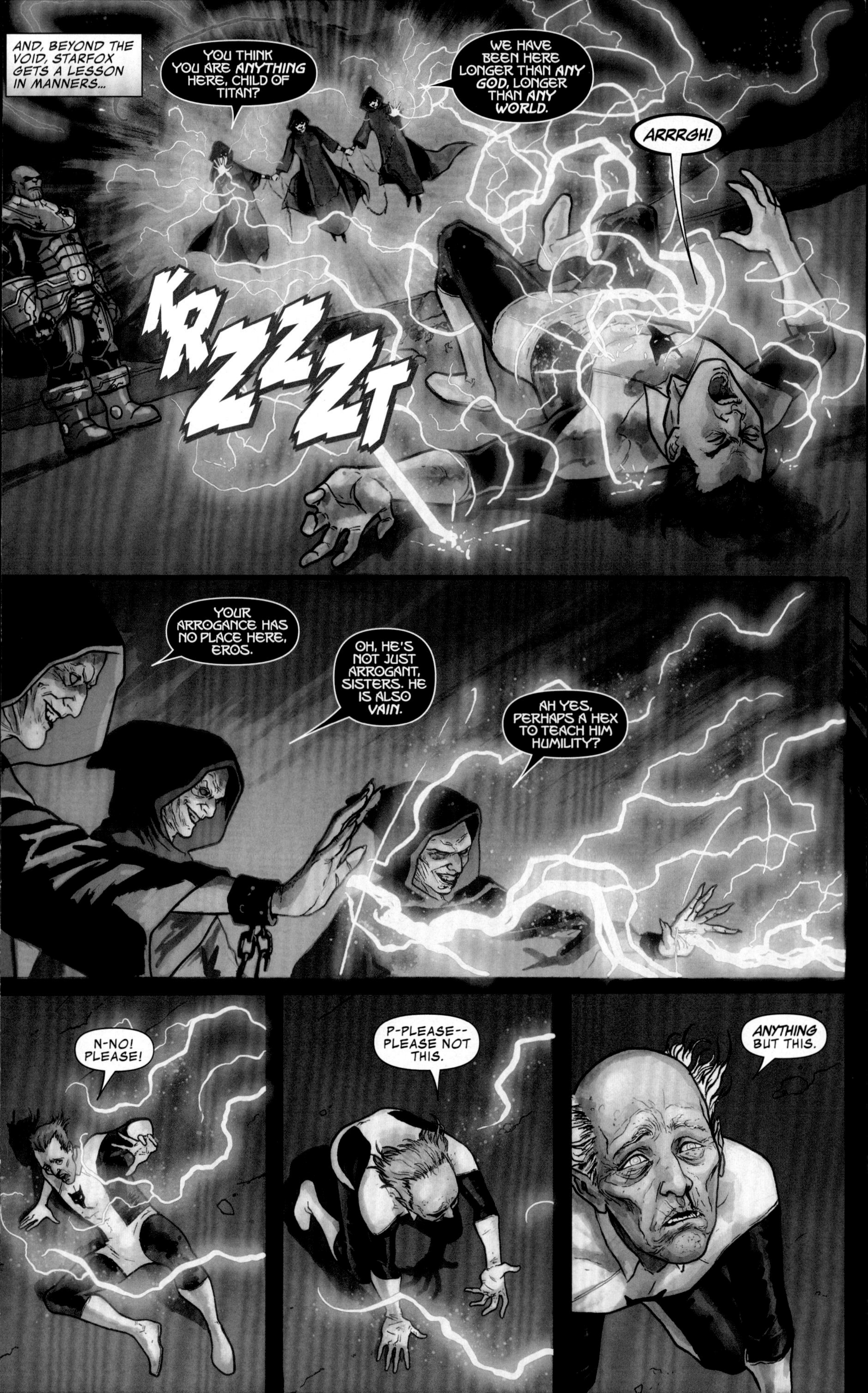
AND, BEYOND THE VOID, STARFOX GETS A LESSON IN MANNERS...
YOU THINK YOU ARE ANYTHING HERE, CHILD OF TITAN?
WE HAVE BEEN HERE LONGER THAN ANY GOD, LONGER THAN ANY WORLD.
ARRRGH!
KRZZZT
YOUR ARROGANCE HAS NO PLACE HERE, EROS.
OH, HE'S NOT JUST ARROGANT, SISTERS. HE IS ALSO VAIN.
AH YES, PERHAPS A HEX TO TEACH HIM HUMILITY?
N-NO! PLEASE!
P-PLEASE-- PLEASE NOT THIS.
ANYTHING BUT THIS.

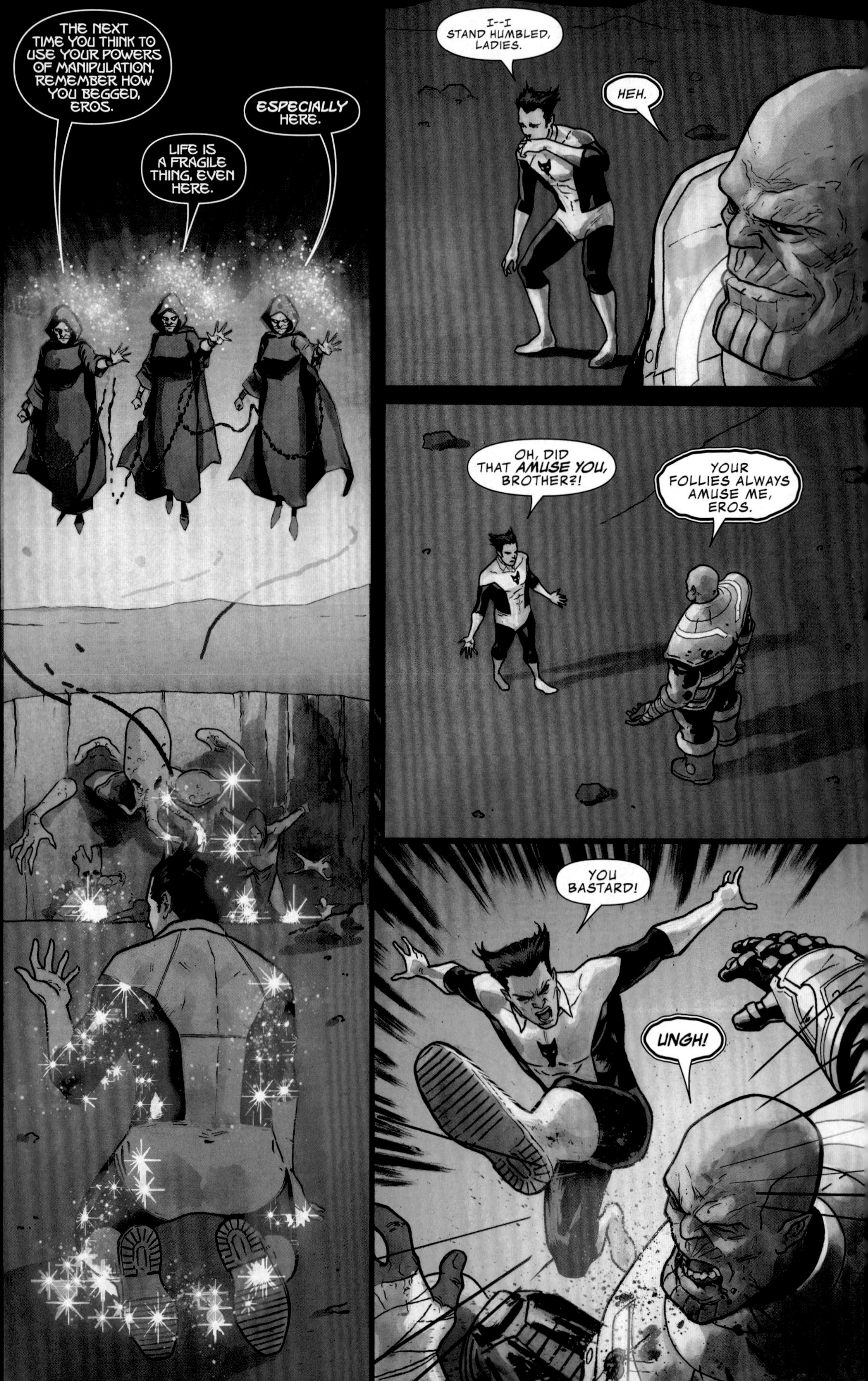
THE NEXT TIME YOU THINK TO USE YOUR POWERS OF MANIPULATION, REMEMBER HOW YOU BEGGED, EROS.
LIFE IS A FRAGILE THING, EVEN HERE.
ESPECIALLY HERE.
I--I STAND HUMBLED, LADIES.
HEH.
OH, DID THAT AMUSE YOU, BROTHER?!
YOUR FOLLIES ALWAYS AMUSE ME, EROS.
YOU BASTARD!
UNGH!

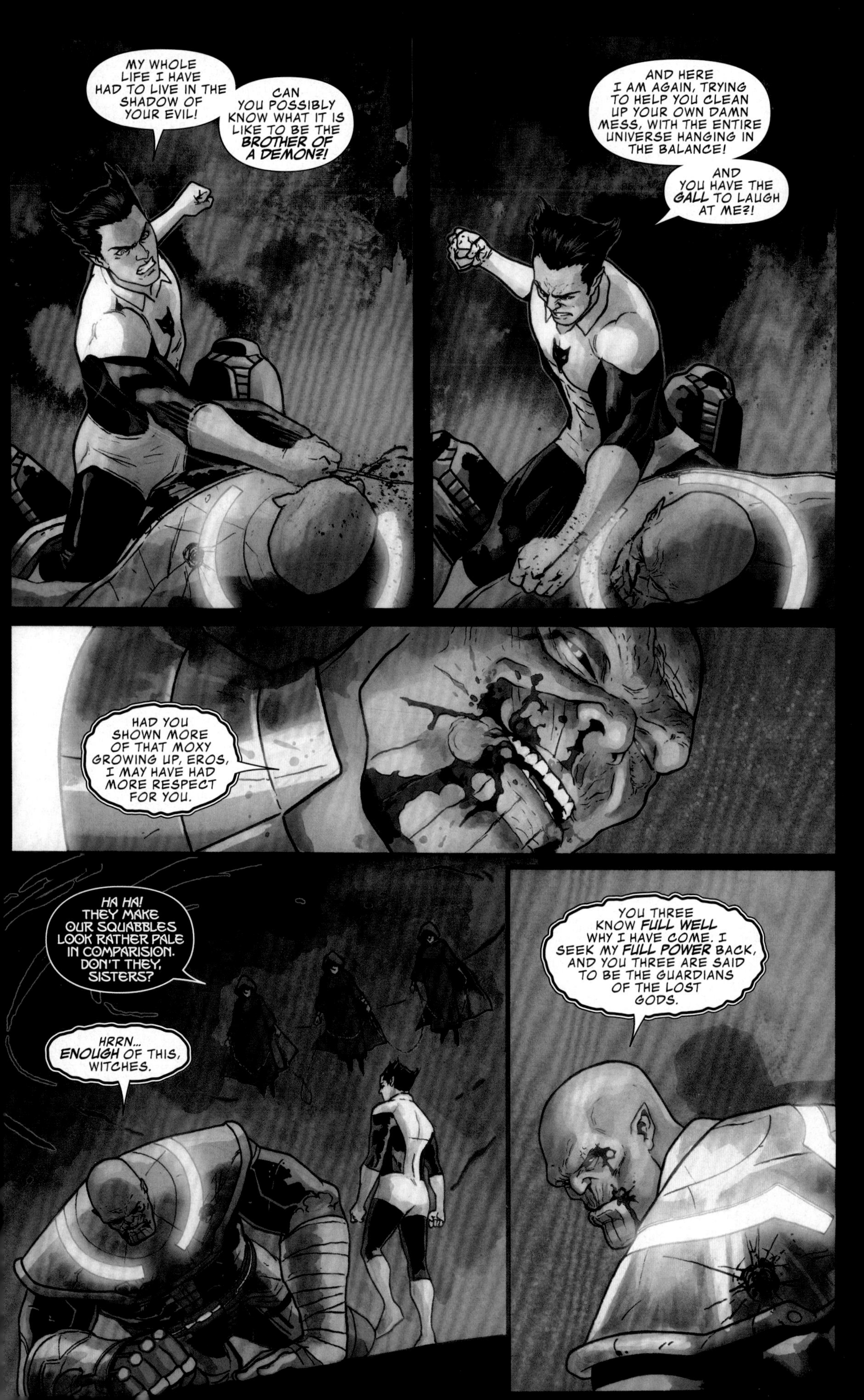
MY WHOLE LIFE I HAVE HAD TO LIVE IN THE SHADOW OF YOUR EVIL!
CAN YOU POSSIBLY KNOW WHAT IT IS LIKE TO BE THE BROTHER OF A DEMON?!
AND HERE I AM AGAIN, TRYING TO HELP YOU CLEAN UP YOUR OWN DAMN MESS, WITH THE ENTIRE UNIVERSE HANGING IN THE BALANCE!
AND YOU HAVE THE GALL TO LAUGH AT ME?!
HAD YOU SHOWN MORE OF THAT MOXY GROWING UP, EROS, I MAY HAVE HAD MORE RESPECT FOR YOU.
HA HA! THEY MAKE OUR SQUABBLES LOOK RATHER PALE IN COMPARISION. DON'T THEY, SISTERS?
HRRN... ENOUGH OF THIS, WITCHES.
YOU THREE KNOW FULL WELL WHY I HAVE COME. I SEEK MY FULL POWER BACK, AND YOU THREE ARE SAID TO BE THE GUARDIANS OF THE LOST GODS.

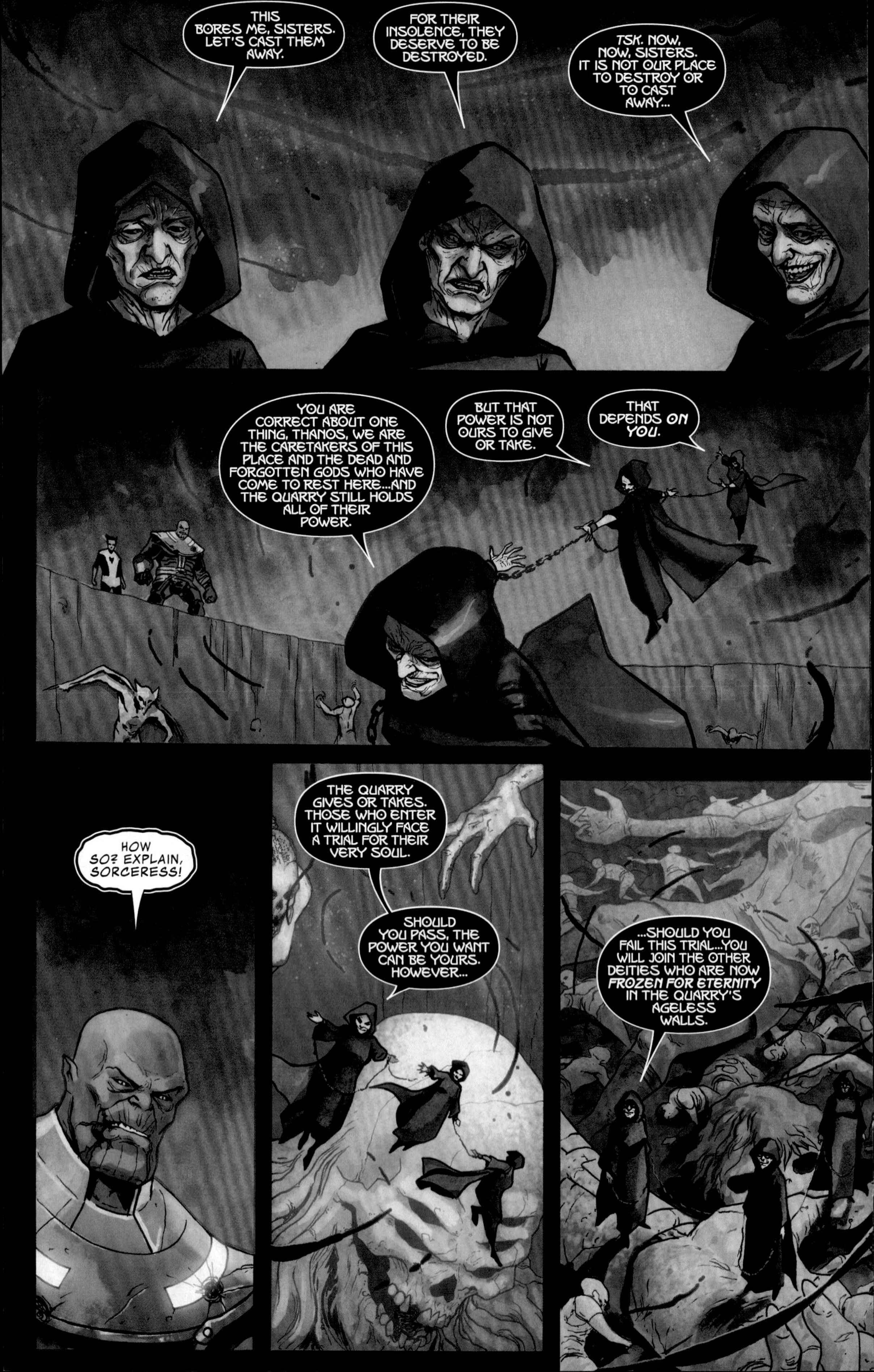
THIS BORES ME, SISTERS. LET'S CAST THEM AWAY.
FOR THEIR INSOLENCE, THEY DESERVE TO BE DESTROYED.
TSK. NOW, NOW, SISTERS. IT IS NOT OUR PLACE TO DESTROY OR TO CAST AWAY...
YOU ARE CORRECT ABOUT ONE THING, THANOS. WE ARE THE CARETAKERS OF THIS PLACE AND THE DEAD AND FORGOTTEN GODS WHO HAVE COME TO REST HERE...AND THE QUARRY STILL HOLDS ALL OF THEIR POWER.
BUT THAT POWER IS NOT OURS TO GIVE OR TAKE.
THAT DEPENDS ON YOU.
HOW SO? EXPLAIN, SORCERESS!
THE QUARRY GIVES OR TAKES. THOSE WHO ENTER IT WILLINGLY FACE A TRIAL FOR THEIR VERY SOUL.
SHOULD YOU PASS, THE POWER YOU WANT CAN BE YOURS. HOWEVER...
...SHOULD YOU FAIL THIS TRIAL...YOU WILL JOIN THE OTHER DEITIES WHO ARE NOW FROZEN FOR ETERNITY IN THE QUARRY'S AGELESS WALLS.

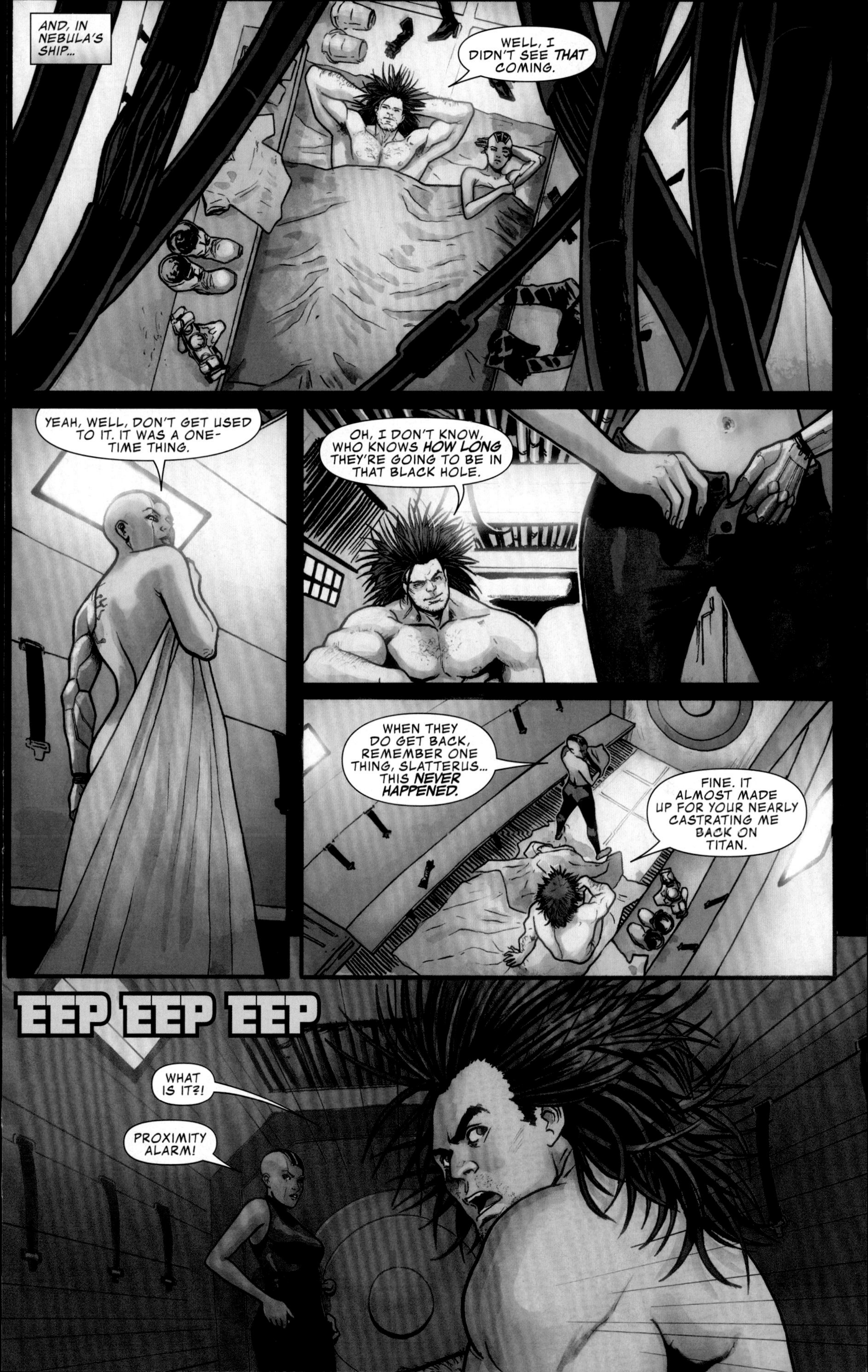
AND, IN NEBULA'S SHIP...
WELL, I DIDN'T SEE THAT COMING.
YEAH, WELL, DON'T GET USED TO IT. IT WAS A ONE-TIME THING.
OH, I DON'T KNOW, WHO KNOWS HOW LONG THEY'RE GOING TO BE IN THAT BLACK HOLE.
WHEN THEY DO GET BACK, REMEMBER ONE THING, SLATTERUS... THIS NEVER HAPPENED.
FINE. IT ALMOST MADE UP FOR YOUR NEARLY CASTRATING ME BACK ON TITAN.
EEP EEP EEP
WHAT IS IT?!
PROXIMITY ALARM!

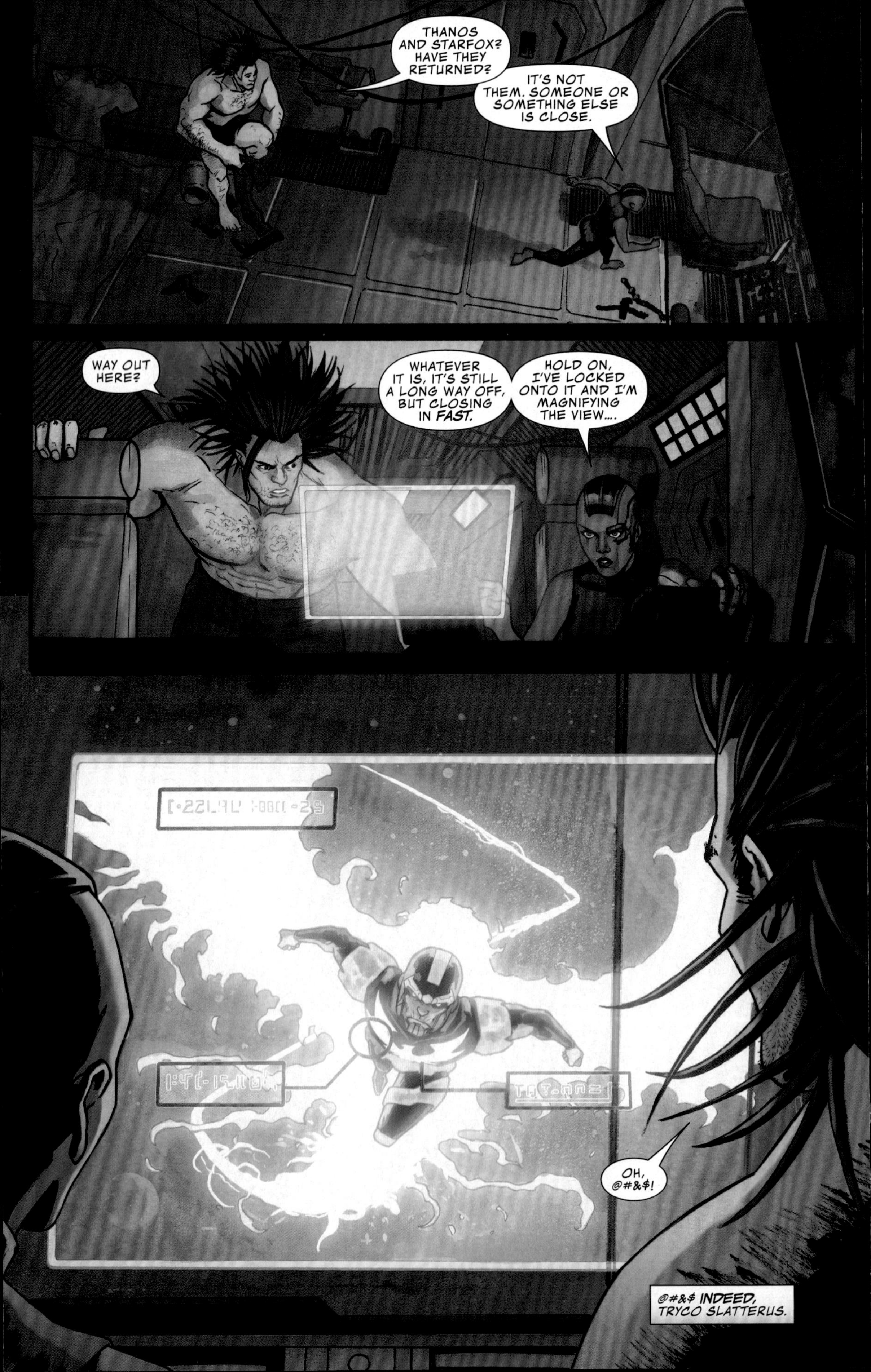
THANOS AND STARFOX? HAVE THEY RETURNED?
IT'S NOT THEM. SOMEONE OR SOMETHING ELSE IS CLOSE.
WAY OUT HERE?
WHATEVER IT IS, IT'S STILL A LONG WAY OFF, BUT CLOSING IN FAST.
HOLD ON, I'VE LOCKED ONTO IT AND I'M MAGNIFYING THE VIEW....
OH, @#&$!
@#&$ INDEED, TRYCO SLATTERUS.

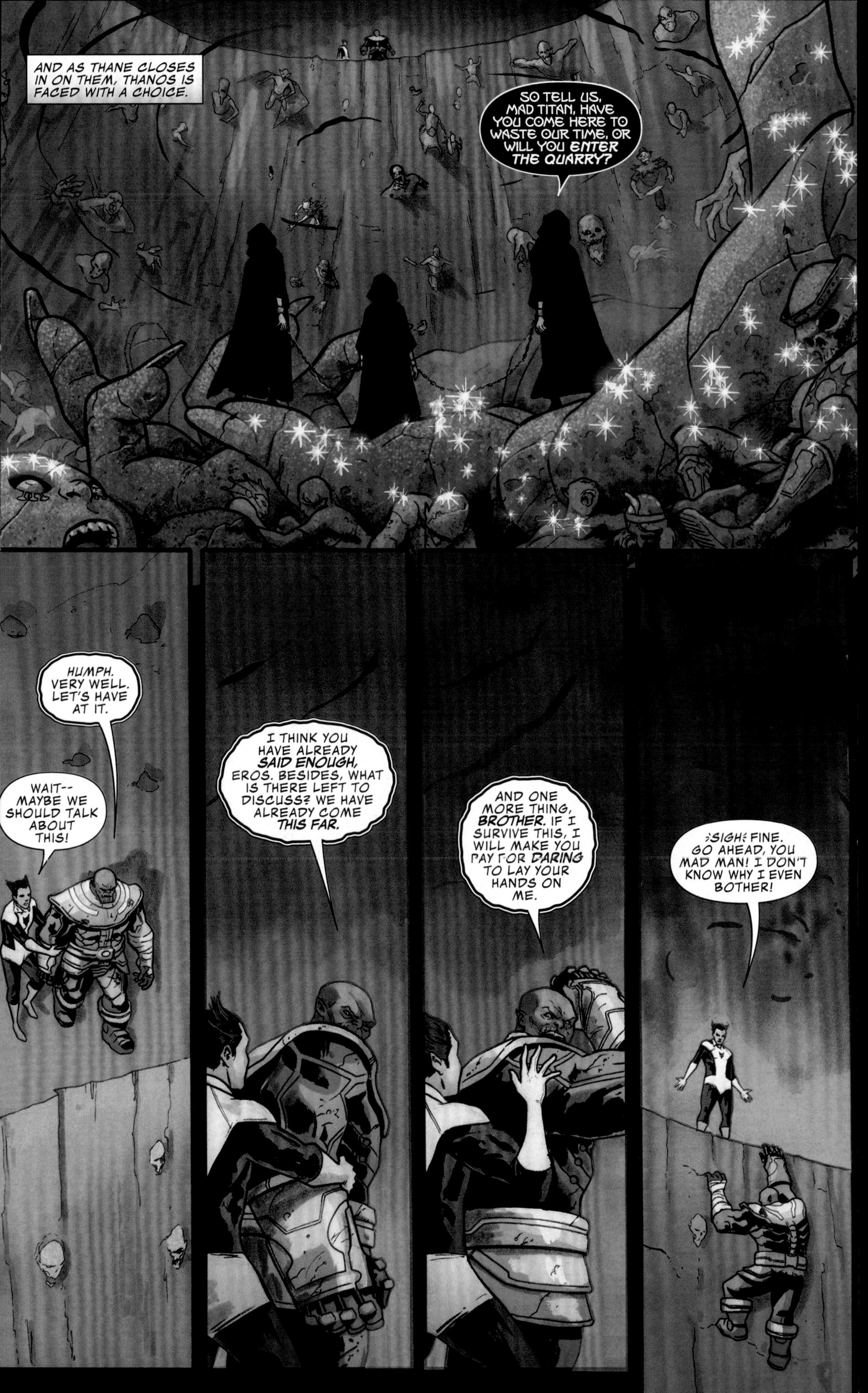
AND AS THANE CLOSES IN ON THEM, THANOS IS FACED WITH A CHOICE.
SO TELL US, MAD TITAN, HAVE YOU COME HERE TO WASTE OUR TIME, OR WILL YOU ENTER THE QUARRY?
HUMPH. VERY WELL. LET'S HAVE AT IT.
WAIT-- MAYBE WE SHOULD TALK ABOUT THIS!
I THINK YOU HAVE ALREADY SAID ENOUGH, EROS. BESIDES, WHAT IS THERE LEFT TO DISCUSS? WE HAVE ALREADY COME THIS FAR.
AND ONE MORE THING, BROTHER. IF I SURVIVE THIS, I WILL MAKE YOU PAY FOR DARING TO LAY YOUR HANDS ON ME.
SIGH FINE. GO AHEAD, YOU MAD MAN! I DON'T KNOW WHY I EVEN BOTHER!

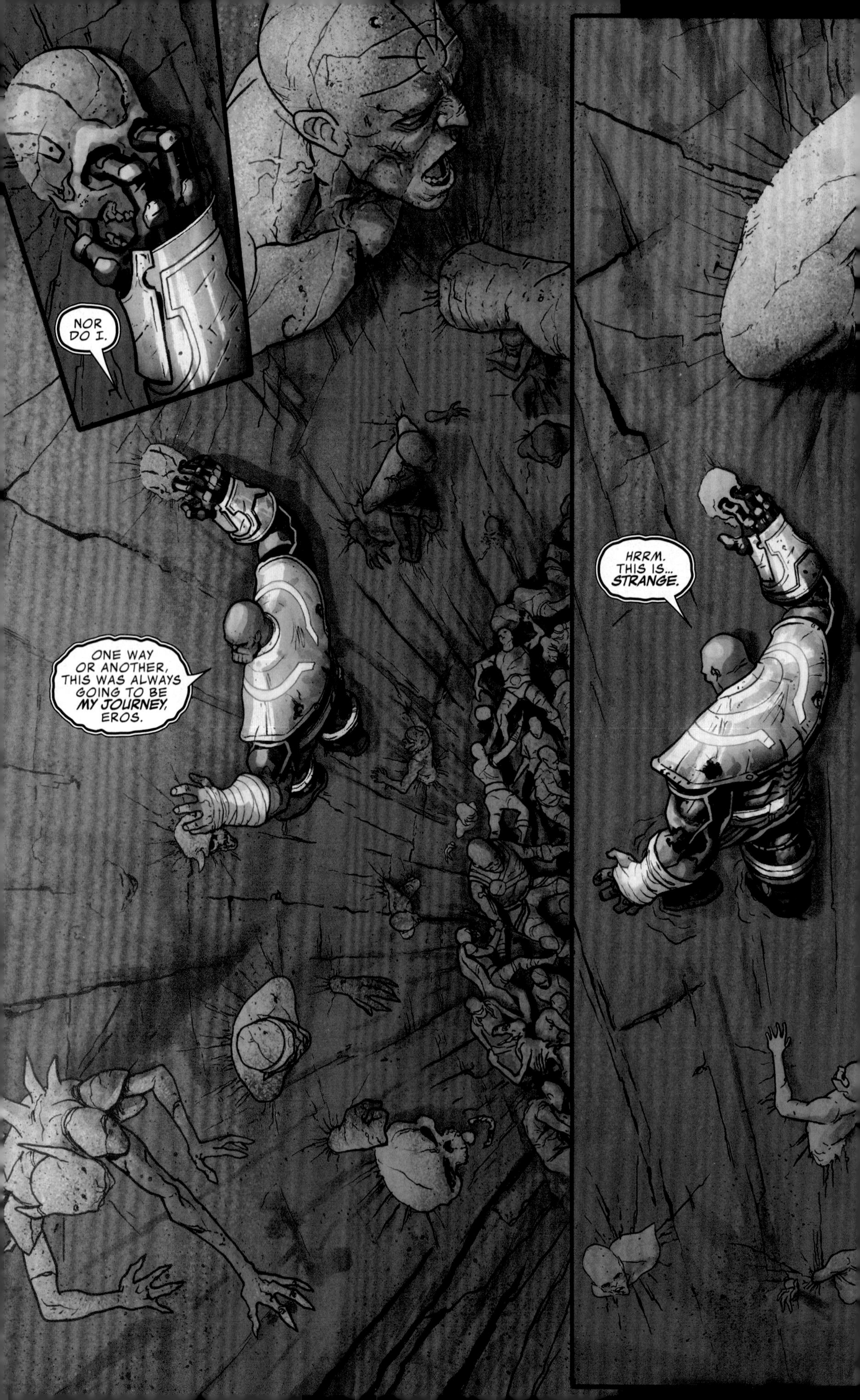
NOR DO I.
ONE WAY OR ANOTHER, THIS WAS ALWAYS GOING TO BE MY JOURNEY, EROS.
HRRM. THIS IS... STRANGE.

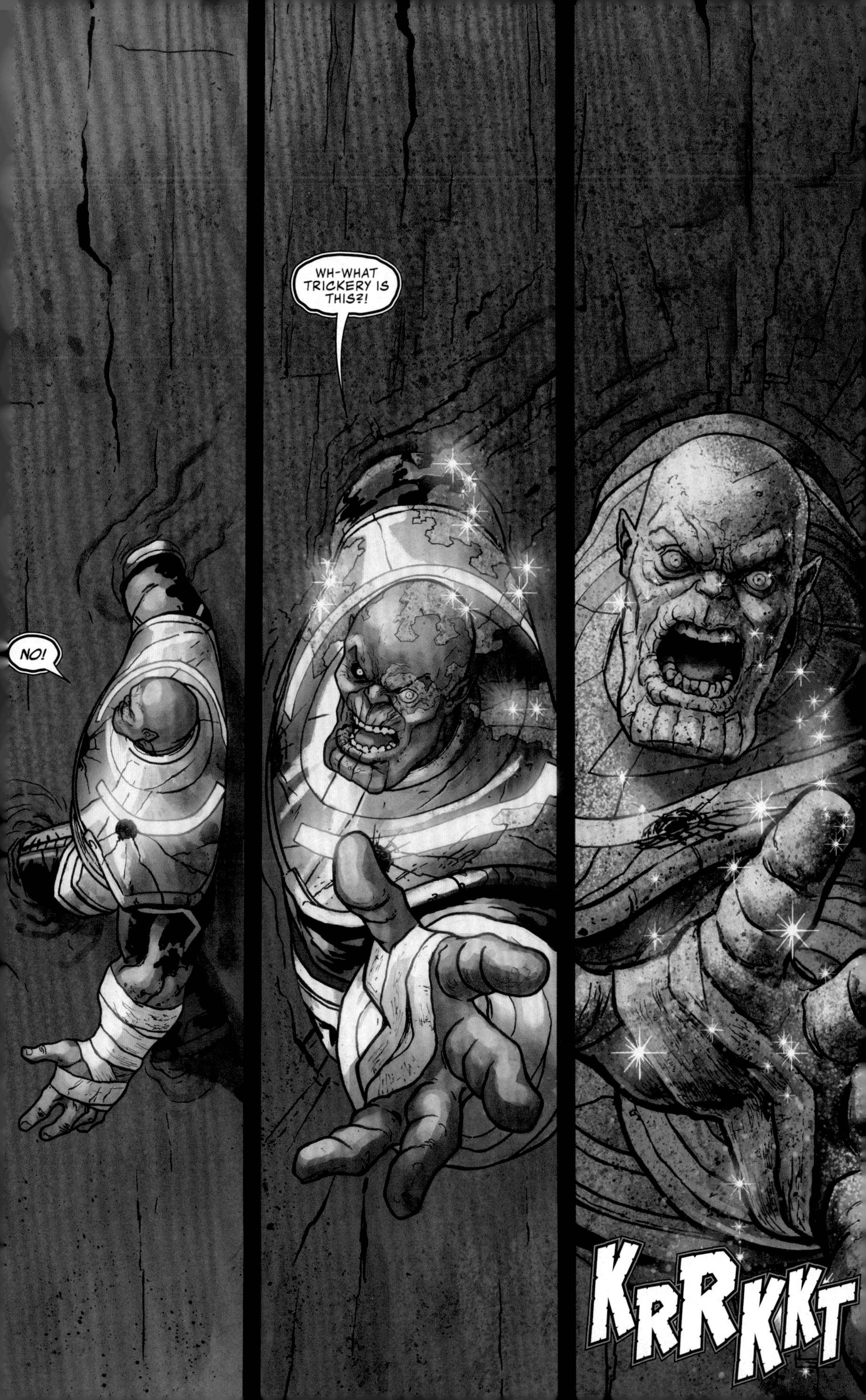
NO!
WH-WHAT TRICKERY IS THIS?!
KRRKKT

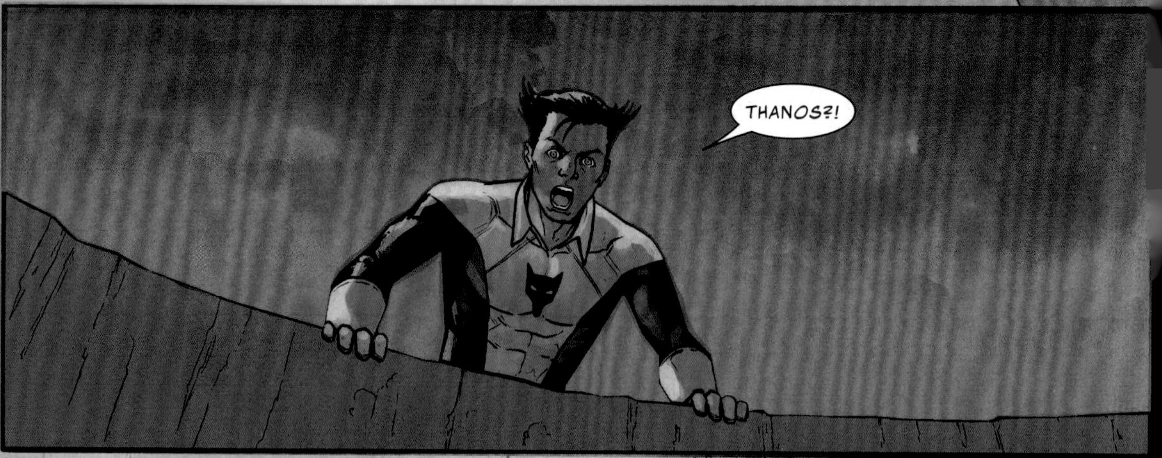
THANOS?!

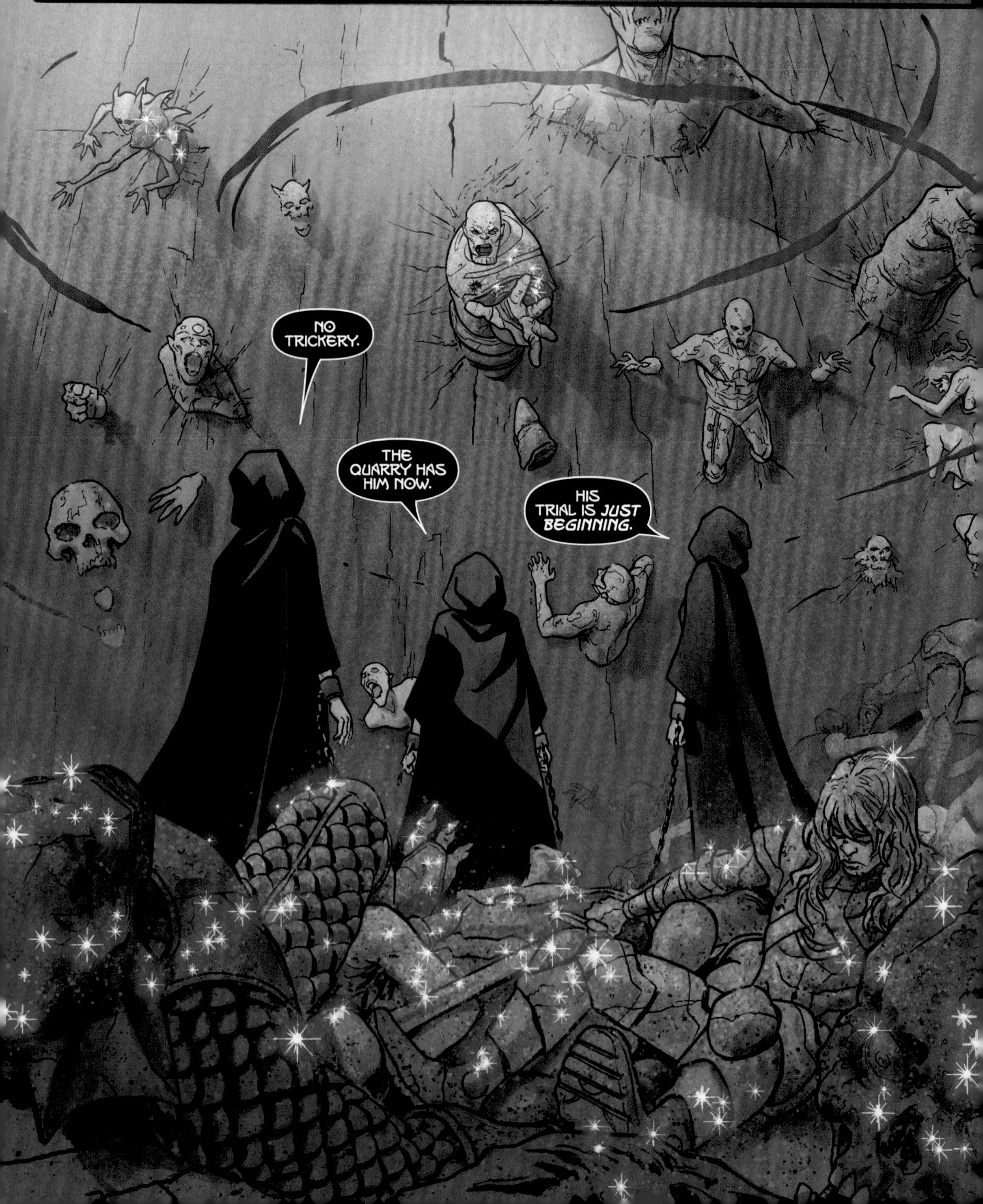
NO TRICKERY.
THE QUARRY HAS HIM NOW.
HIS TRIAL IS JUST BEGINNING.

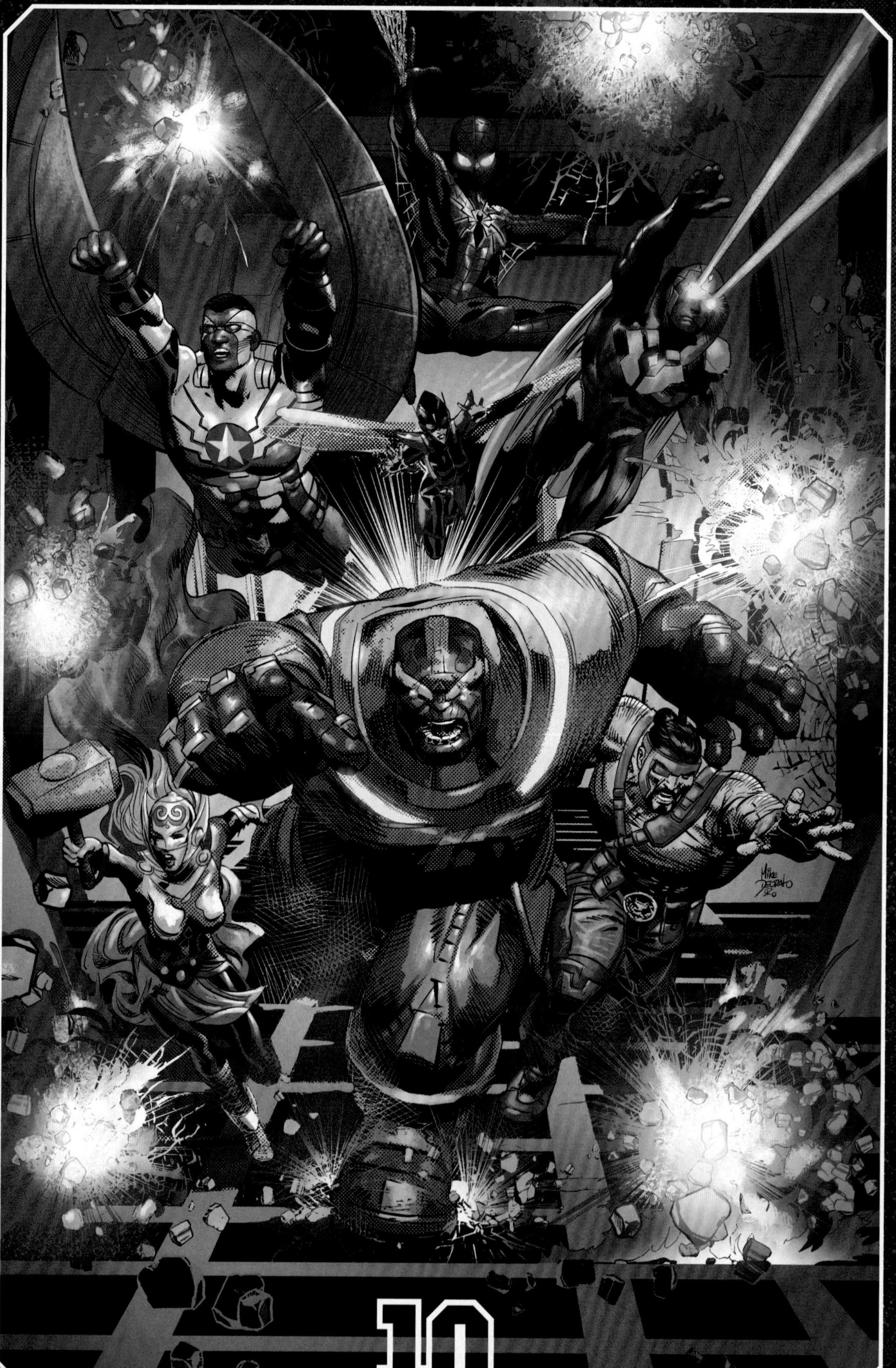
10

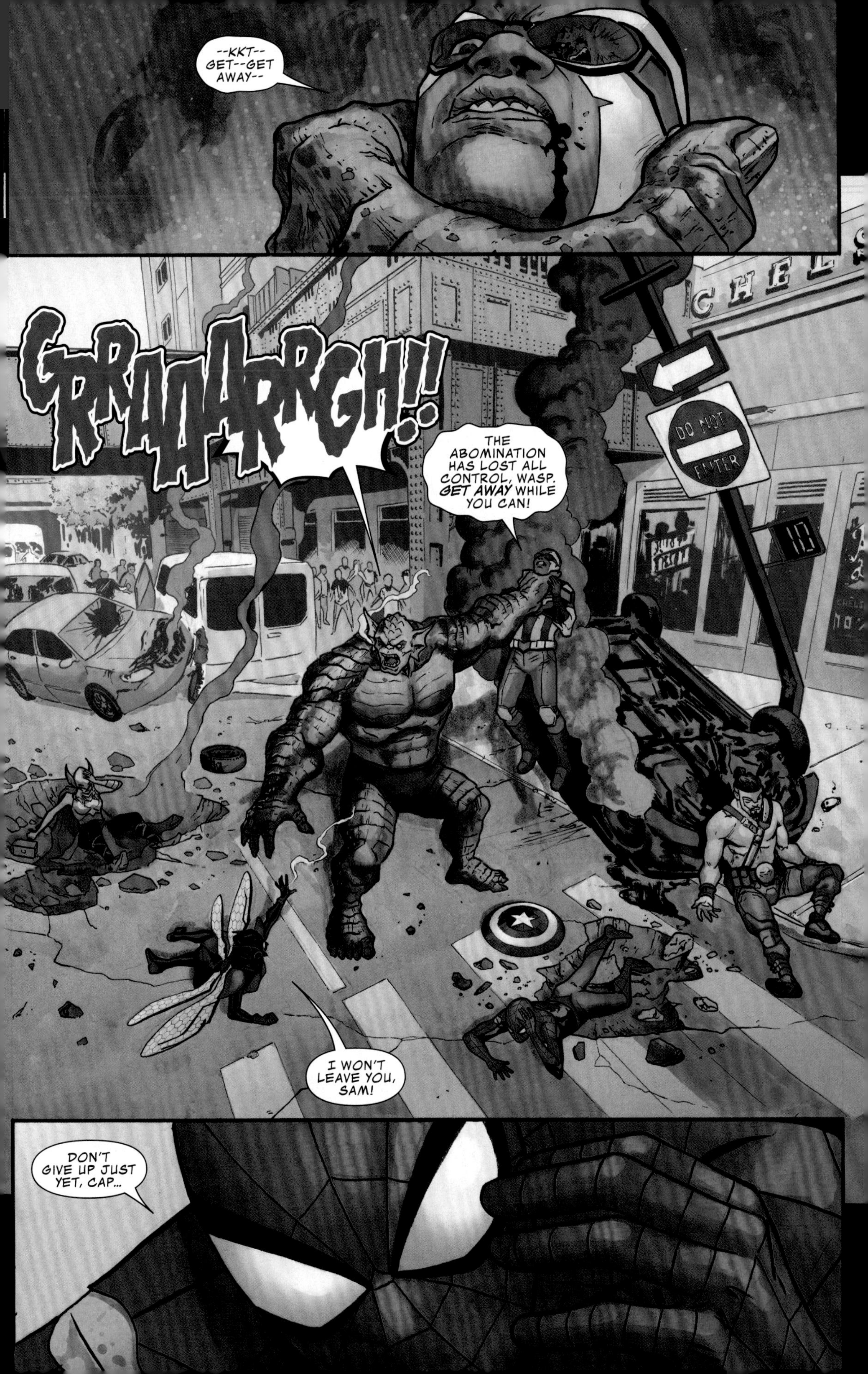
--KKT-- GET--GET AWAY--
GRAAARRGH!!
THE ABOMINATION HAS LOST ALL CONTROL, WASP. GET AWAY WHILE YOU CAN!
DO NOT ENTER
I WON'T LEAVE YOU, SAM!
DON'T GIVE UP JUST YET, CAP...

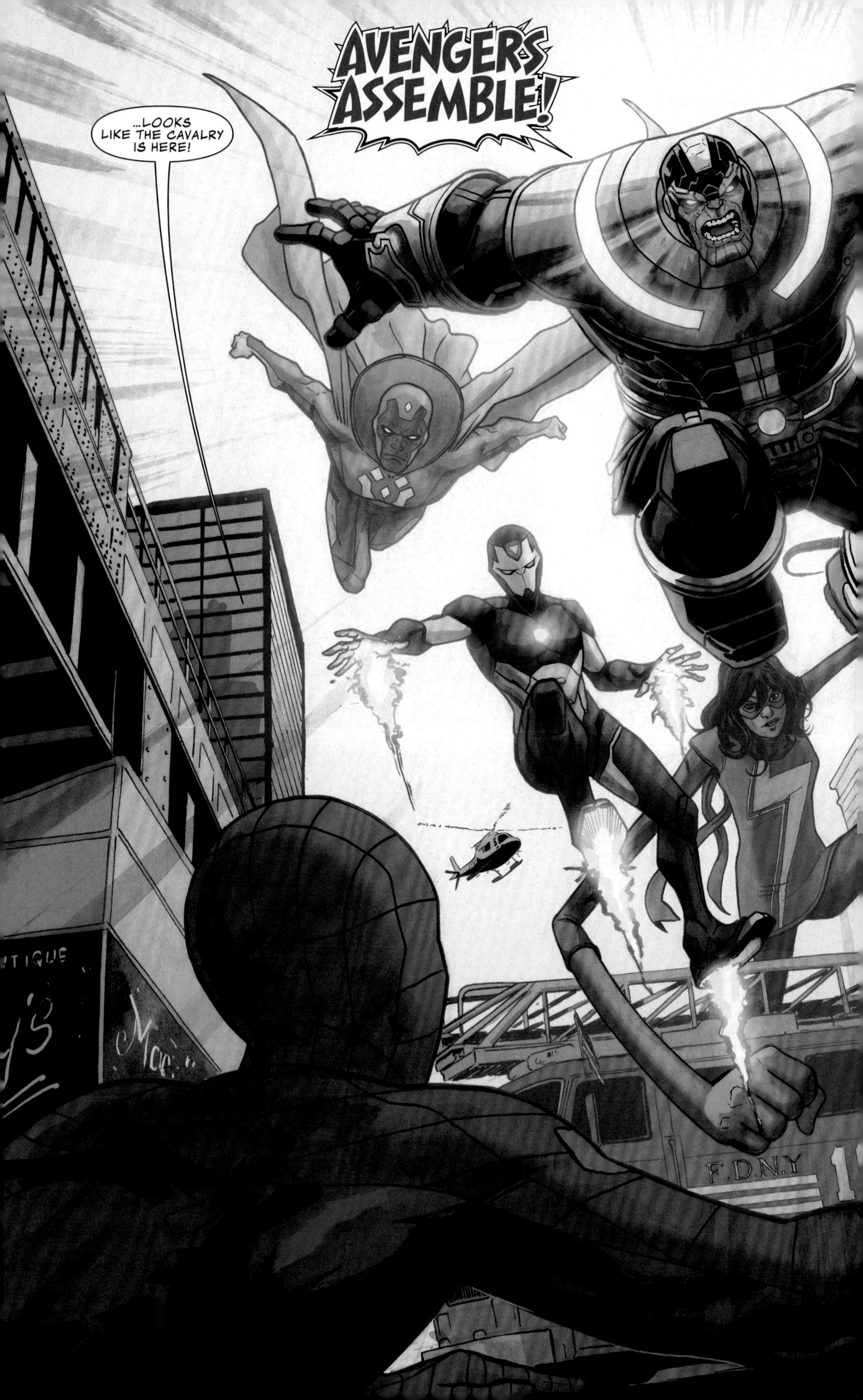
...LOOKS LIKE THE CAVALRY IS HERE!
AVENGERS ASSEMBLE!
F.D.N.Y

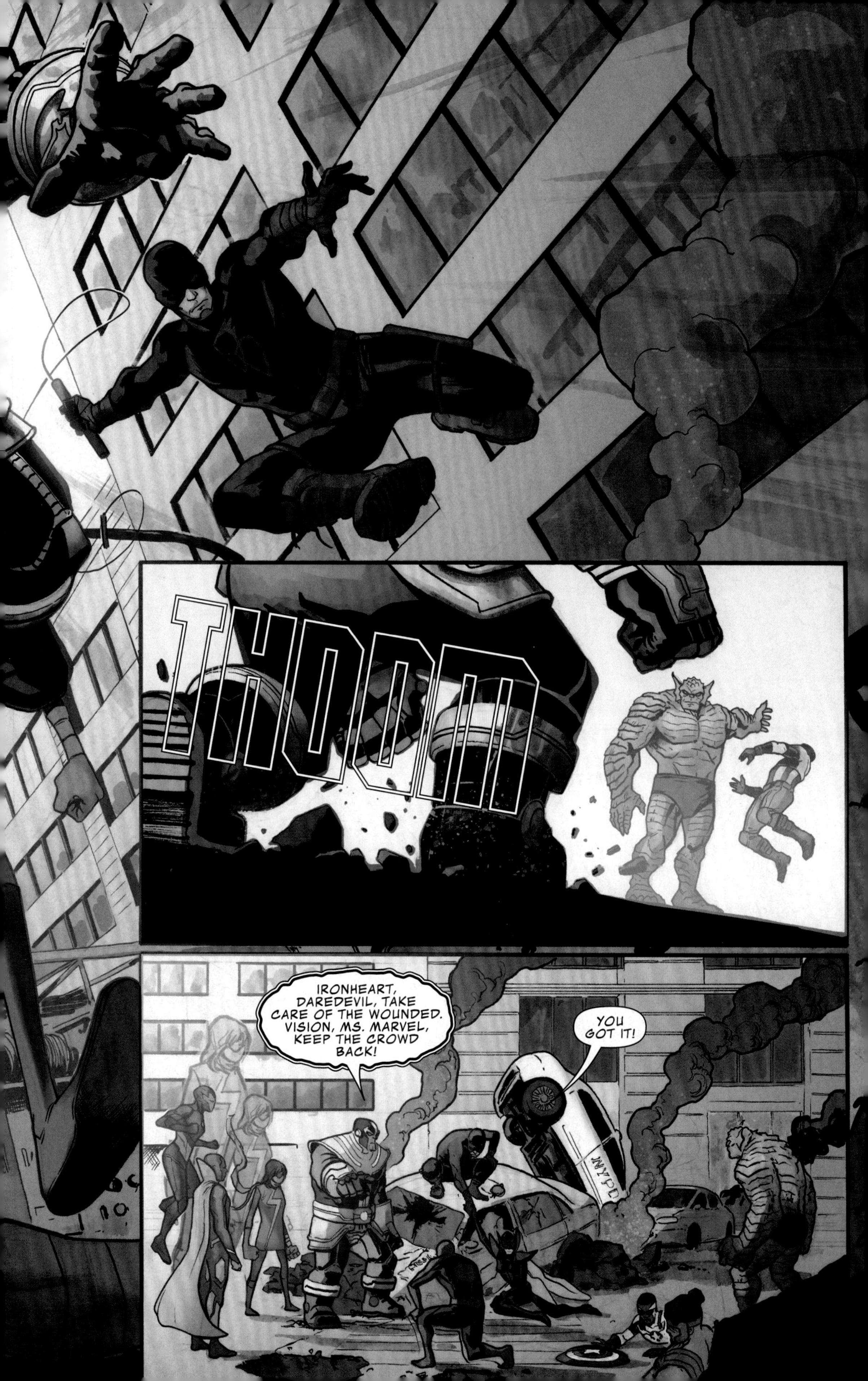
THOOM
IRONHEART, DAREDEVIL, TAKE CARE OF THE WOUNDED. VISION, MS. MARVEL, KEEP THE CROWD BACK!
YOU GOT IT!
NYPD

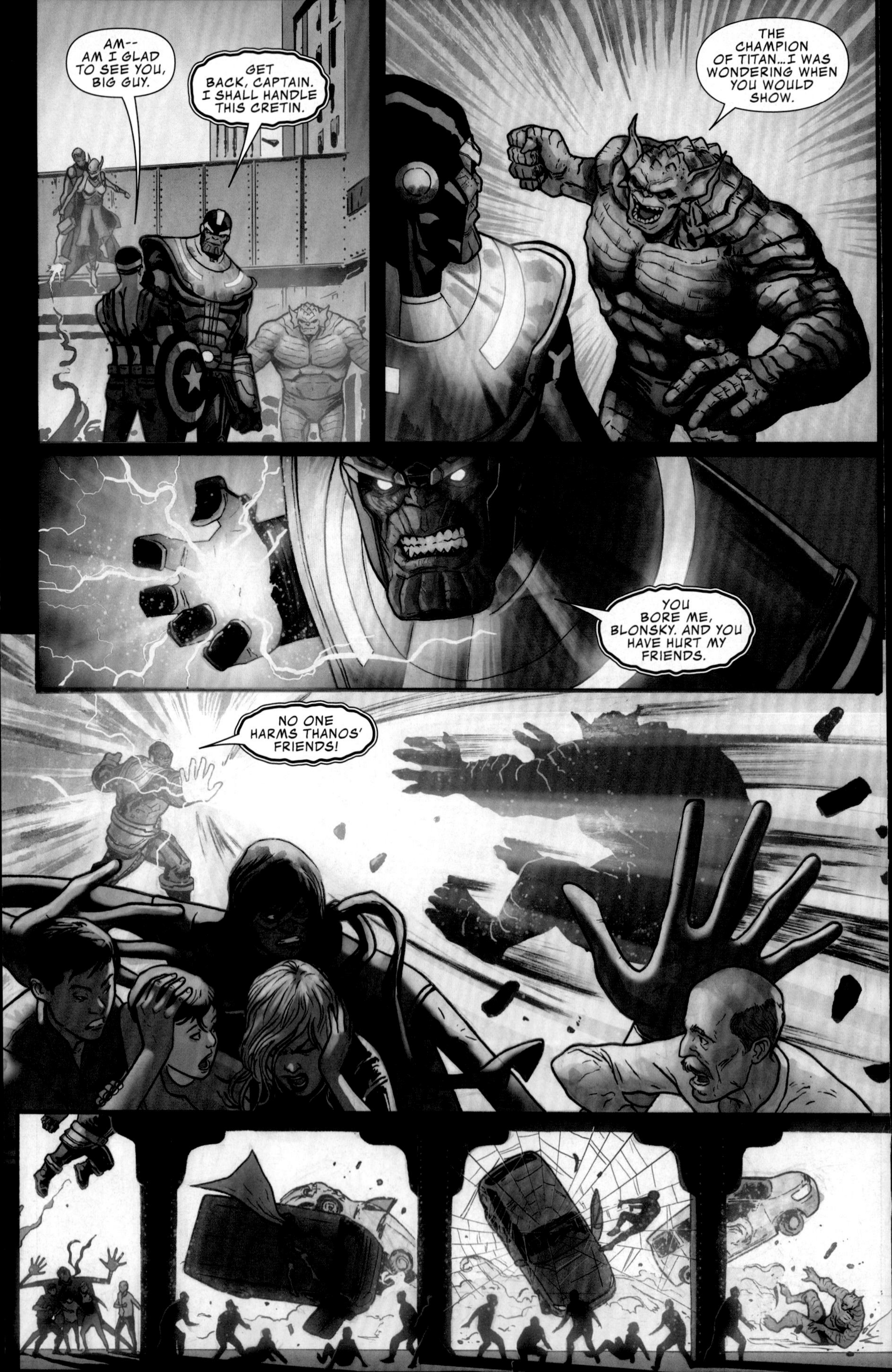
AM-- AM I GLAD TO SEE YOU, BIG GUY.
GET BACK, CAPTAIN. I SHALL HANDLE THIS CRETIN.
THE CHAMPION OF TITAN...I WAS WONDERING WHEN YOU WOULD SHOW.
YOU BORE ME, BLONSKY. AND YOU HAVE HURT MY FRIENDS.
NO ONE HARMS THANOS' FRIENDS!

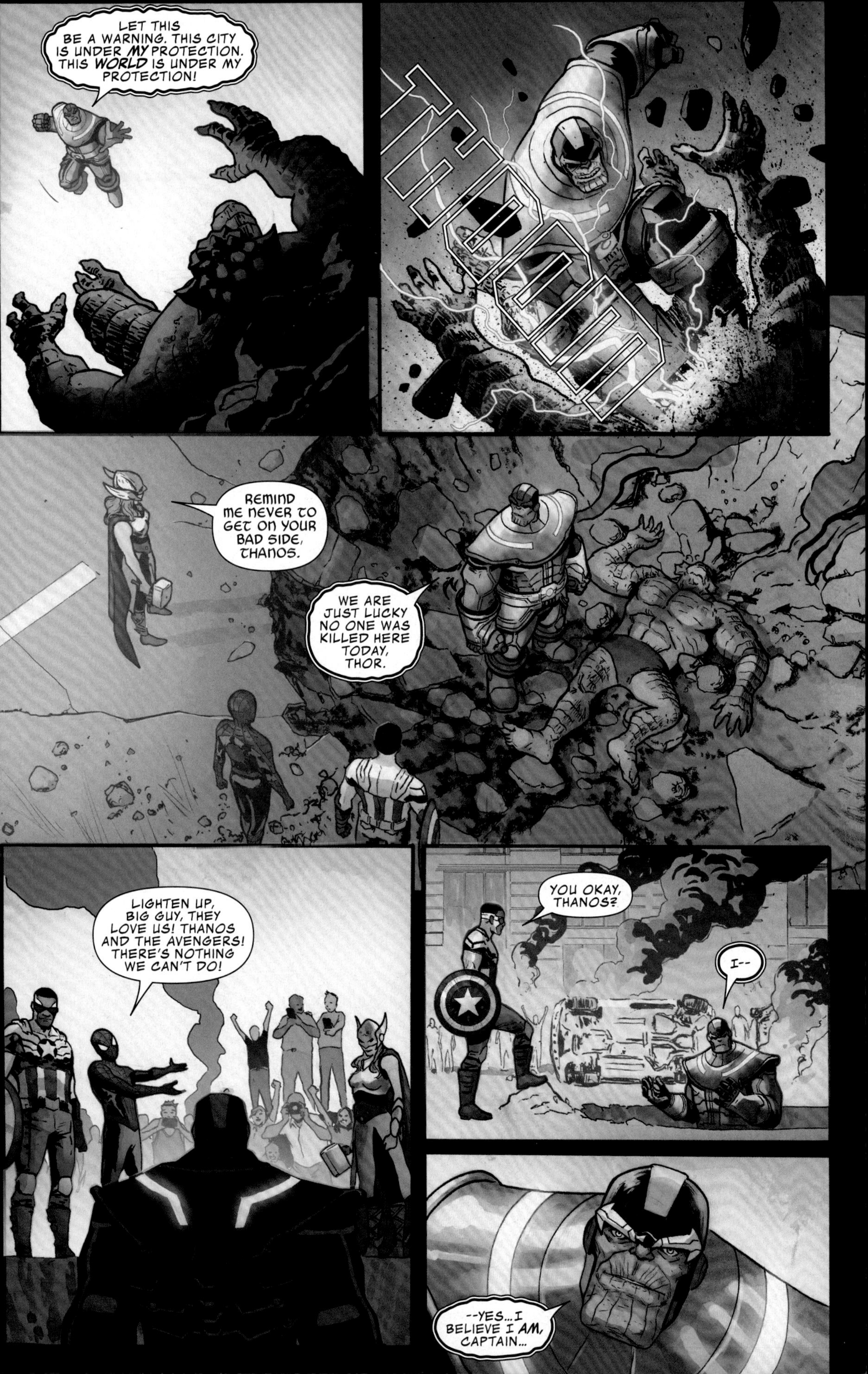
LET THIS BE A WARNING. THIS CITY IS UNDER MY PROTECTION. THIS WORLD IS UNDER MY PROTECTION!
THOOM
REMIND ME NEVER TO GET ON YOUR BAD SIDE, THANOS.
WE ARE JUST LUCKY NO ONE WAS KILLED HERE TODAY, THOR.
LIGHTEN UP, BIG GUY, THEY LOVE US! THANOS AND THE AVENGERS! THERE'S NOTHING WE CAN'T DO!
YOU OKAY, THANOS?
I--
--YES...I BELIEVE I AM, CAPTAIN...

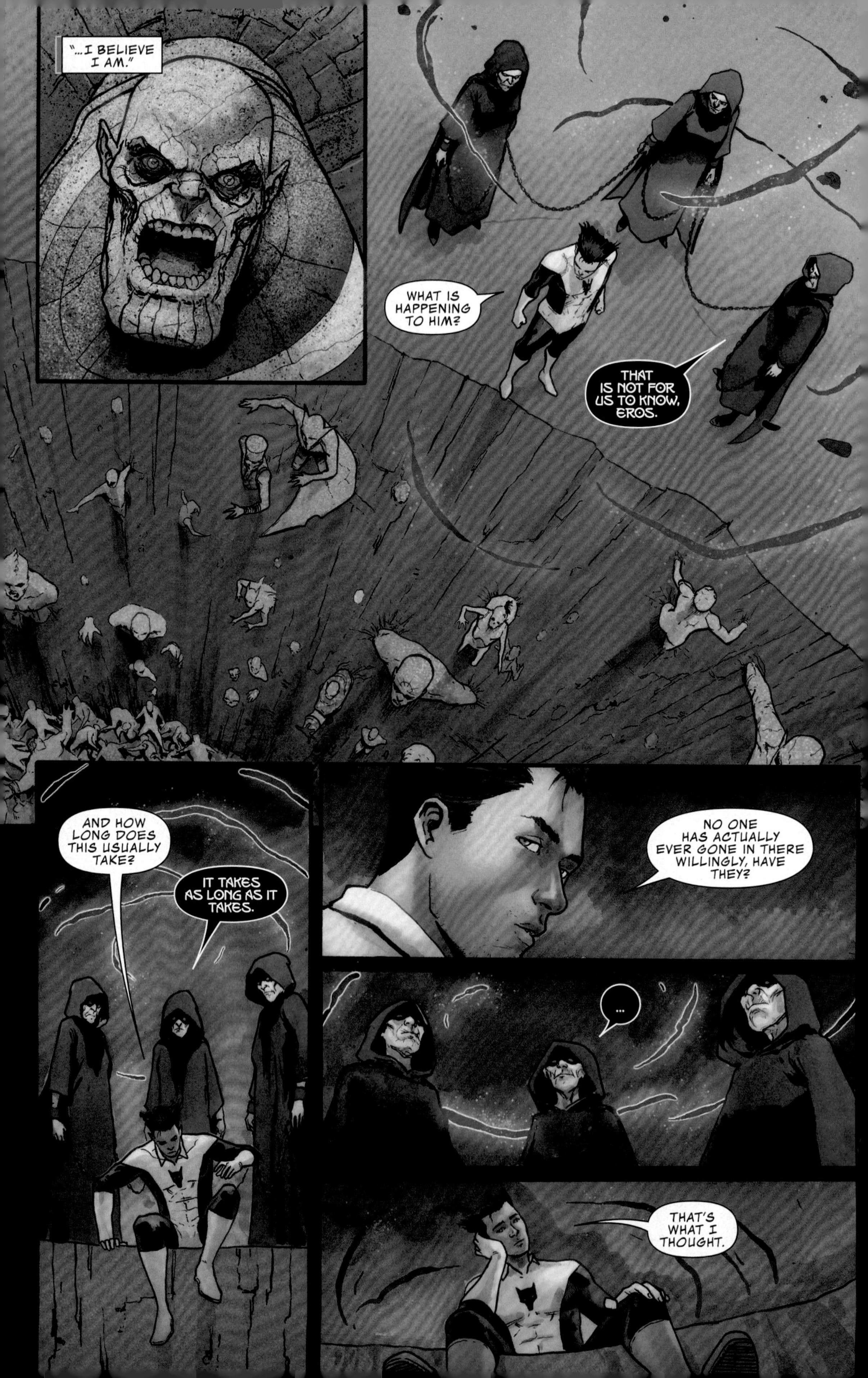
"...I BELIEVE I AM."
WHAT IS HAPPENING TO HIM?
THAT IS NOT FOR US TO KNOW, EROS.
AND HOW LONG DOES THIS USUALLY TAKE?
IT TAKES AS LONG AS IT TAKES.
NO ONE HAS ACTUALLY EVER GONE IN THERE WILLINGLY, HAVE THEY?
...
THAT'S WHAT I THOUGHT.

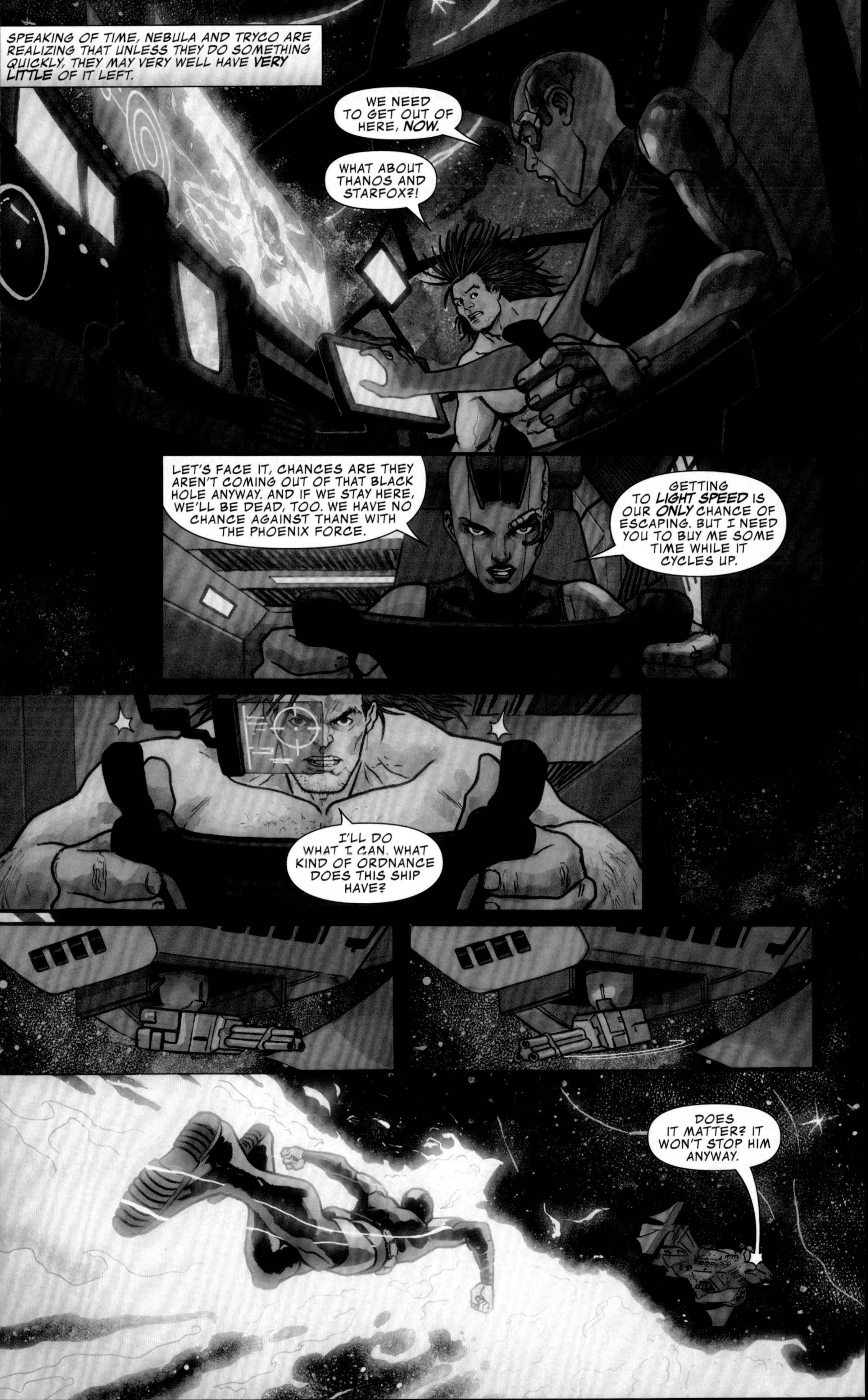
SPEAKING OF TIME, NEBULA AND TRYCO ARE REALIZING THAT UNLESS THEY DO SOMETHING QUICKLY, THEY MAY VERY WELL HAVE **VERY LITTLE** OF IT LEFT.
WE NEED TO GET OUT OF HERE, **NOW.**
WHAT ABOUT THANOS AND STARFOX?!
LET'S FACE IT, CHANCES ARE THEY AREN'T COMING OUT OF THAT BLACK HOLE ANYWAY. AND IF WE STAY HERE, WE'LL BE DEAD, TOO. WE HAVE NO CHANCE AGAINST THANE WITH THE PHOENIX FORCE.
GETTING TO **LIGHT SPEED** IS OUR **ONLY** CHANCE OF ESCAPING. BUT I NEED YOU TO BUY ME SOME TIME WHILE IT CYCLES UP.
I'LL DO WHAT I CAN. WHAT KIND OF ORDNANCE DOES THIS SHIP HAVE?
DOES IT MATTER? IT WON'T STOP HIM ANYWAY.

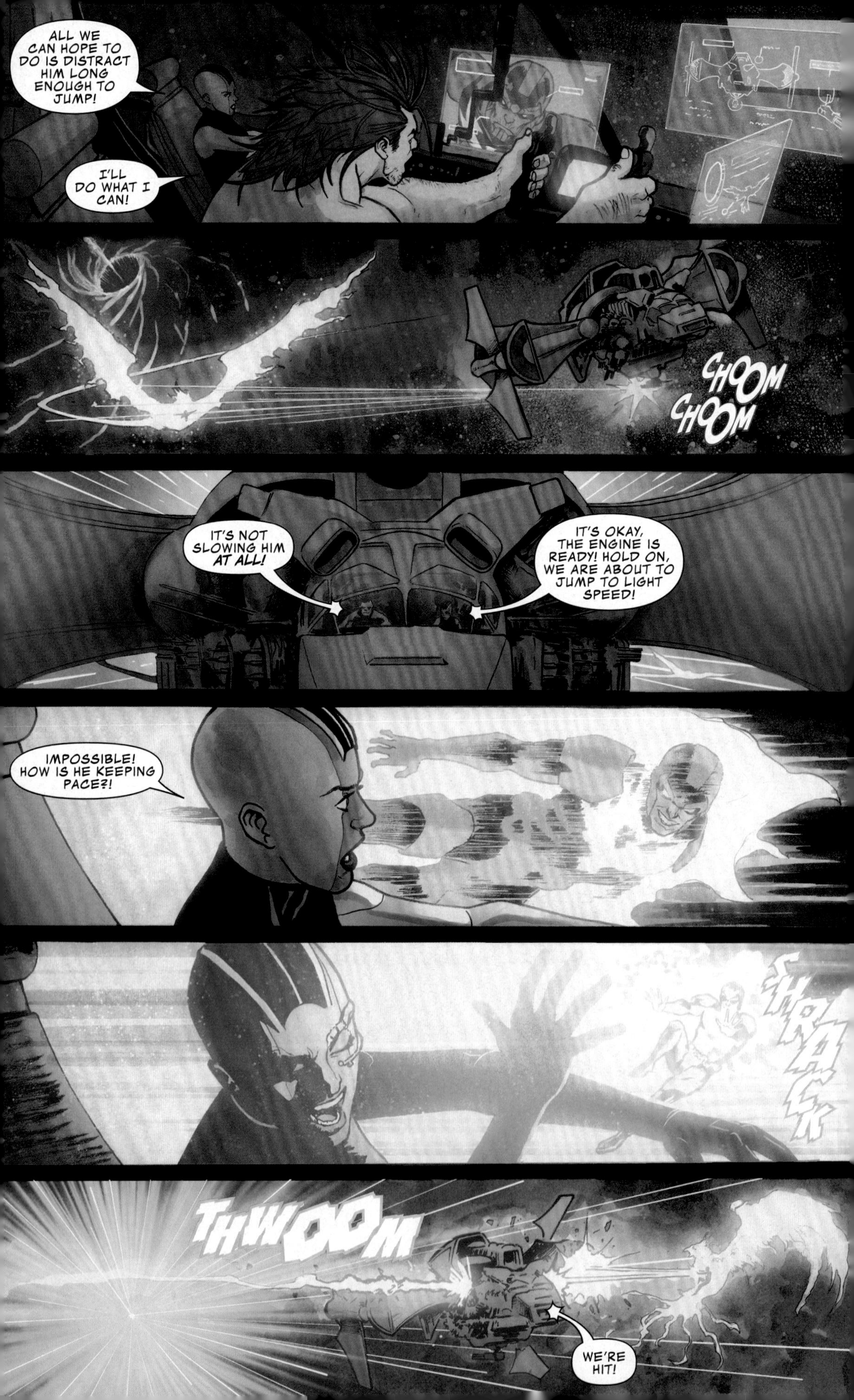
ALL WE CAN HOPE TO DO IS DISTRACT HIM LONG ENOUGH TO JUMP!
I'LL DO WHAT I CAN!
CHOOM CHOOM
IT'S NOT SLOWING HIM AT ALL!
IT'S OKAY, THE ENGINE IS READY! HOLD ON, WE ARE ABOUT TO JUMP TO LIGHT SPEED!
IMPOSSIBLE! HOW IS HE KEEPING PACE?!
SHRACK
THWOOM
WE'RE HIT!

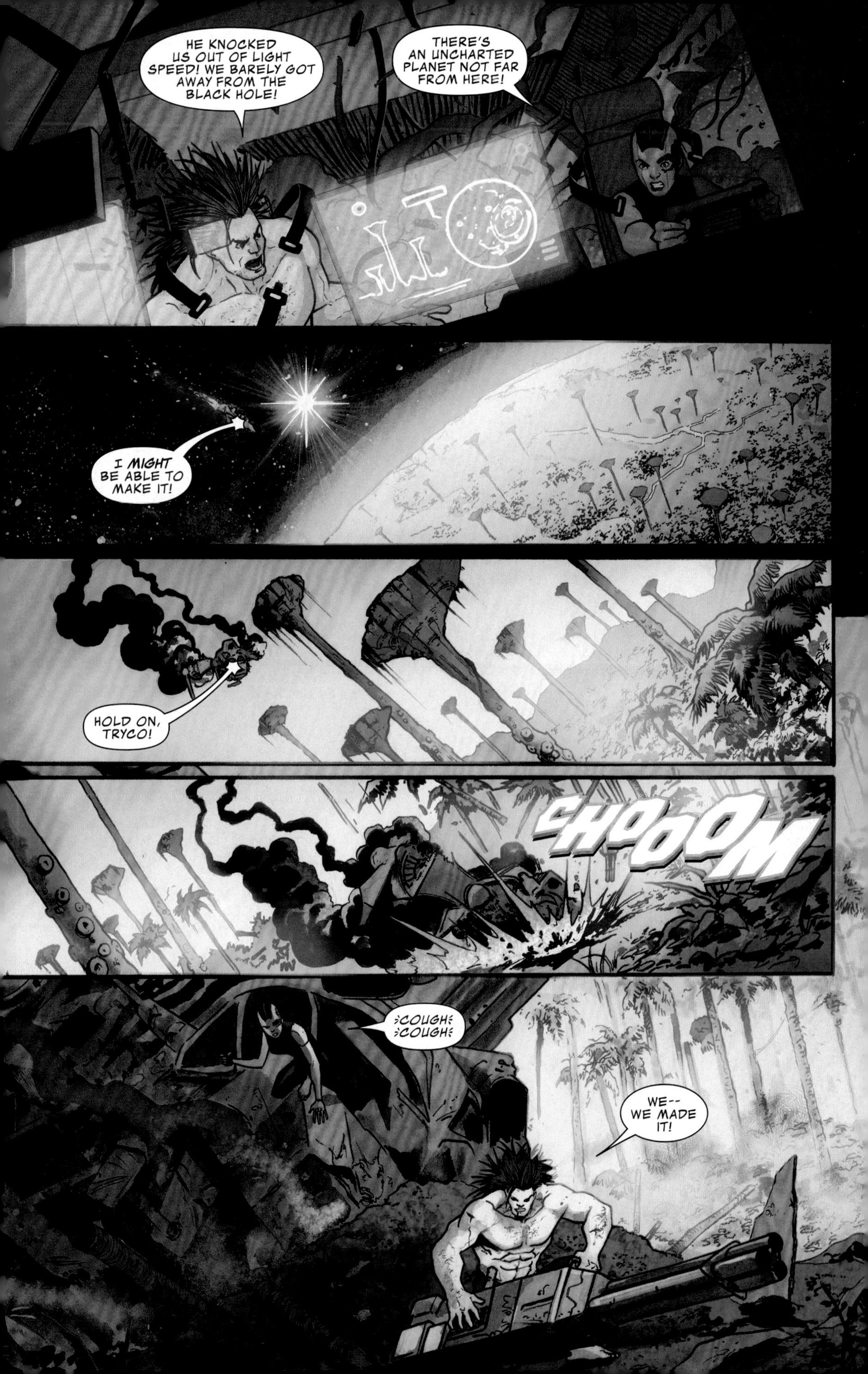
HE KNOCKED US OUT OF LIGHT SPEED! WE BARELY GOT AWAY FROM THE BLACK HOLE!
THERE'S AN UNCHARTED PLANET NOT FAR FROM HERE!
I MIGHT BE ABLE TO MAKE IT!
HOLD ON, TRYCO!
CHOOOM
COUGH COUGH
WE-- WE MADE IT!

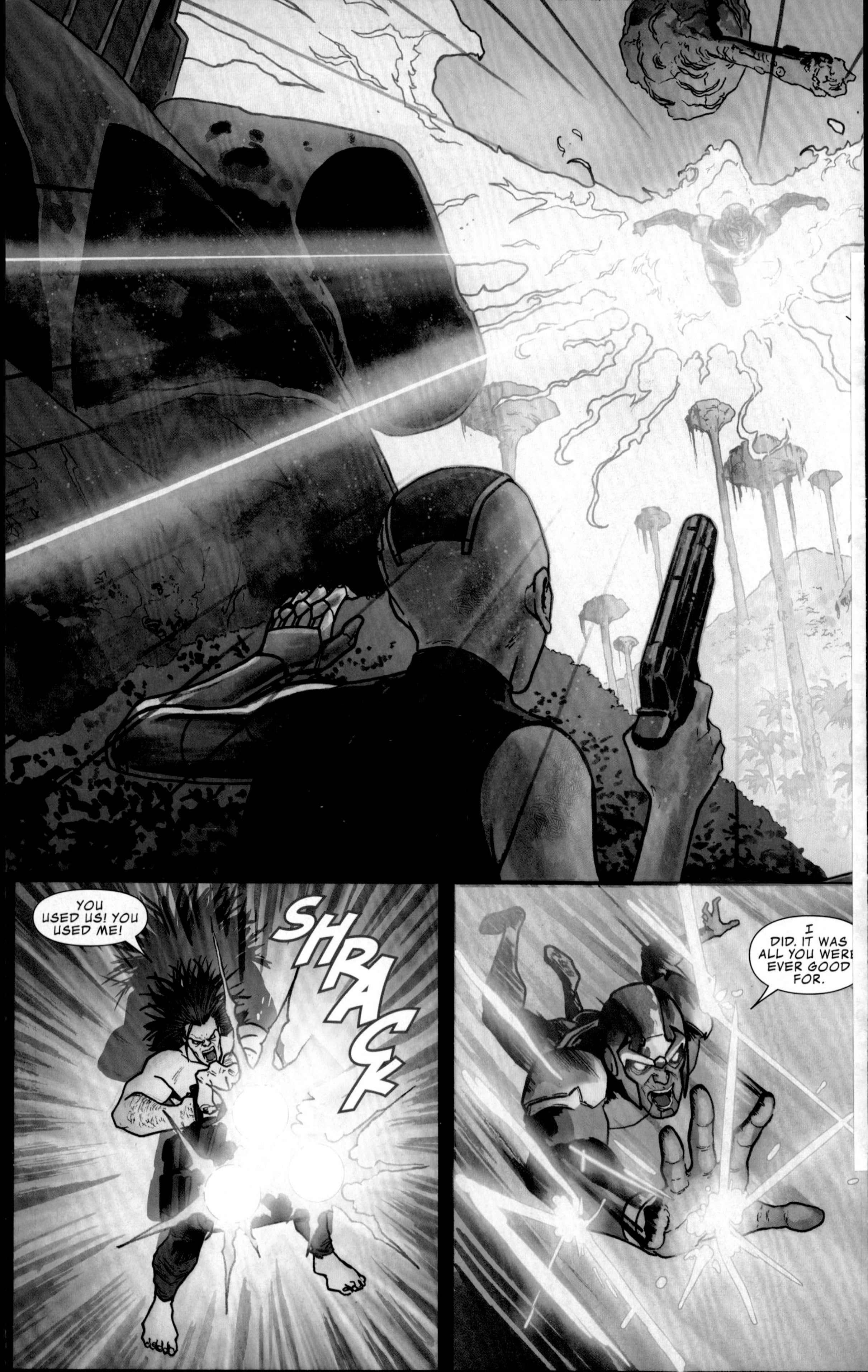
YOU USED US! YOU USED ME!
SHRACK
I DID. IT WAS ALL YOU WERE EVER GOOD FOR.

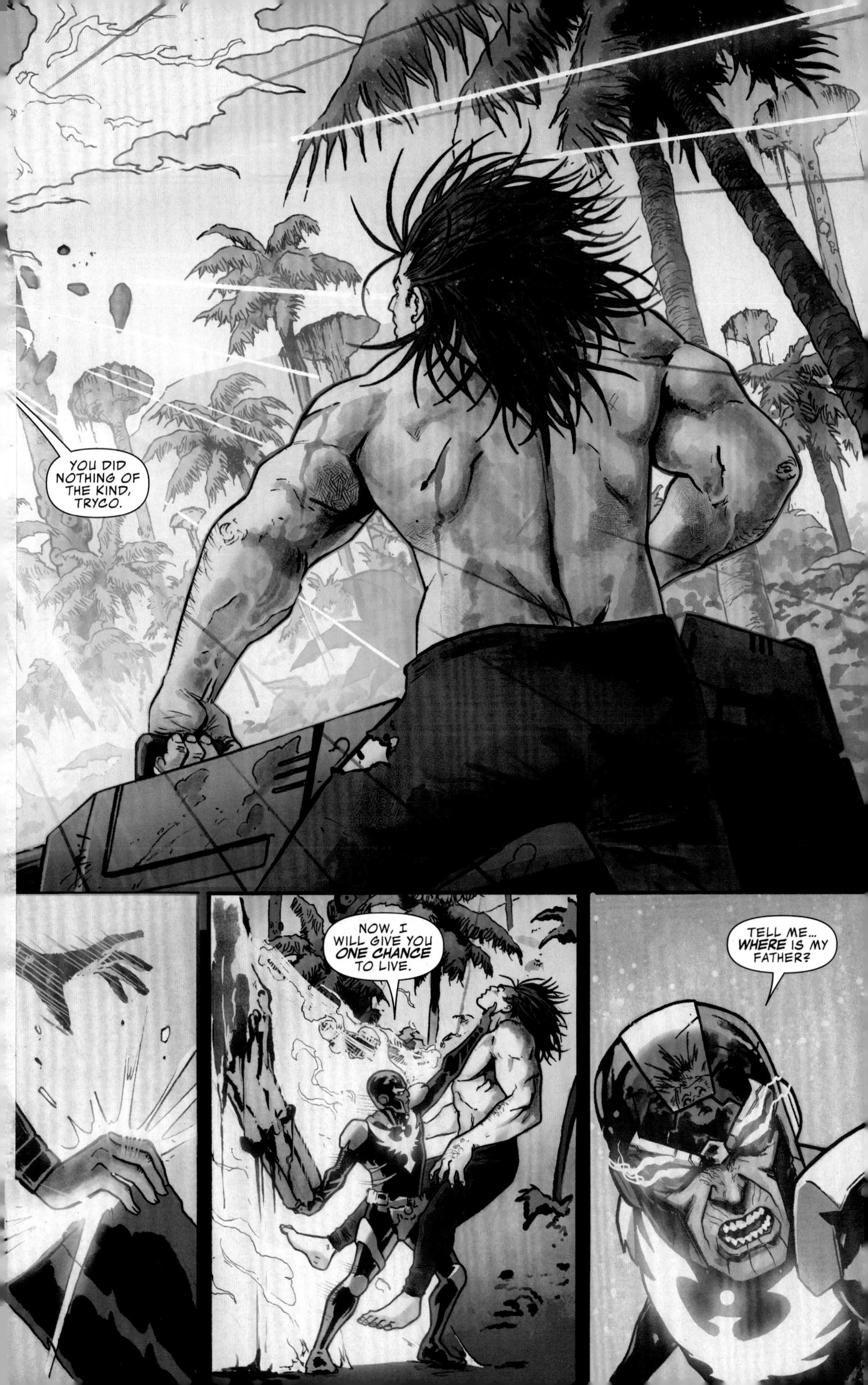
YOU DID NOTHING OF THE KIND, TRYCO.
NOW, I WILL GIVE YOU ONE CHANCE TO LIVE.
TELL ME... WHERE IS MY FATHER?

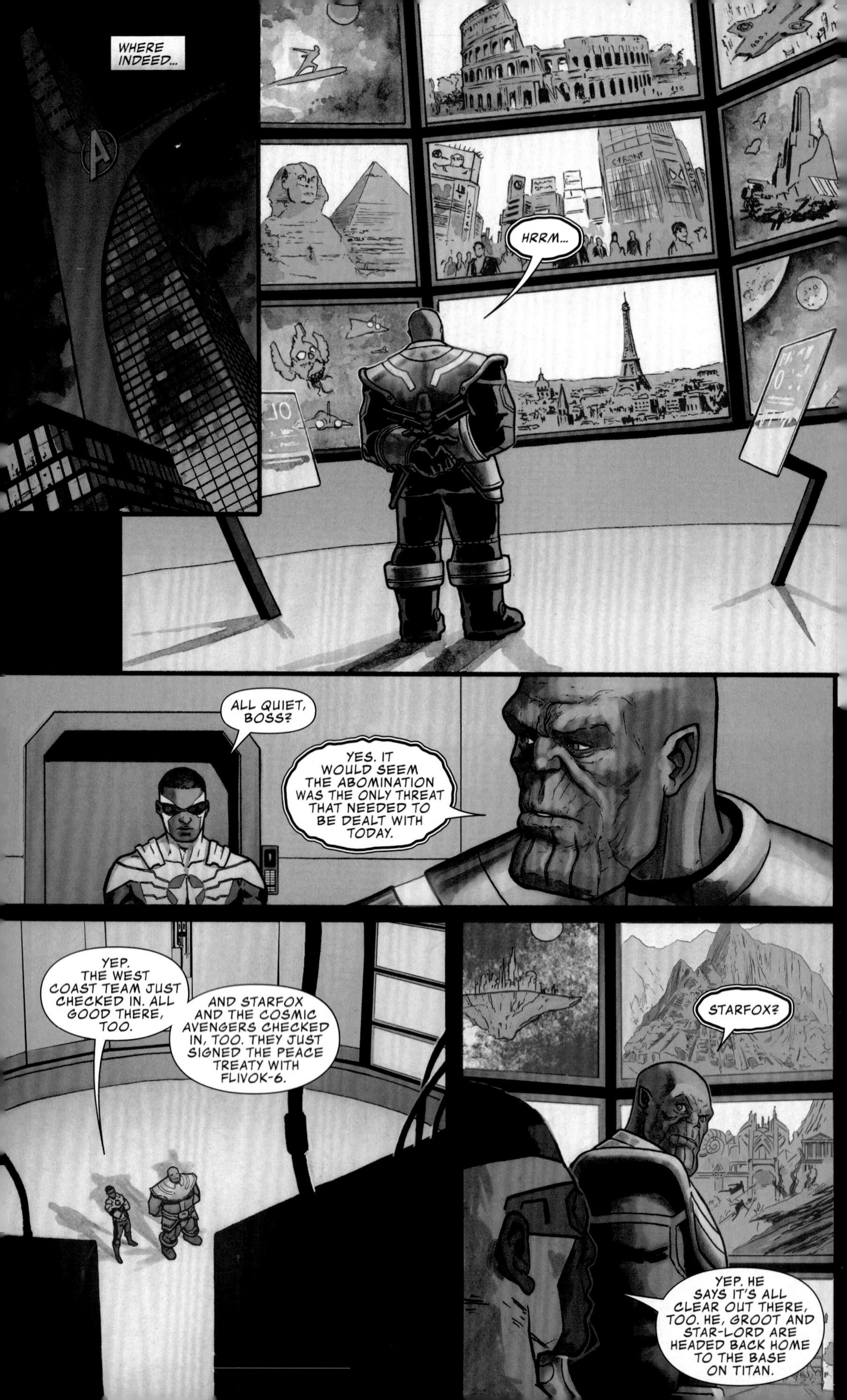
WHERE INDEED...
HRRM...
ALL QUIET, BOSS?
YES. IT WOULD SEEM THE ABOMINATION WAS THE ONLY THREAT THAT NEEDED TO BE DEALT WITH TODAY.
YEP. THE WEST COAST TEAM JUST CHECKED IN. ALL GOOD THERE, TOO.
AND STARFOX AND THE COSMIC AVENGERS CHECKED IN, TOO. THEY JUST SIGNED THE PEACE TREATY WITH FLIVOK-6.
STARFOX?
YEP. HE SAYS IT'S ALL CLEAR OUT THERE, TOO. HE, GROOT AND STAR-LORD ARE HEADED BACK HOME TO THE BASE ON TITAN.

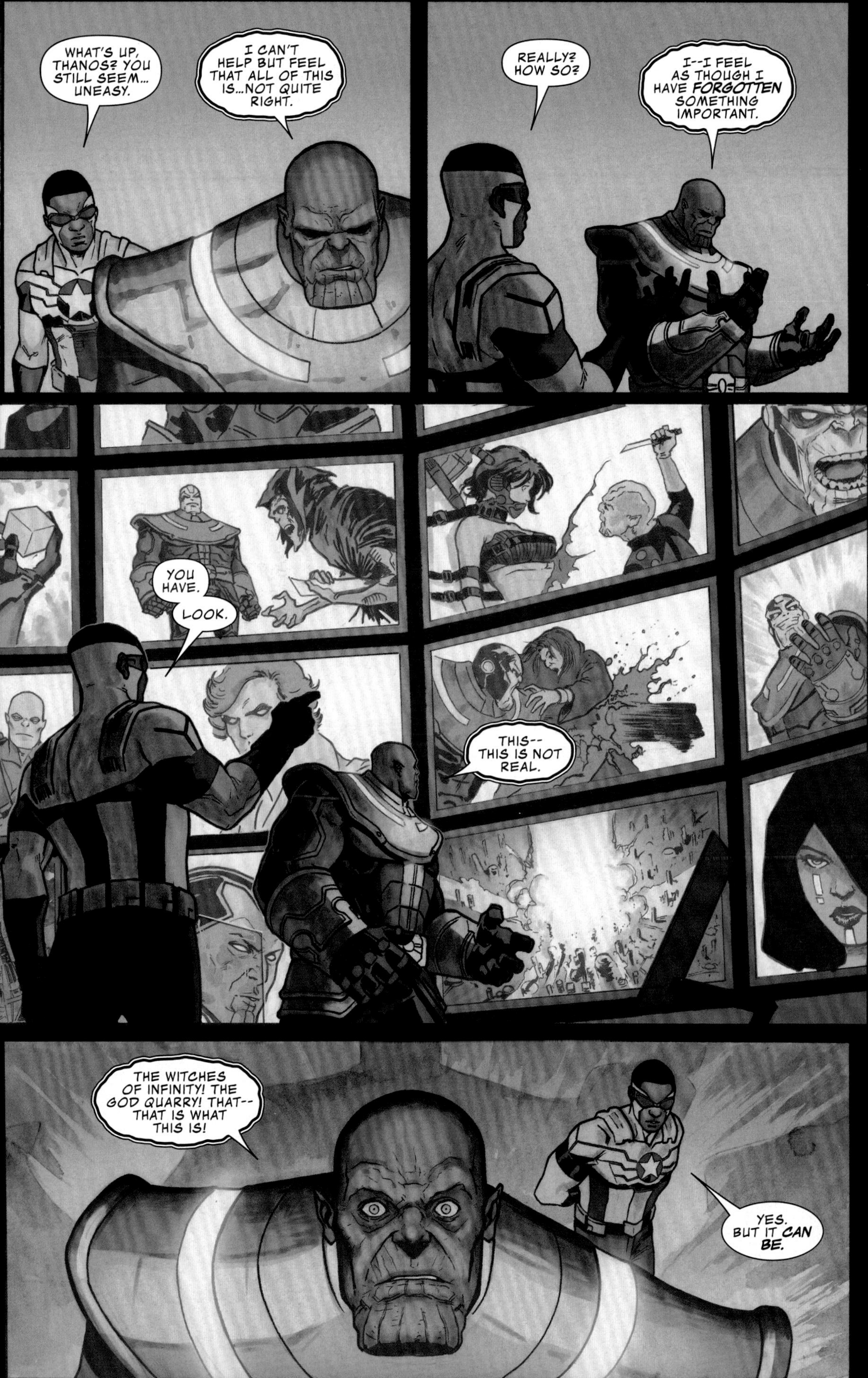
WHAT'S UP, THANOS? YOU STILL SEEM... UNEASY.
I CAN'T HELP BUT FEEL THAT ALL OF THIS IS...NOT QUITE RIGHT.
REALLY? HOW SO?
I--I FEEL AS THOUGH I HAVE FORGOTTEN SOMETHING IMPORTANT.
YOU HAVE.
LOOK.
THIS-- THIS IS NOT REAL.
THE WITCHES OF INFINITY! THE GOD QUARRY! THAT-- THAT IS WHAT THIS IS!
YES. BUT IT CAN BE.

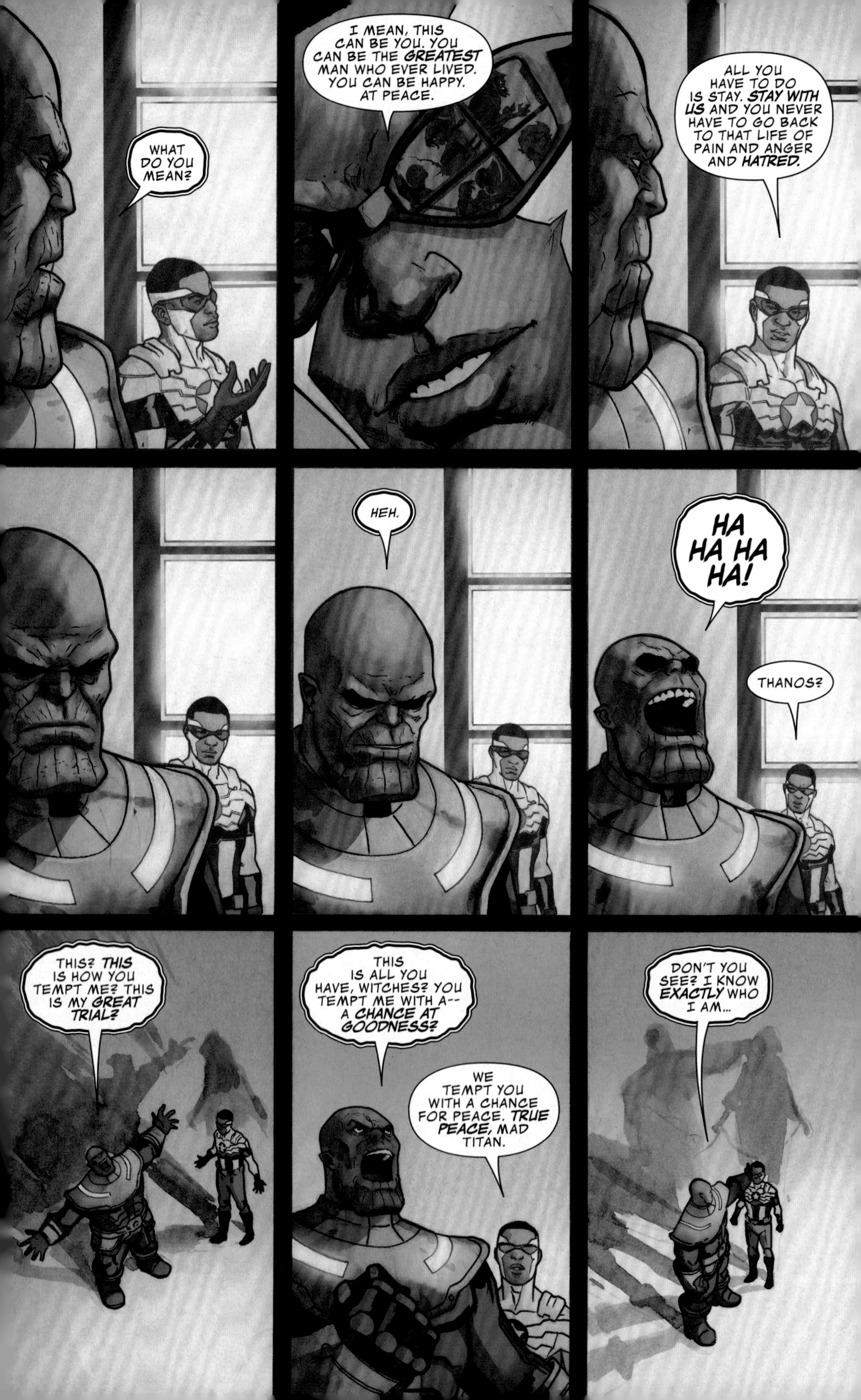
WHAT DO YOU MEAN?
I MEAN, THIS CAN BE YOU. YOU CAN BE THE GREATEST MAN WHO EVER LIVED. YOU CAN BE HAPPY. AT PEACE.
ALL YOU HAVE TO DO IS STAY. STAY WITH US AND YOU NEVER HAVE TO GO BACK TO THAT LIFE OF PAIN AND ANGER AND HATRED.
HEH.
HA HA HA HA!
THANOS?
THIS? THIS IS HOW YOU TEMPT ME? THIS IS MY GREAT TRIAL?
THIS IS ALL YOU HAVE, WITCHES? YOU TEMPT ME WITH A-- A CHANCE AT GOODNESS?
WE TEMPT YOU WITH A CHANCE FOR PEACE. TRUE PEACE, MAD TITAN.
DON'T YOU SEE? I KNOW EXACTLY WHO I AM...

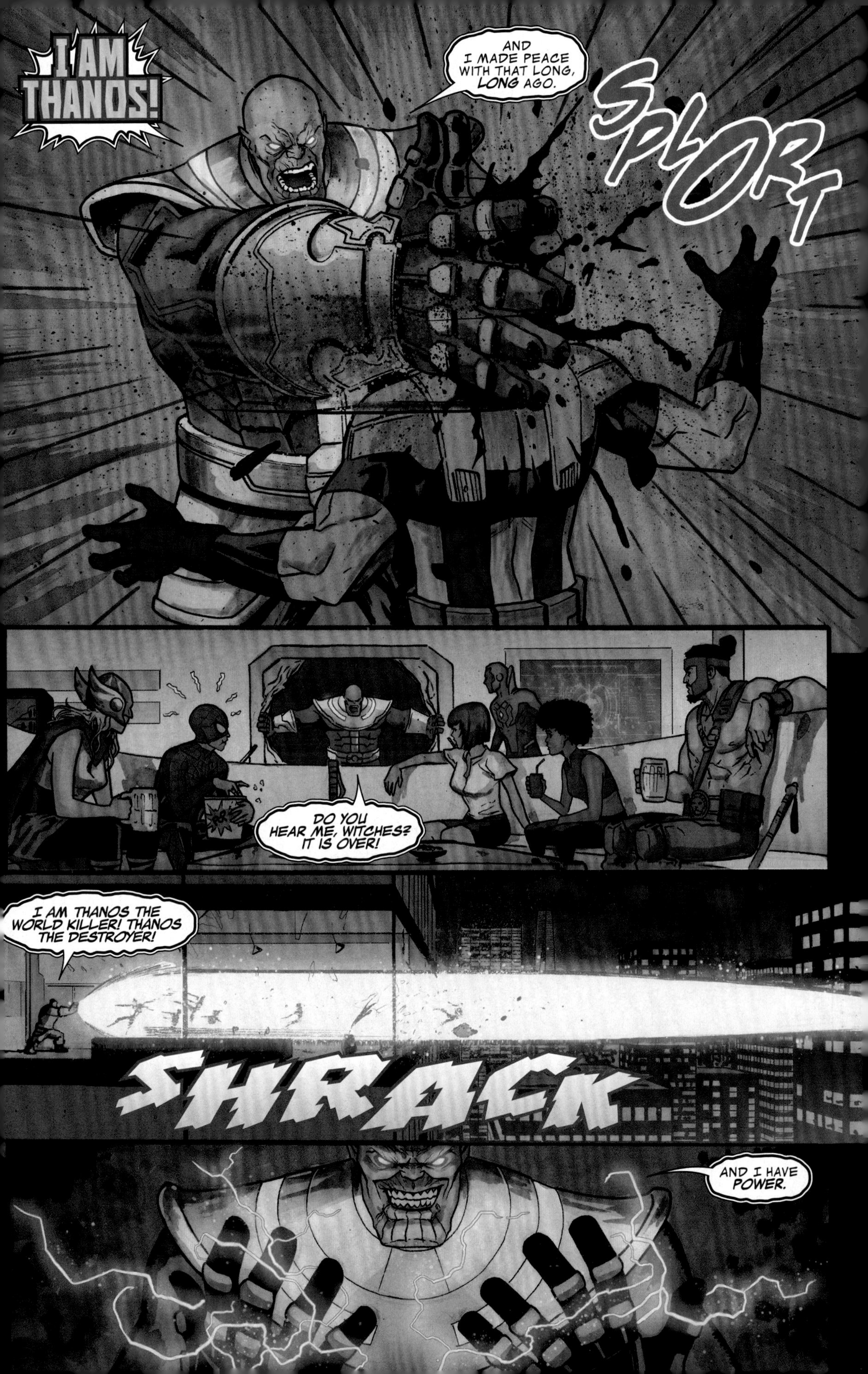
I AM THANOS!
AND I MADE PEACE WITH THAT LONG, LONG AGO.
SPLORT
DO YOU HEAR ME, WITCHES? IT IS OVER!
I AM THANOS THE WORLD KILLER! THANOS THE DESTROYER!
SHRACK
AND I HAVE POWER.

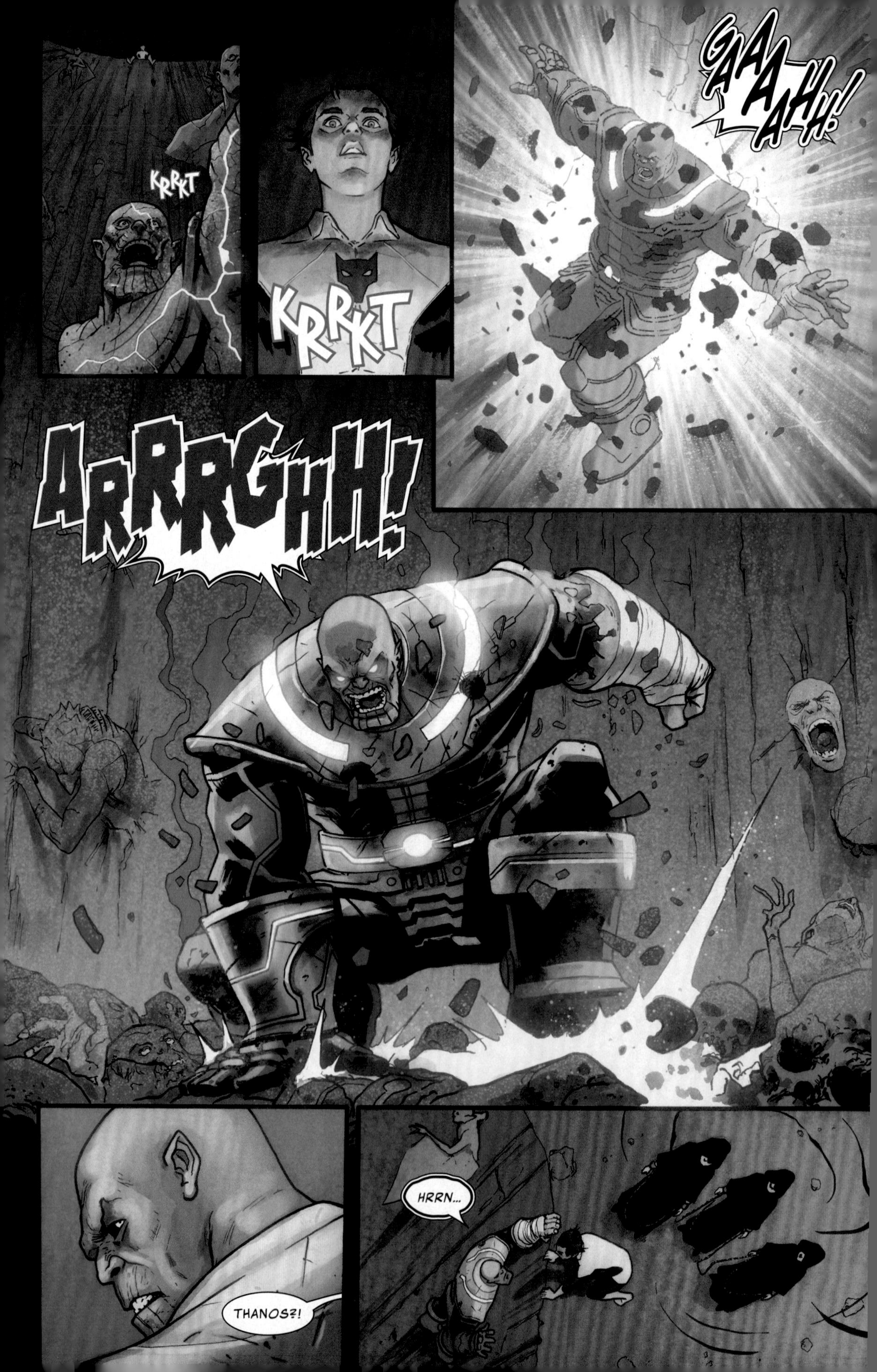

KRRKT
KRRKT
GAAAAHH!
ARRRGHH!
THANOS?!
HRRN...

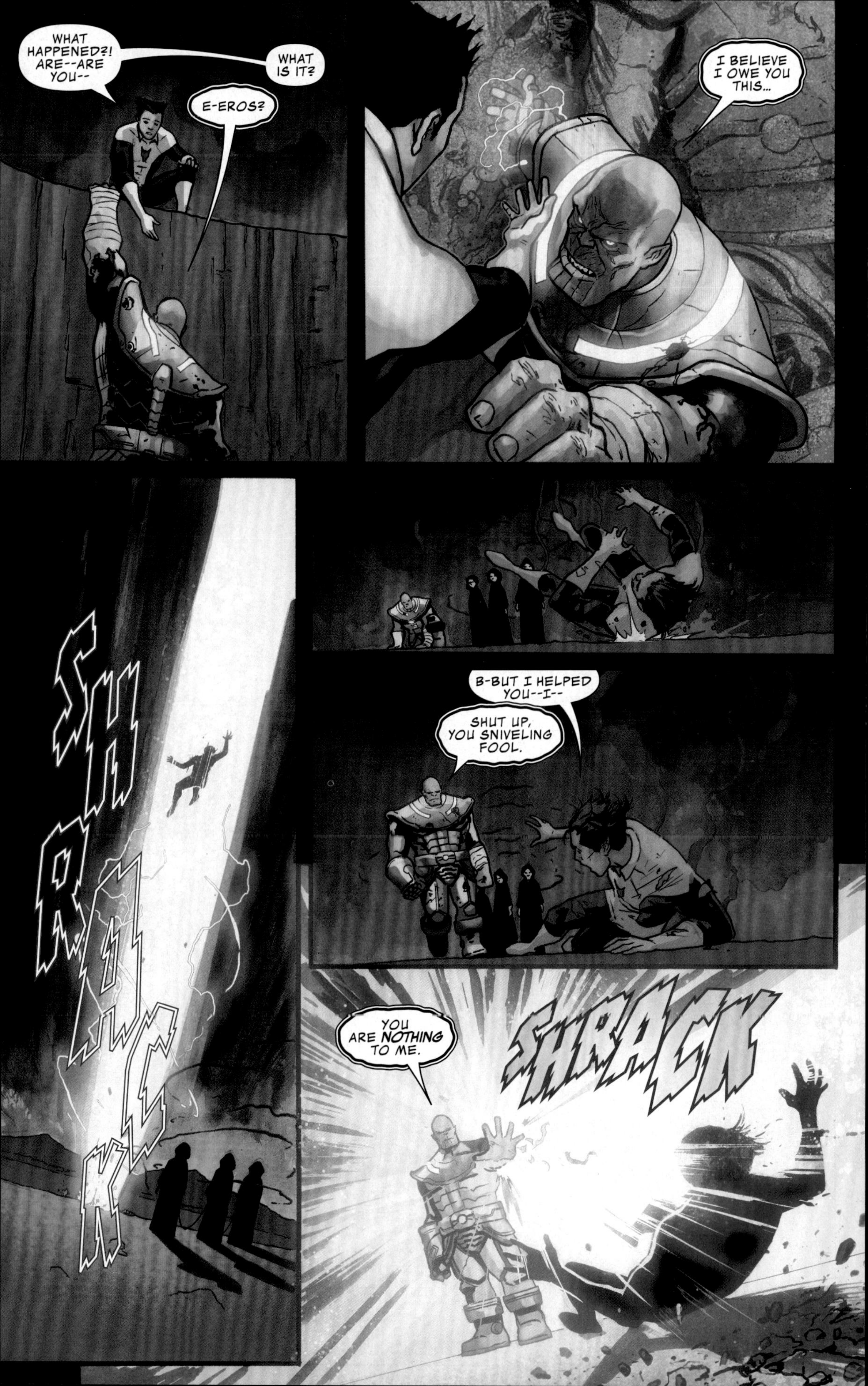
WHAT HAPPENED?! ARE--ARE YOU--
WHAT IS IT?
E-EROS?
I BELIEVE I OWE YOU THIS...
SHRACK
B-BUT I HELPED YOU--I--
SHUT UP, YOU SNIVELING FOOL.
YOU ARE NOTHING TO ME.
SHRACK

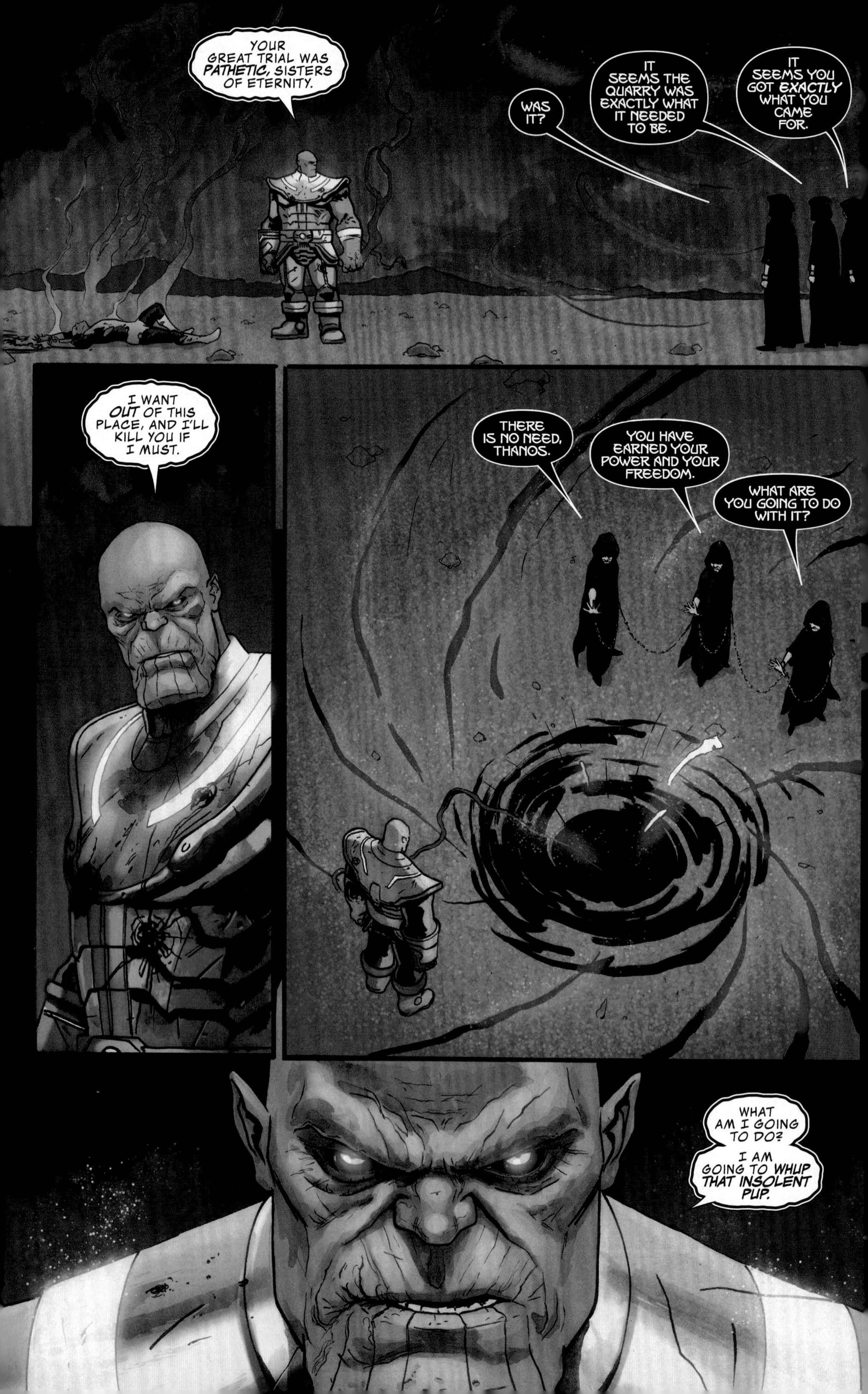
YOUR GREAT TRIAL WAS PATHETIC, SISTERS OF ETERNITY.
WAS IT?
IT SEEMS THE QUARRY WAS EXACTLY WHAT IT NEEDED TO BE.
IT SEEMS YOU GOT EXACTLY WHAT YOU CAME FOR.
I WANT OUT OF THIS PLACE, AND I'LL KILL YOU IF I MUST.
THERE IS NO NEED, THANOS.
YOU HAVE EARNED YOUR POWER AND YOUR FREEDOM.
WHAT ARE YOU GOING TO DO WITH IT?
WHAT AM I GOING TO DO?
I AM GOING TO WHUP THAT INSOLENT PUP.

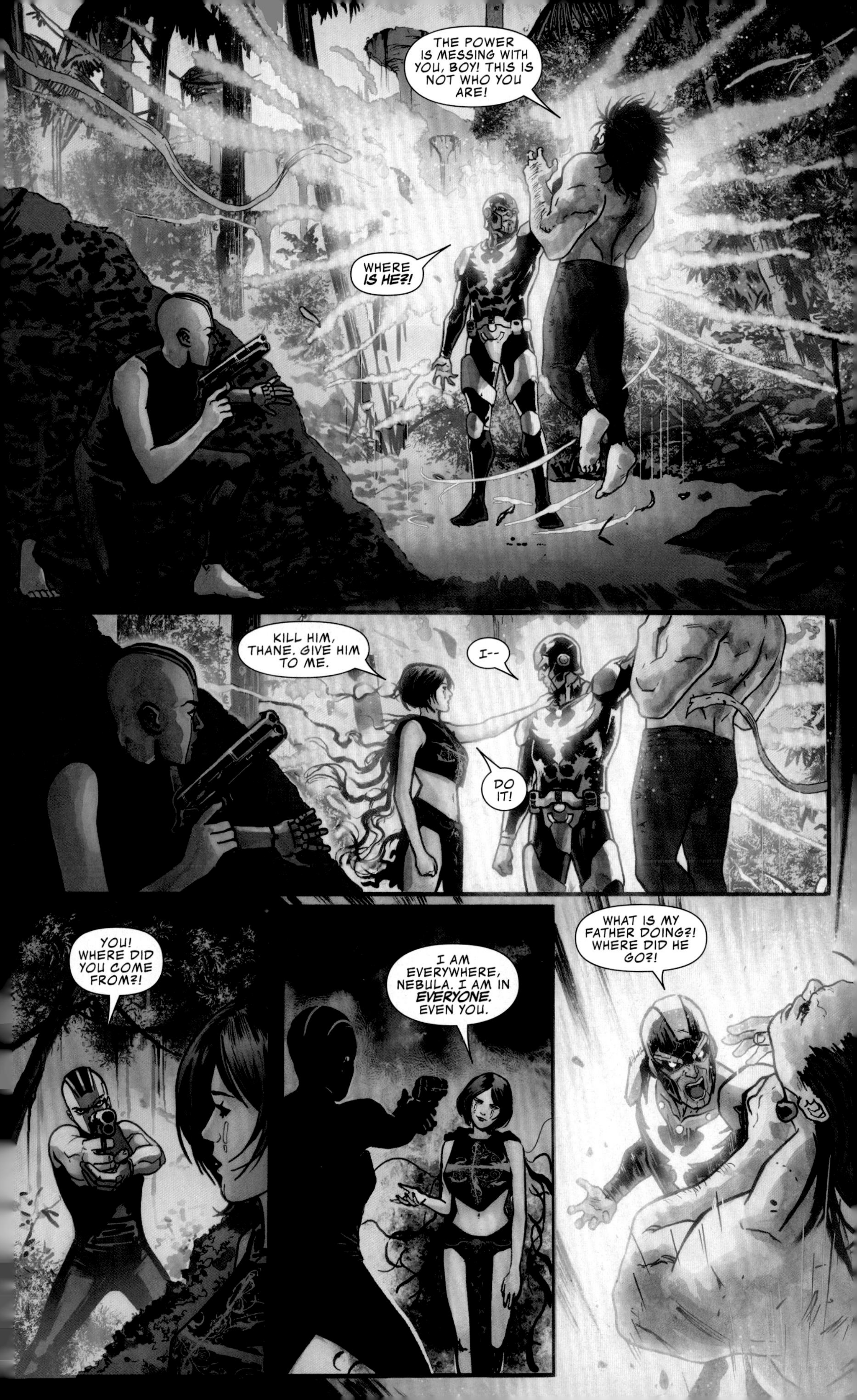
THE POWER IS MESSING WITH YOU, BOY! THIS IS NOT WHO YOU ARE!
WHERE IS HE?!
KILL HIM, THANE. GIVE HIM TO ME.
I--
DO IT!
YOU! WHERE DID YOU COME FROM?!
I AM EVERYWHERE, NEBULA. I AM IN EVERYONE. EVEN YOU.
WHAT IS MY FATHER DOING?! WHERE DID HE GO?!

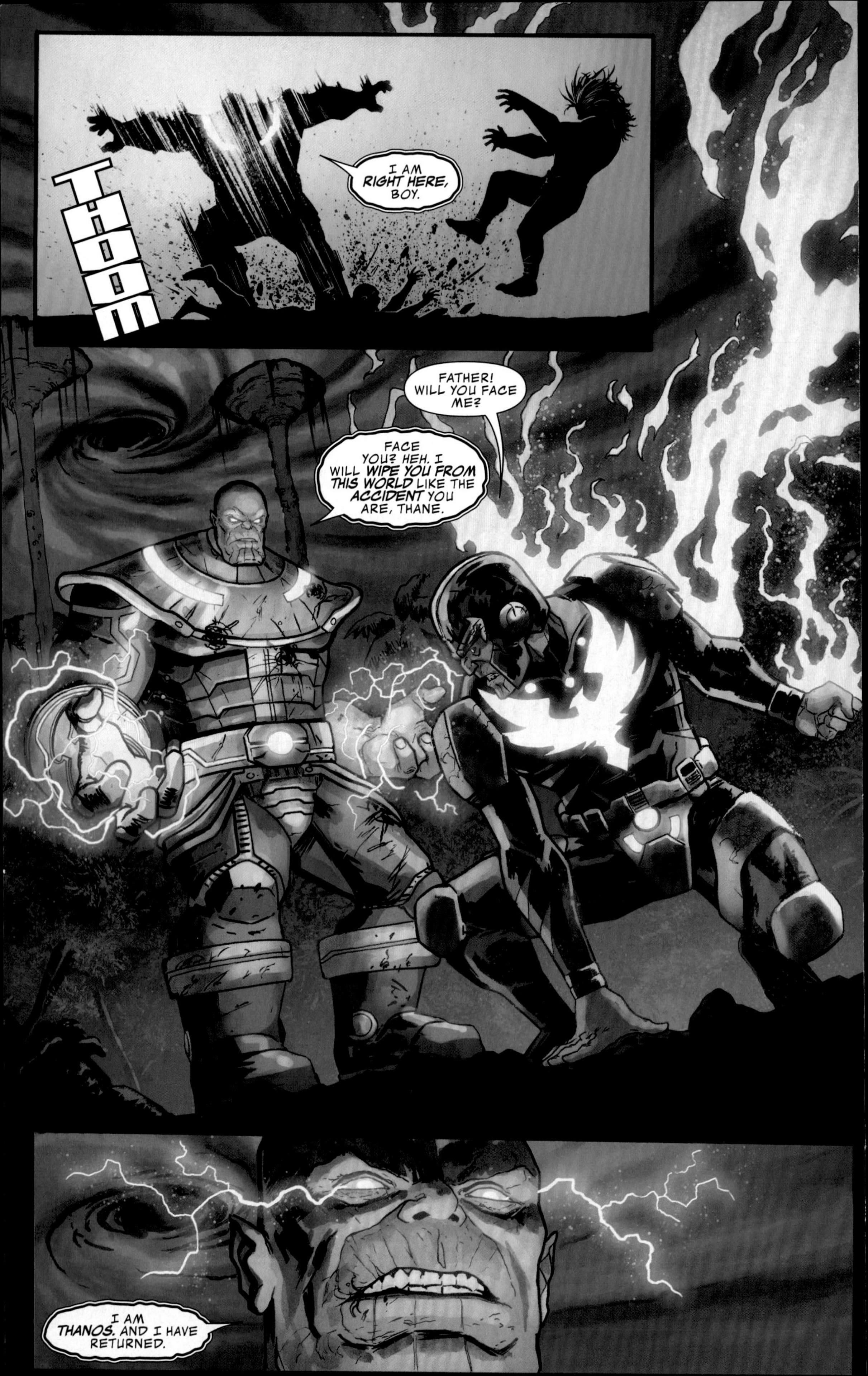
THOOM
I AM RIGHT HERE, BOY.
FATHER! WILL YOU FACE ME?
FACE YOU? HEH. I WILL WIPE YOU FROM THIS WORLD LIKE THE ACCIDENT YOU ARE, THANE.
I AM THANOS. AND I HAVE RETURNED.

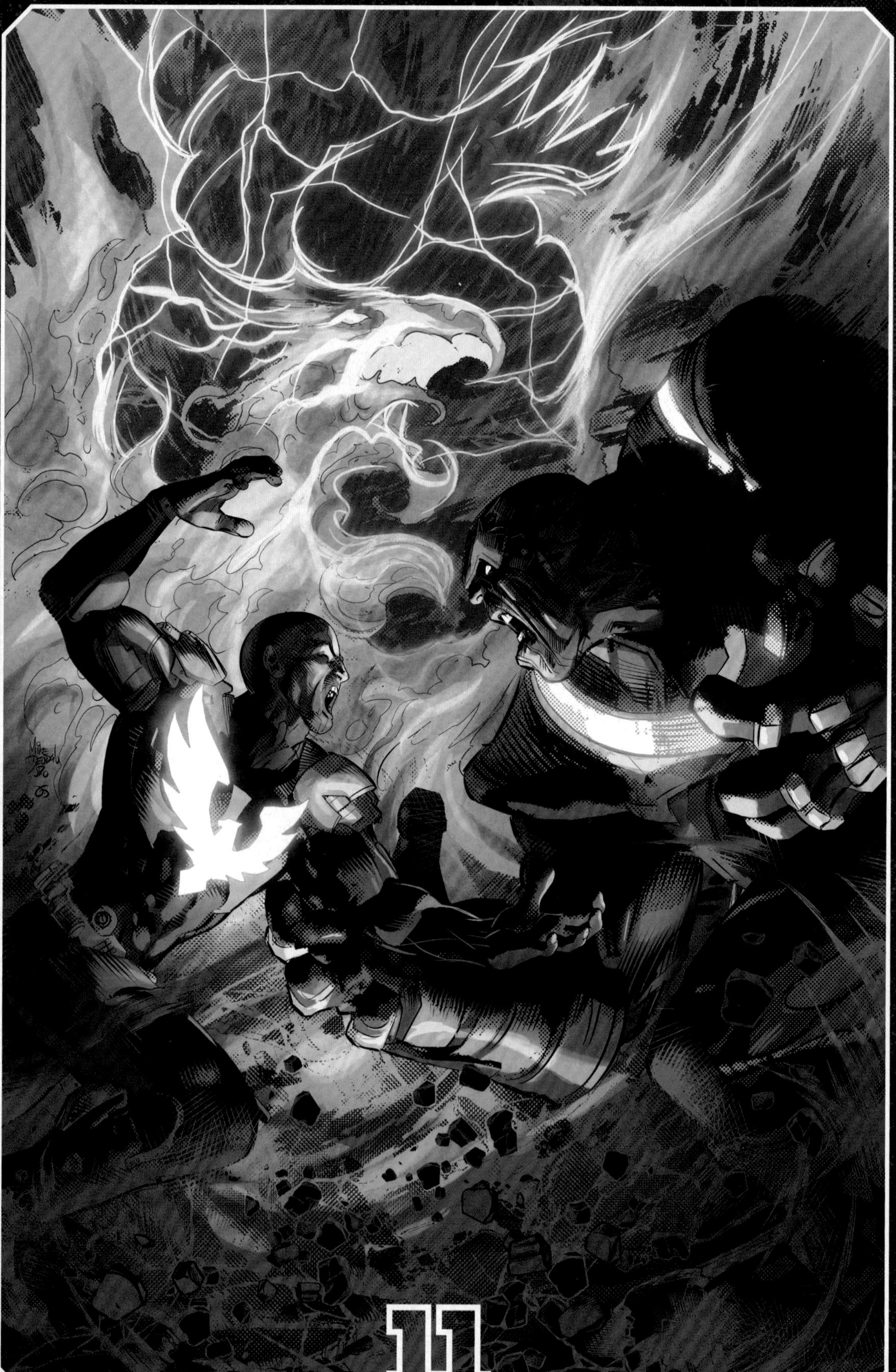
11

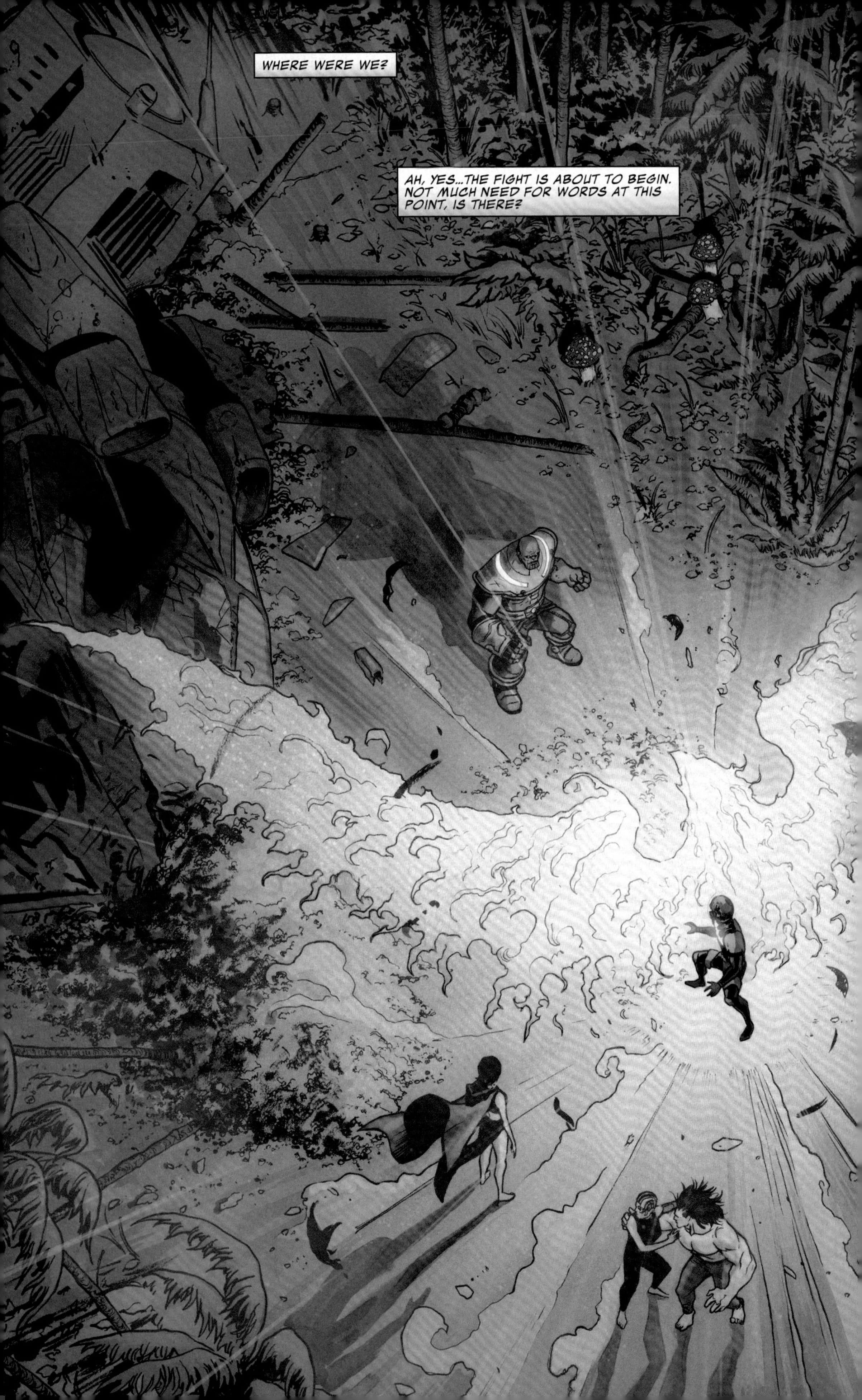
WHERE WERE WE?
AH, YES...THE FIGHT IS ABOUT TO BEGIN. NOT MUCH NEED FOR WORDS AT THIS POINT, IS THERE?

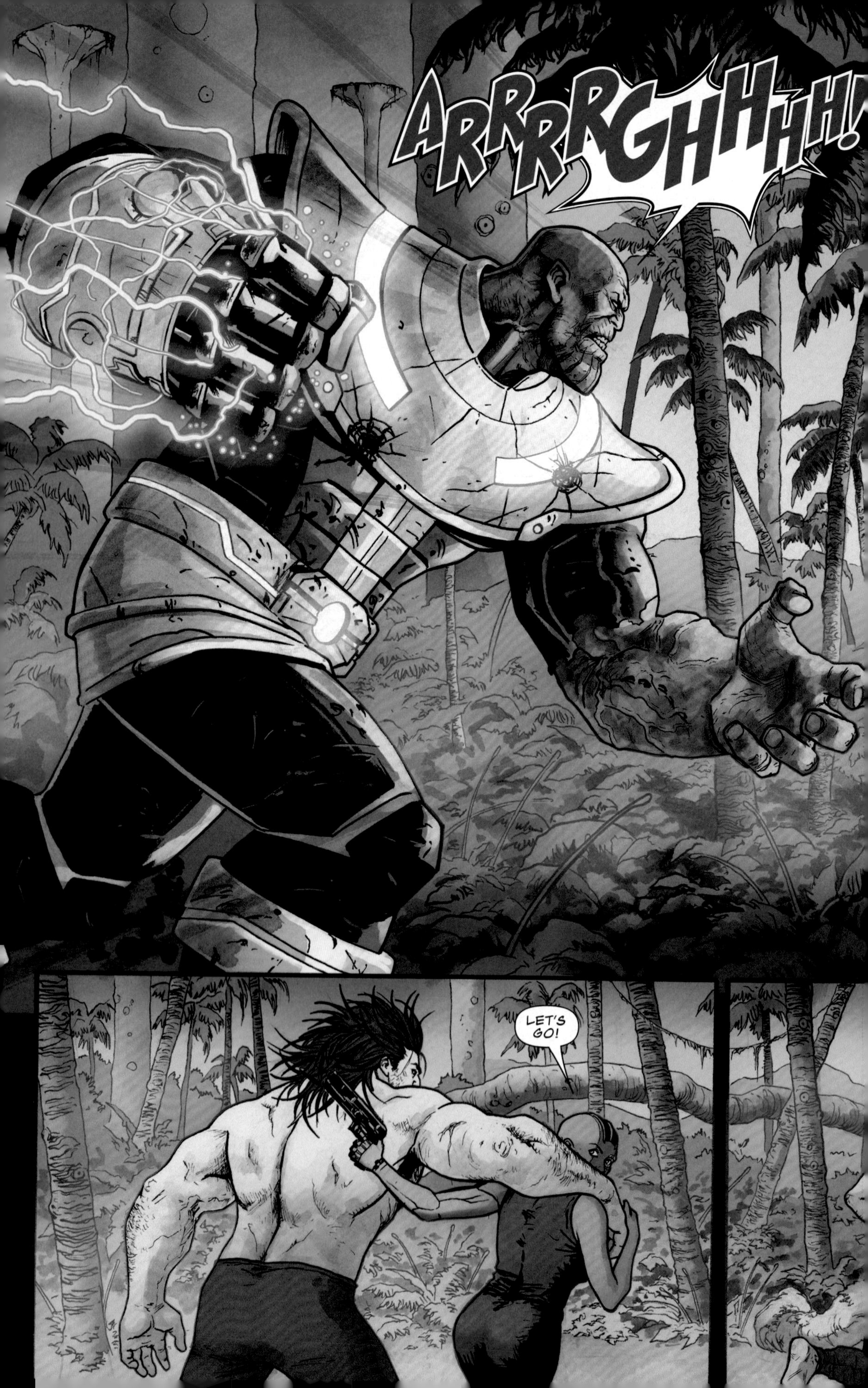
ARRRRGHHHH!
LET'S GO!

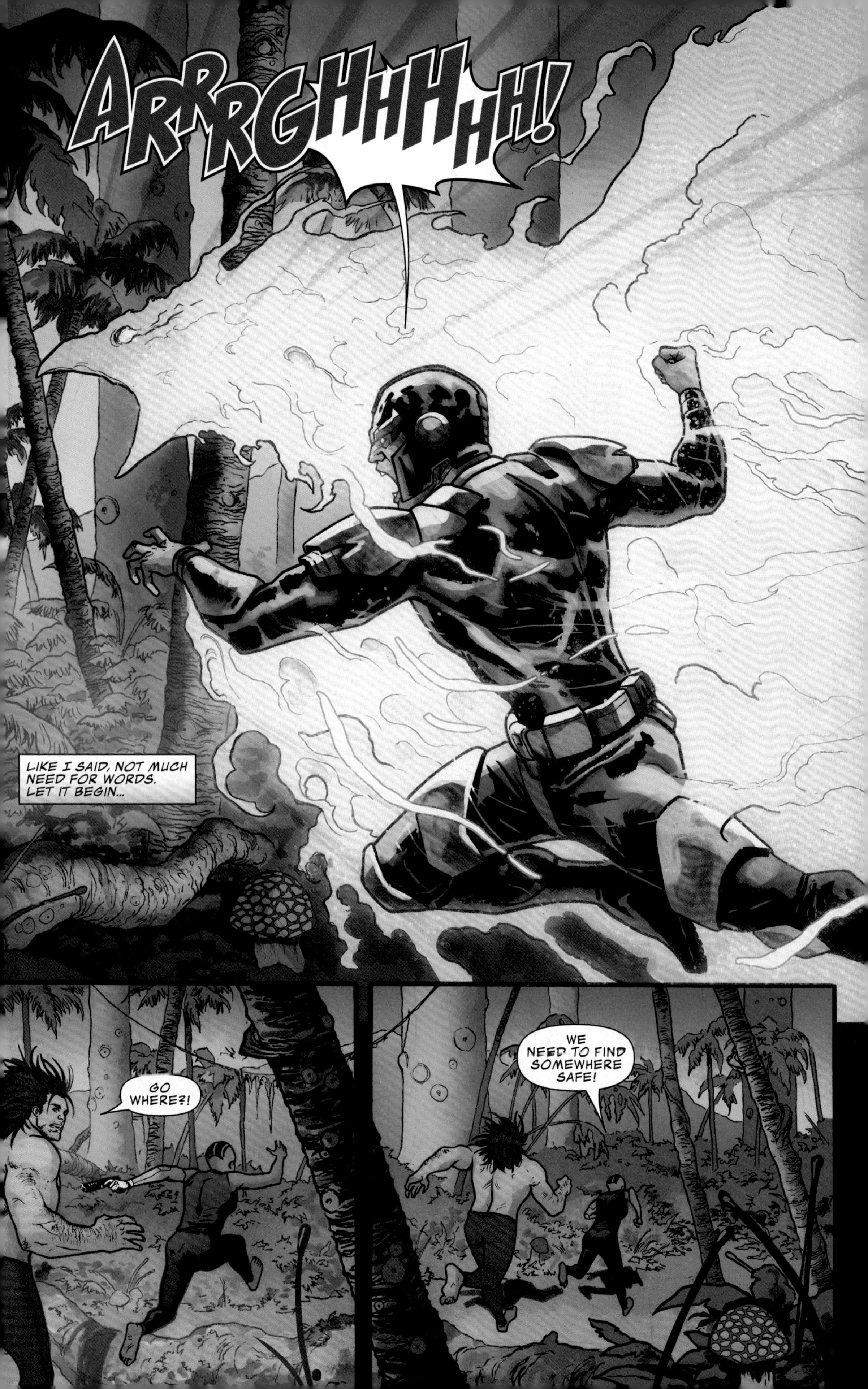
ARRRGHHHHH!
LIKE I SAID, NOT MUCH NEED FOR WORDS. LET IT BEGIN...
GO WHERE?!
WE NEED TO FIND SOMEWHERE SAFE!

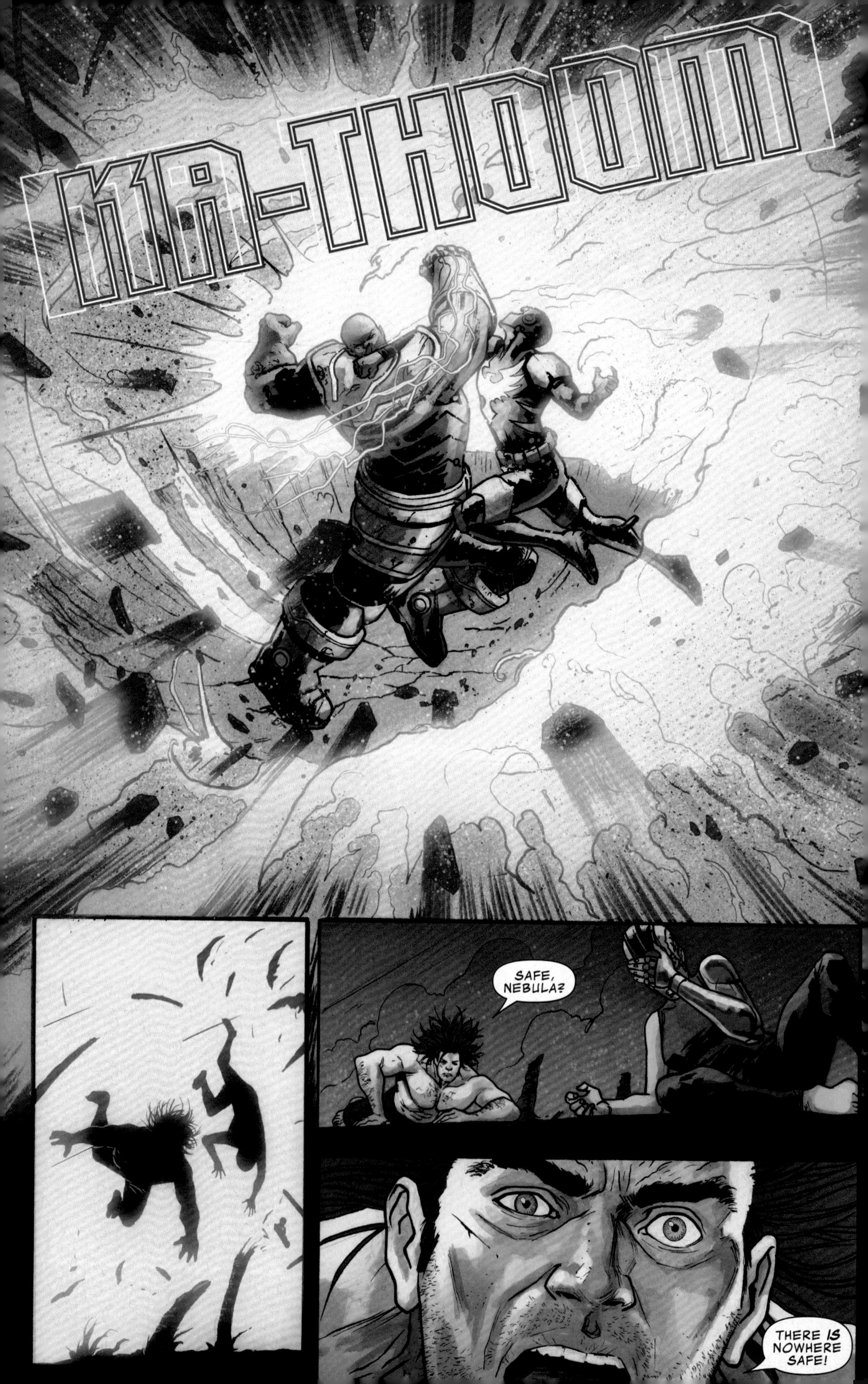
KA-THOOM
SAFE, NEBULA?
THERE IS NOWHERE SAFE!

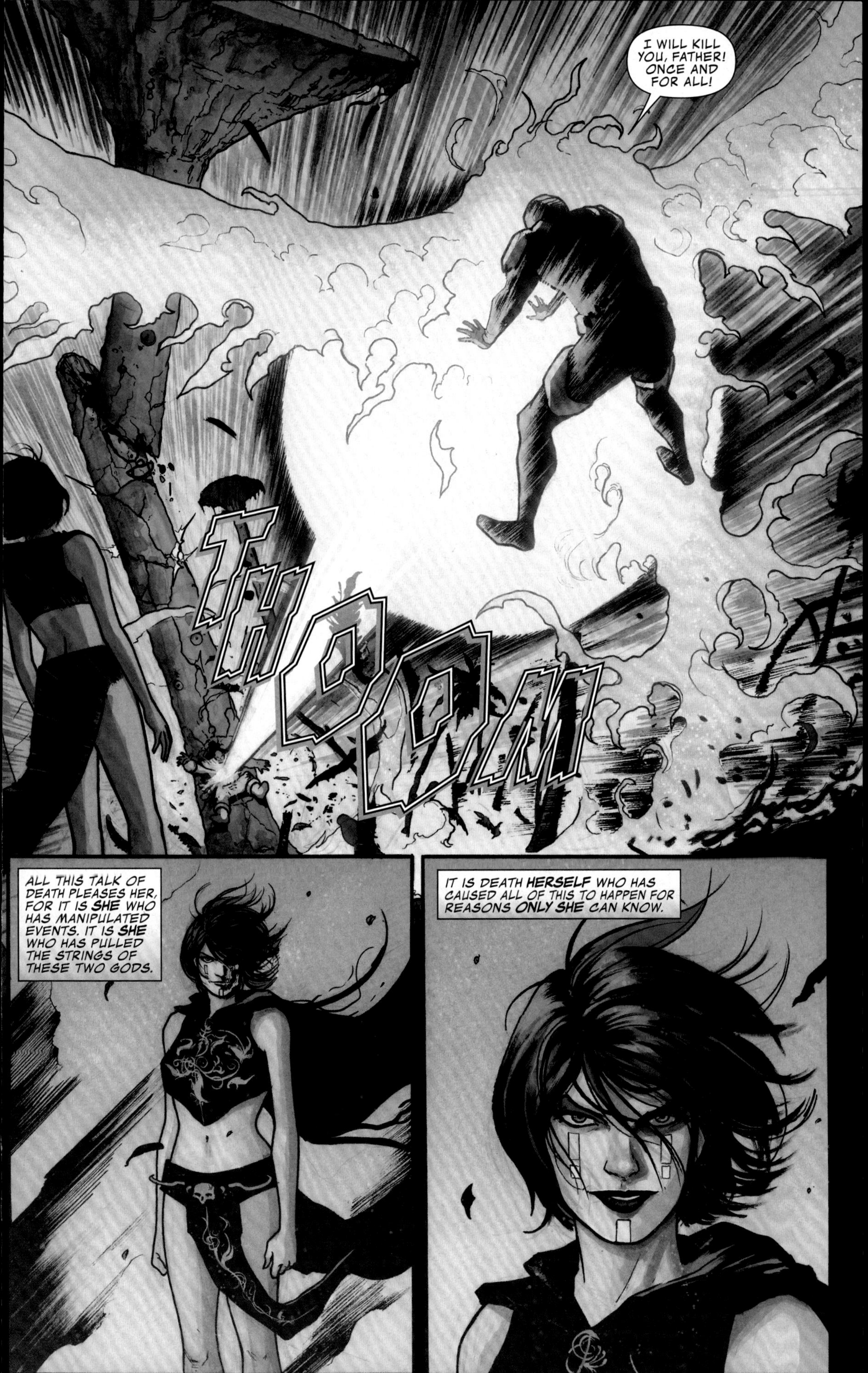
I WILL KILL YOU, FATHER! ONCE AND FOR ALL!
THOOM
ALL THIS TALK OF DEATH PLEASES HER, FOR IT IS SHE WHO HAS MANIPULATED EVENTS. IT IS SHE WHO HAS PULLED THE STRINGS OF THESE TWO GODS.
IT IS DEATH HERSELF WHO HAS CAUSED ALL OF THIS TO HAPPEN FOR REASONS ONLY SHE CAN KNOW.

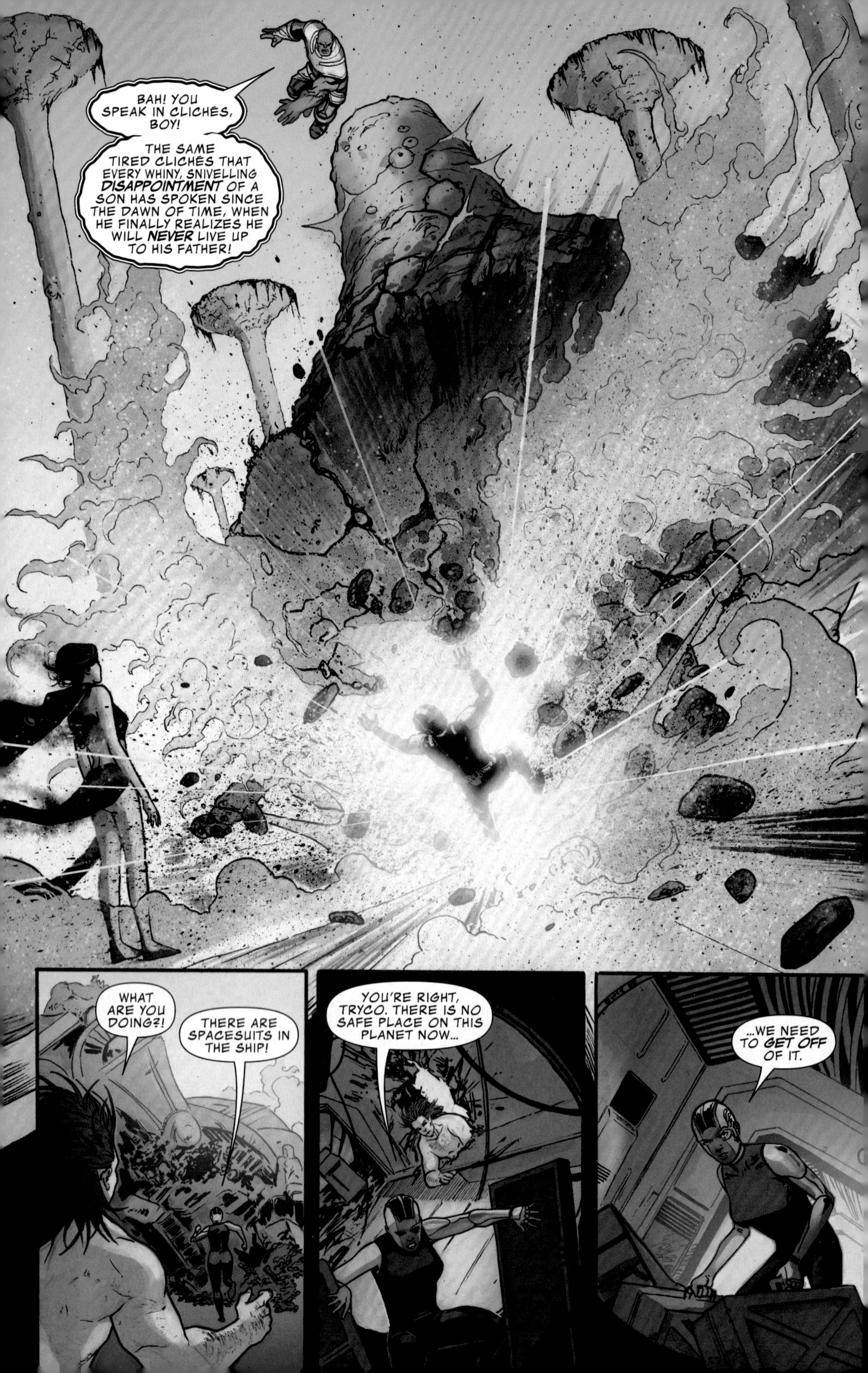
BAH! YOU SPEAK IN CLICHÉS, BOY!
THE SAME TIRED CLICHÉS THAT EVERY WHINY, SNIVELLING DISAPPOINTMENT OF A SON HAS SPOKEN SINCE THE DAWN OF TIME, WHEN HE FINALLY REALIZES HE WILL NEVER LIVE UP TO HIS FATHER!
WHAT ARE YOU DOING?!
THERE ARE SPACESUITS IN THE SHIP!
YOU'RE RIGHT, TRYCO. THERE IS NO SAFE PLACE ON THIS PLANET NOW...
...WE NEED TO GET OFF OF IT.

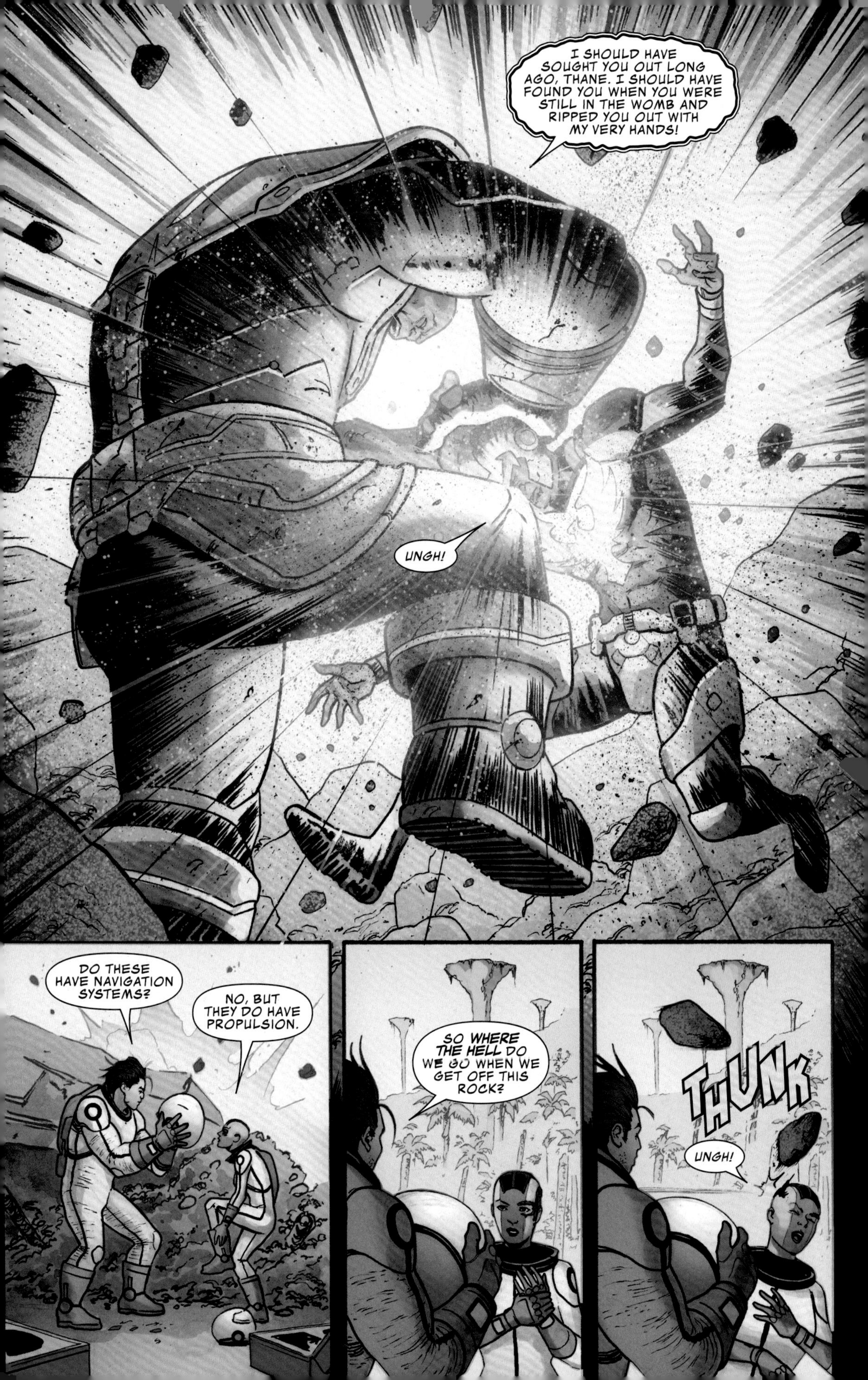
I SHOULD HAVE SOUGHT YOU OUT LONG AGO, THANE. I SHOULD HAVE FOUND YOU WHEN YOU WERE STILL IN THE WOMB AND RIPPED YOU OUT WITH MY VERY HANDS!
UNGH!
DO THESE HAVE NAVIGATION SYSTEMS?
NO, BUT THEY DO HAVE PROPULSION.
SO WHERE THE HELL DO WE GO WHEN WE GET OFF THIS ROCK?
THUNK
UNGH!

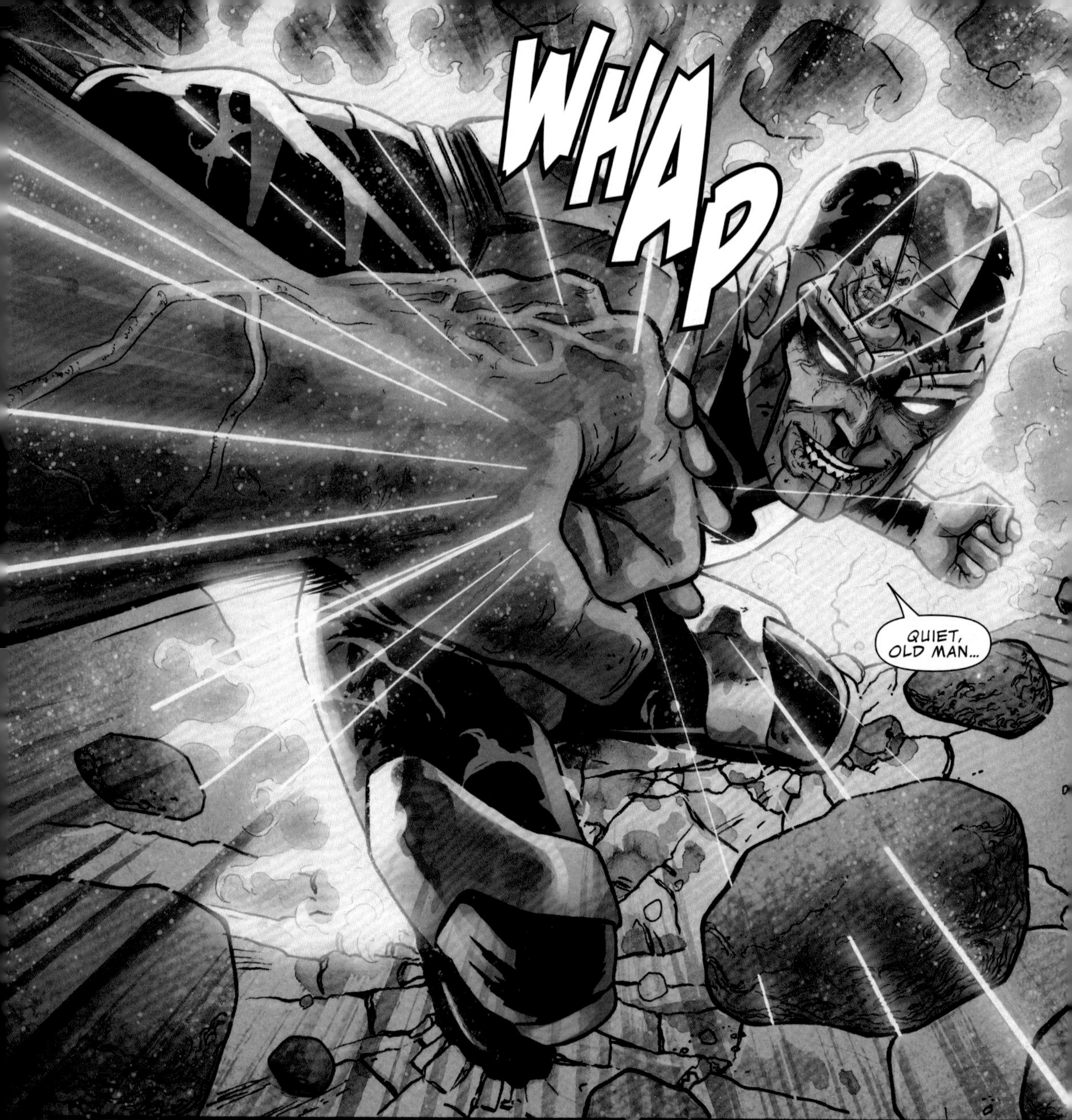
WHAP
QUIET, OLD MAN...

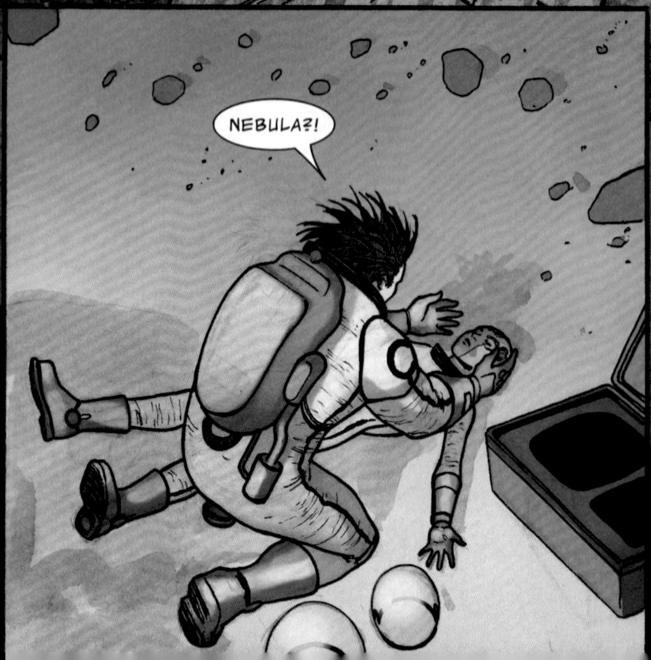
NEBULA?!

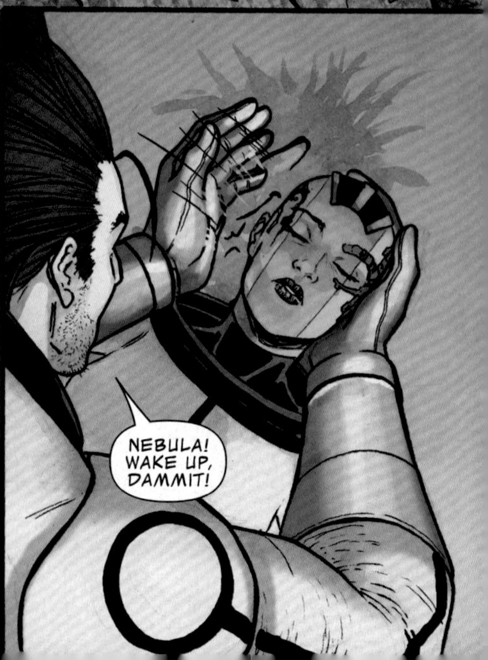
NEBULA! WAKE UP, DAMMIT!

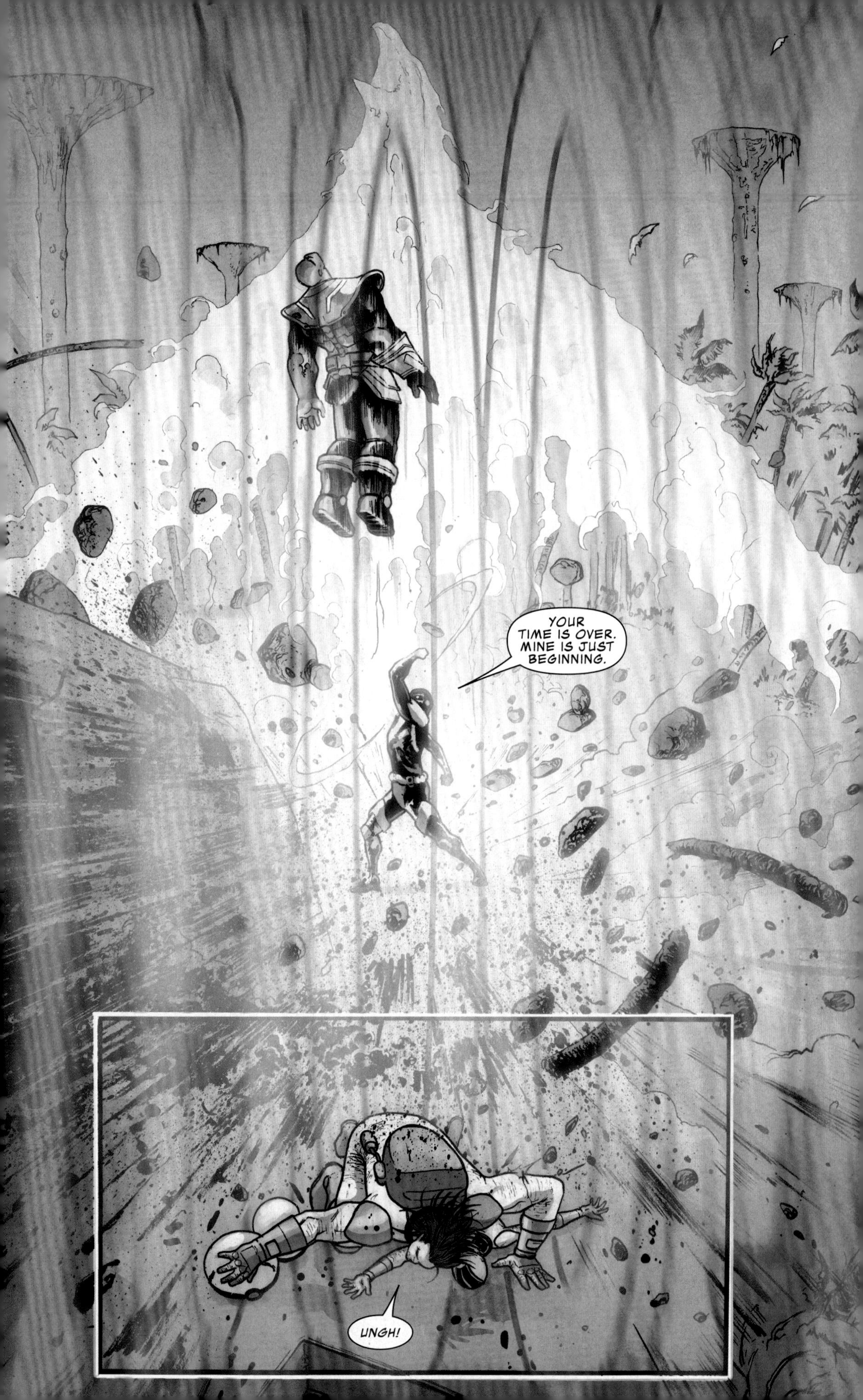
YOUR TIME IS OVER. MINE IS JUST BEGINNING.
UNGH!

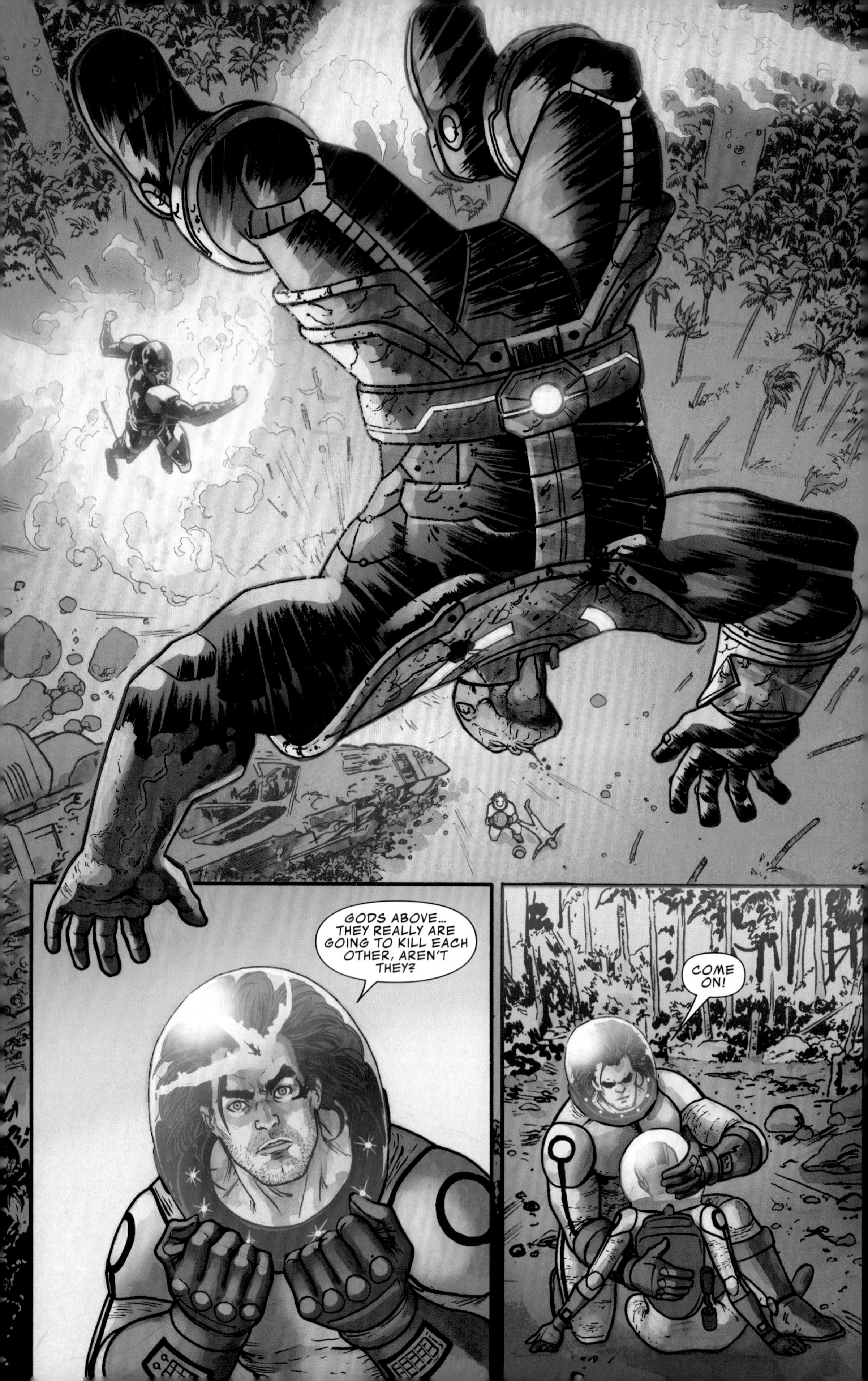
GODS ABOVE... THEY REALLY ARE GOING TO KILL EACH OTHER, AREN'T THEY?
COME ON!

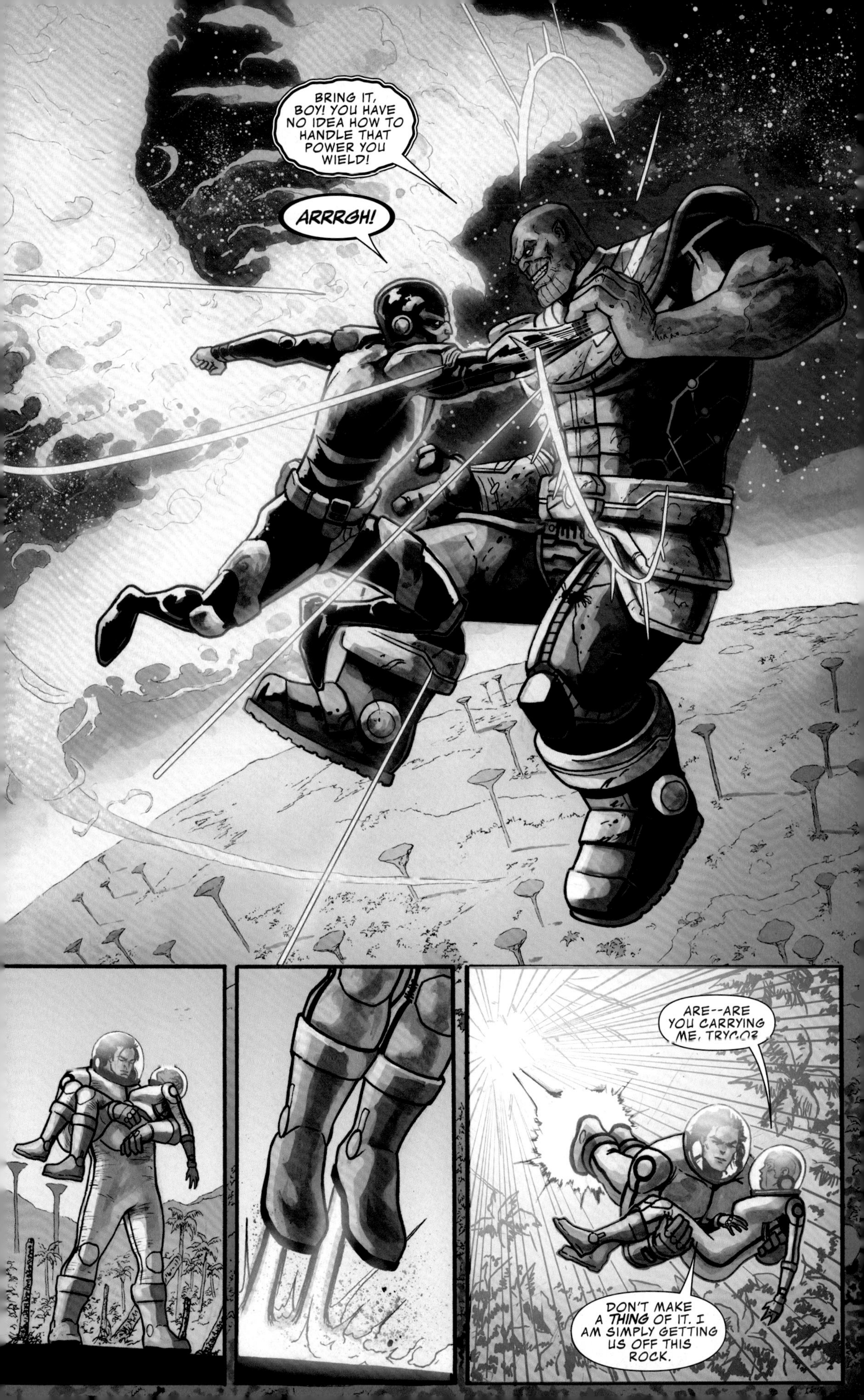
BRING IT, BOY! YOU HAVE NO IDEA HOW TO HANDLE THAT POWER YOU WIELD!
ARRRGH!
ARE--ARE YOU CARRYING ME, TRYCO?
DON'T MAKE A THING OF IT. I AM SIMPLY GETTING US OFF THIS ROCK.

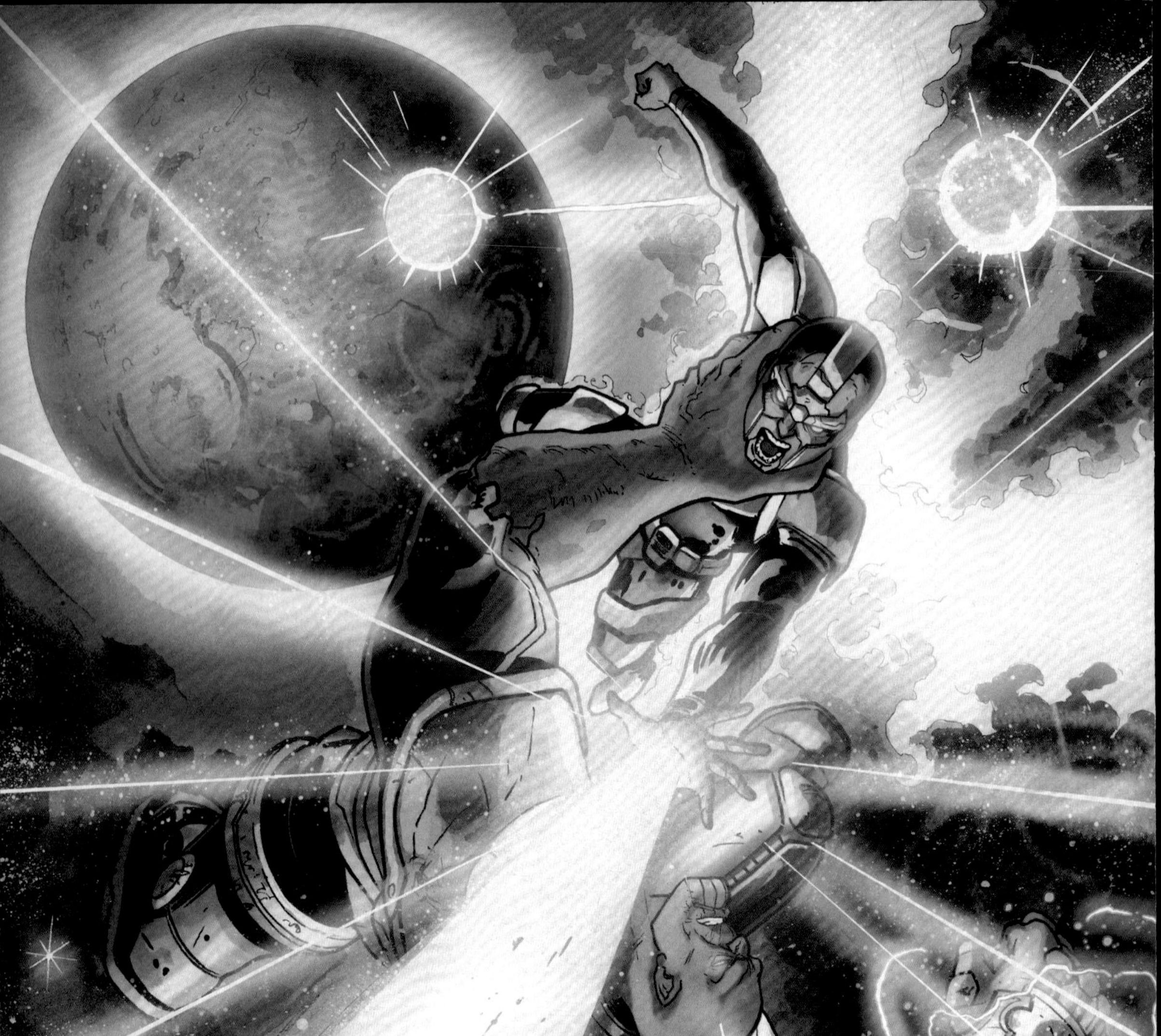

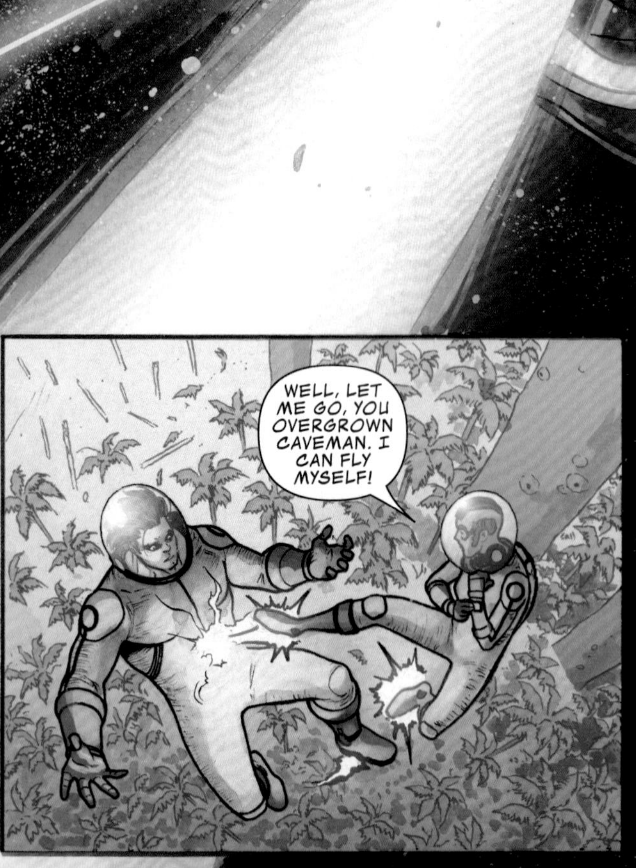
WELL, LET ME GO, YOU OVERGROWN CAVEMAN. I CAN FLY MYSELF!

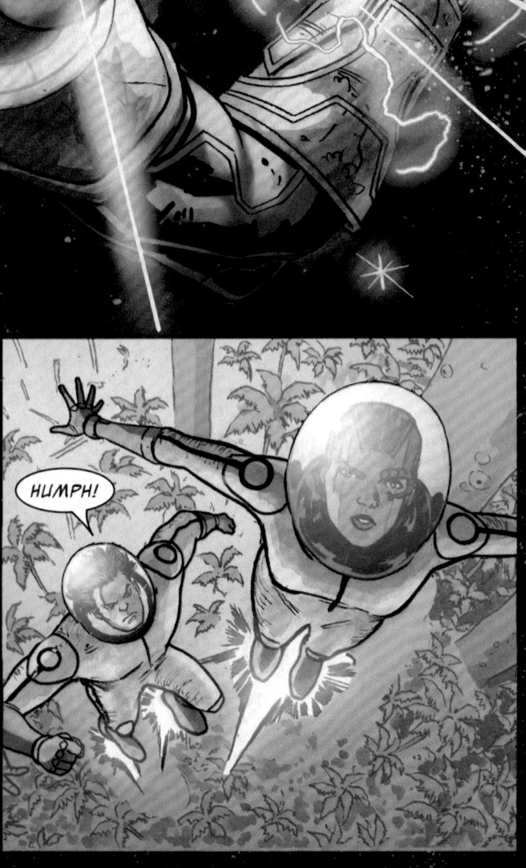
HUMPH!

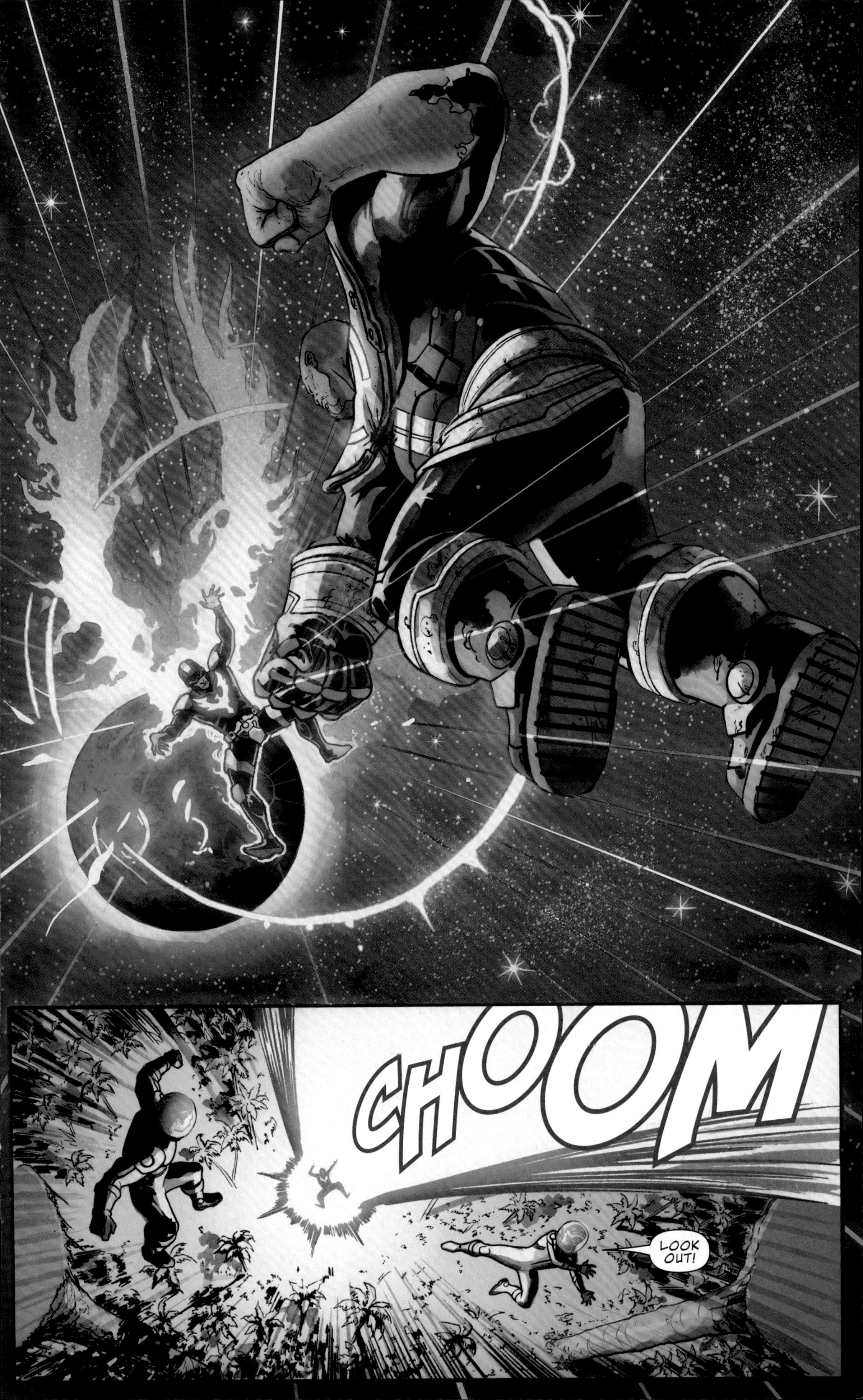
CHOOOM
LOOK OUT!

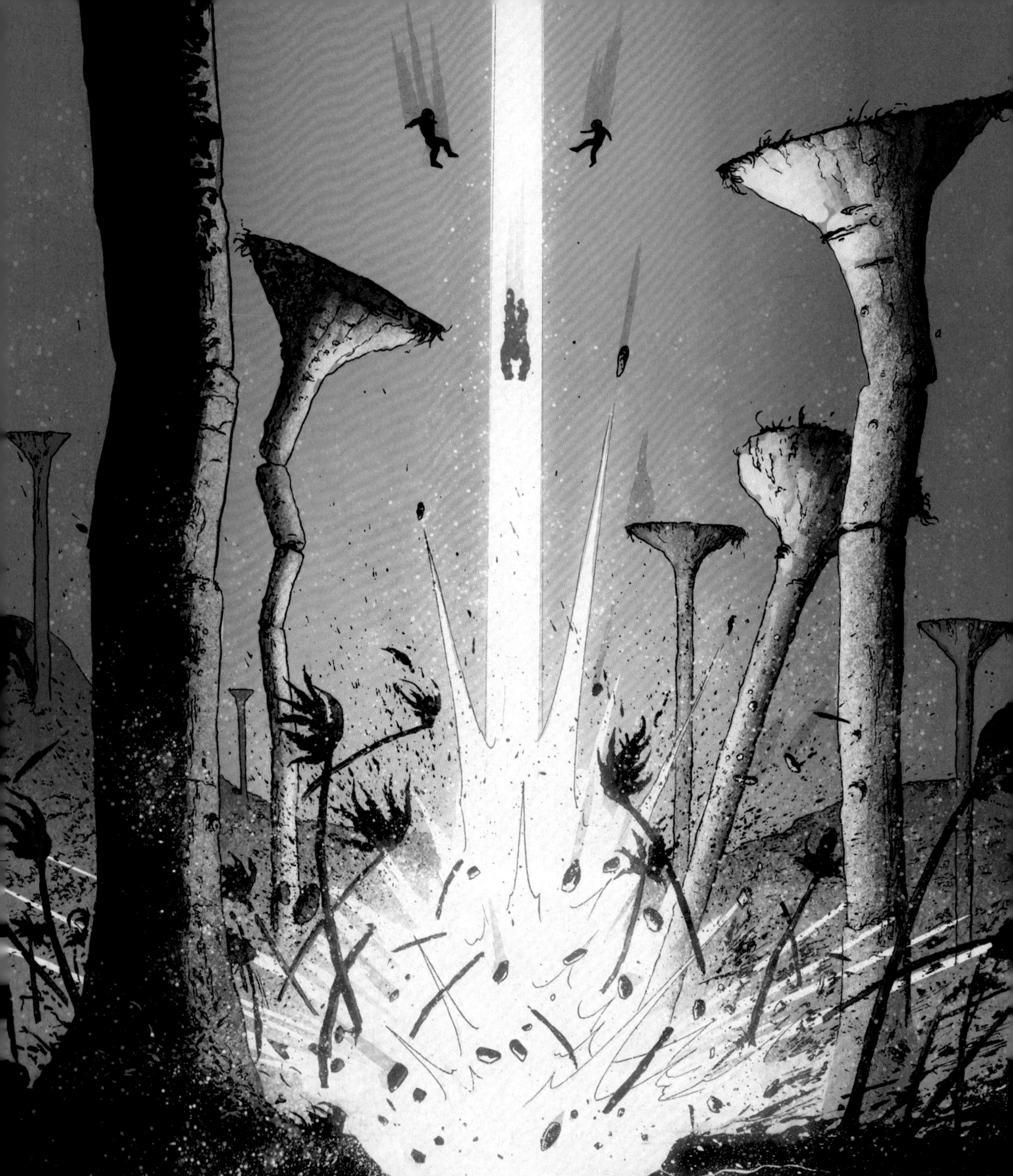

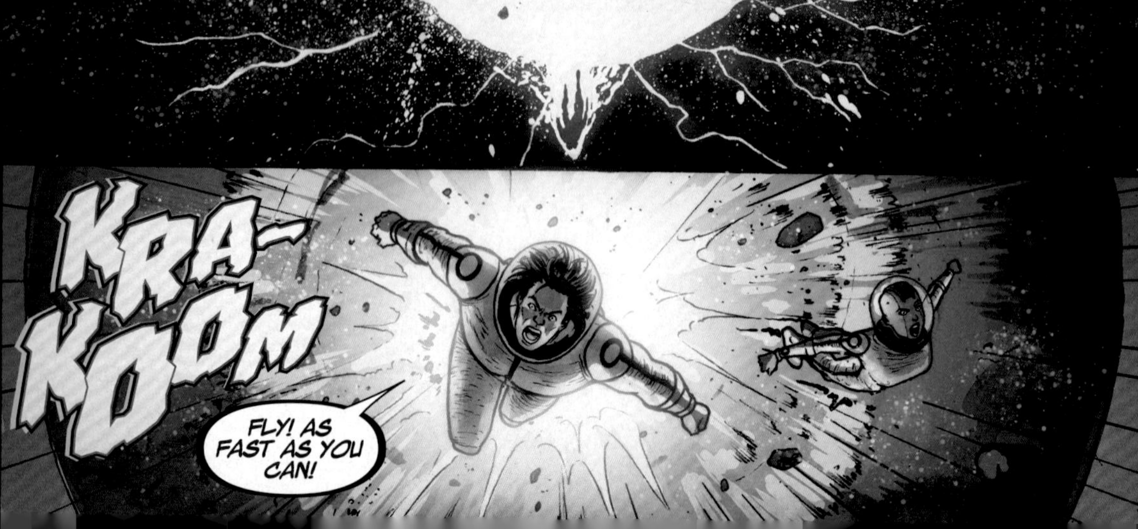
KRA-KOOM
FLY! AS FAST AS YOU CAN!

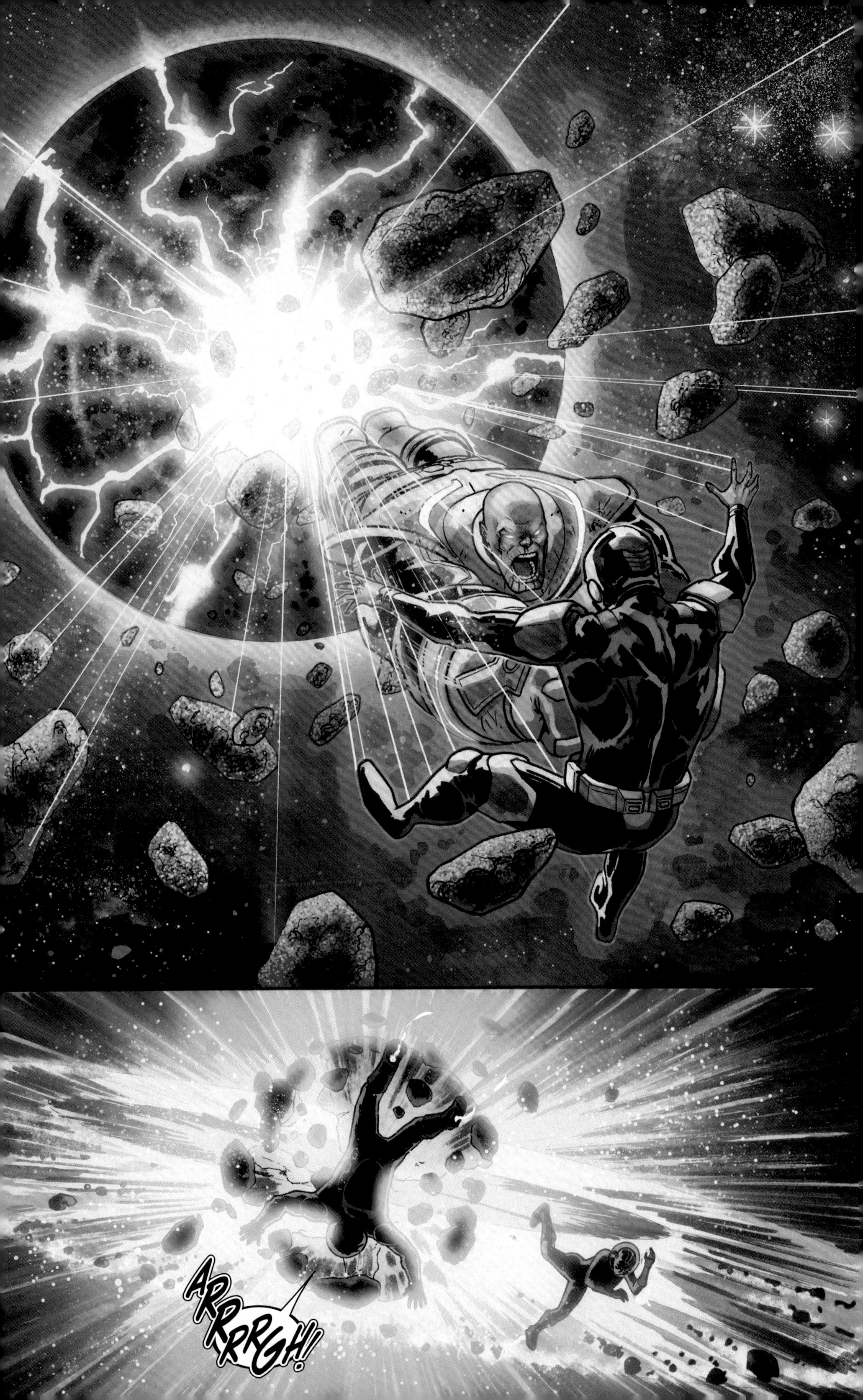
ARRRRGH!

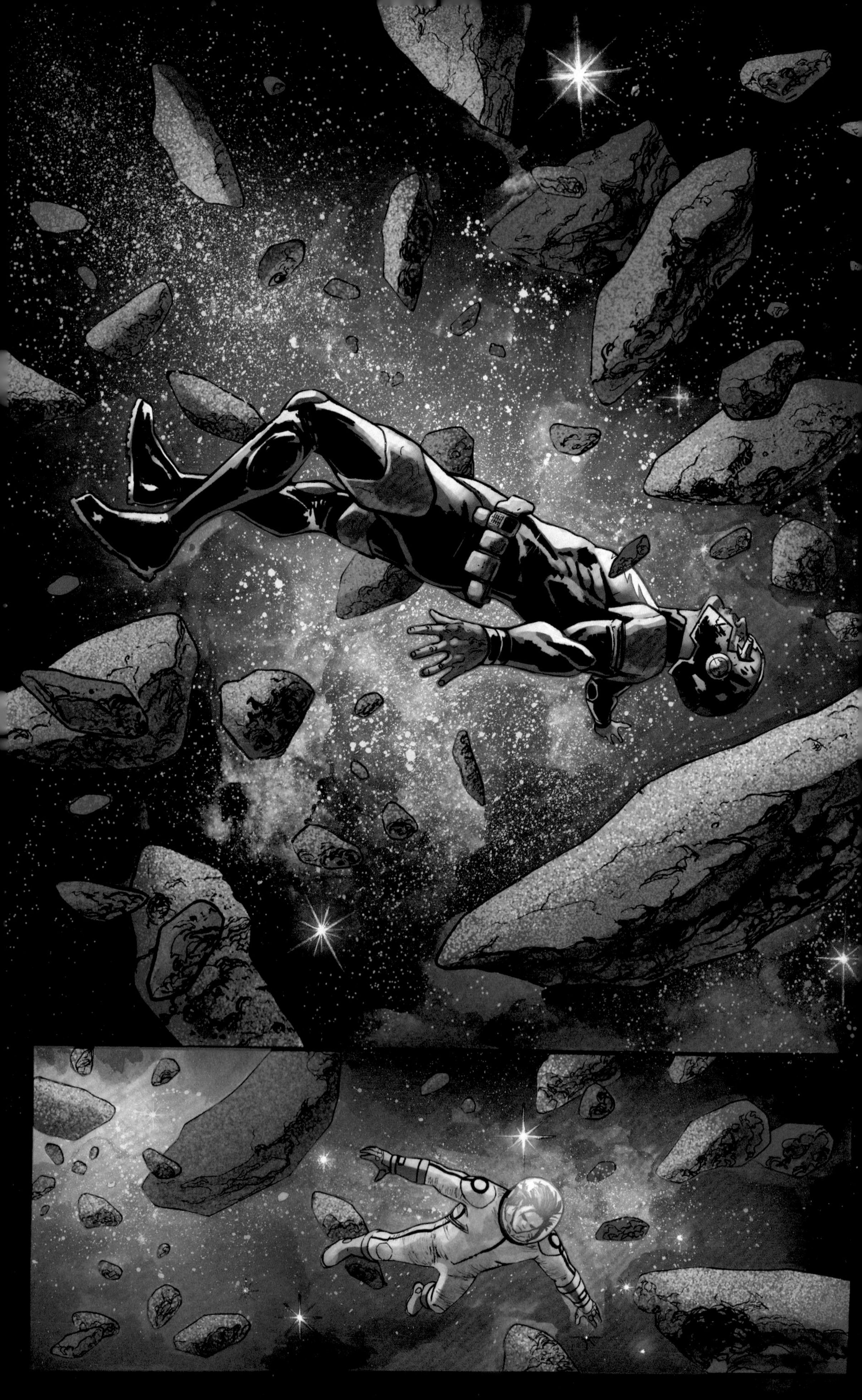

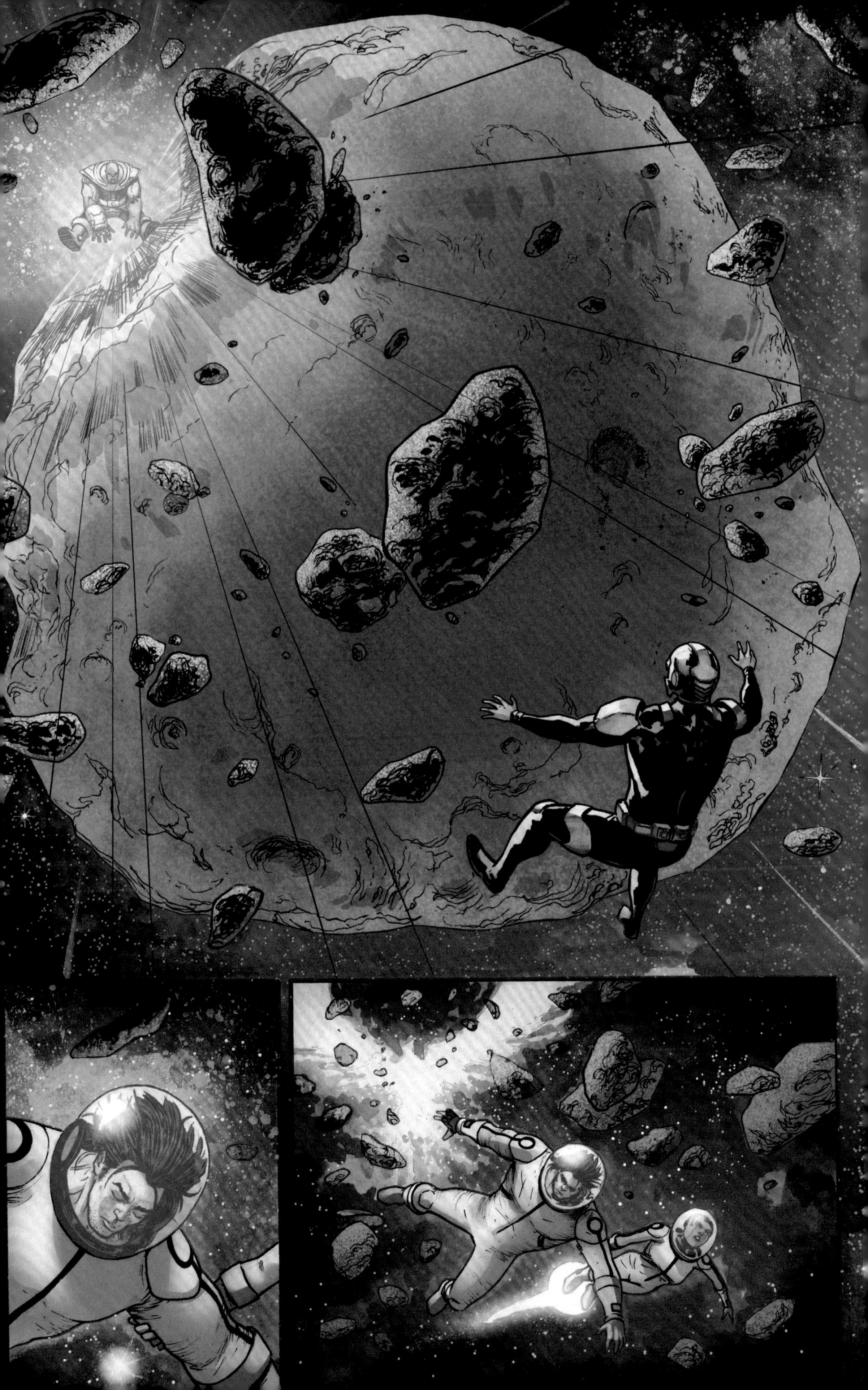

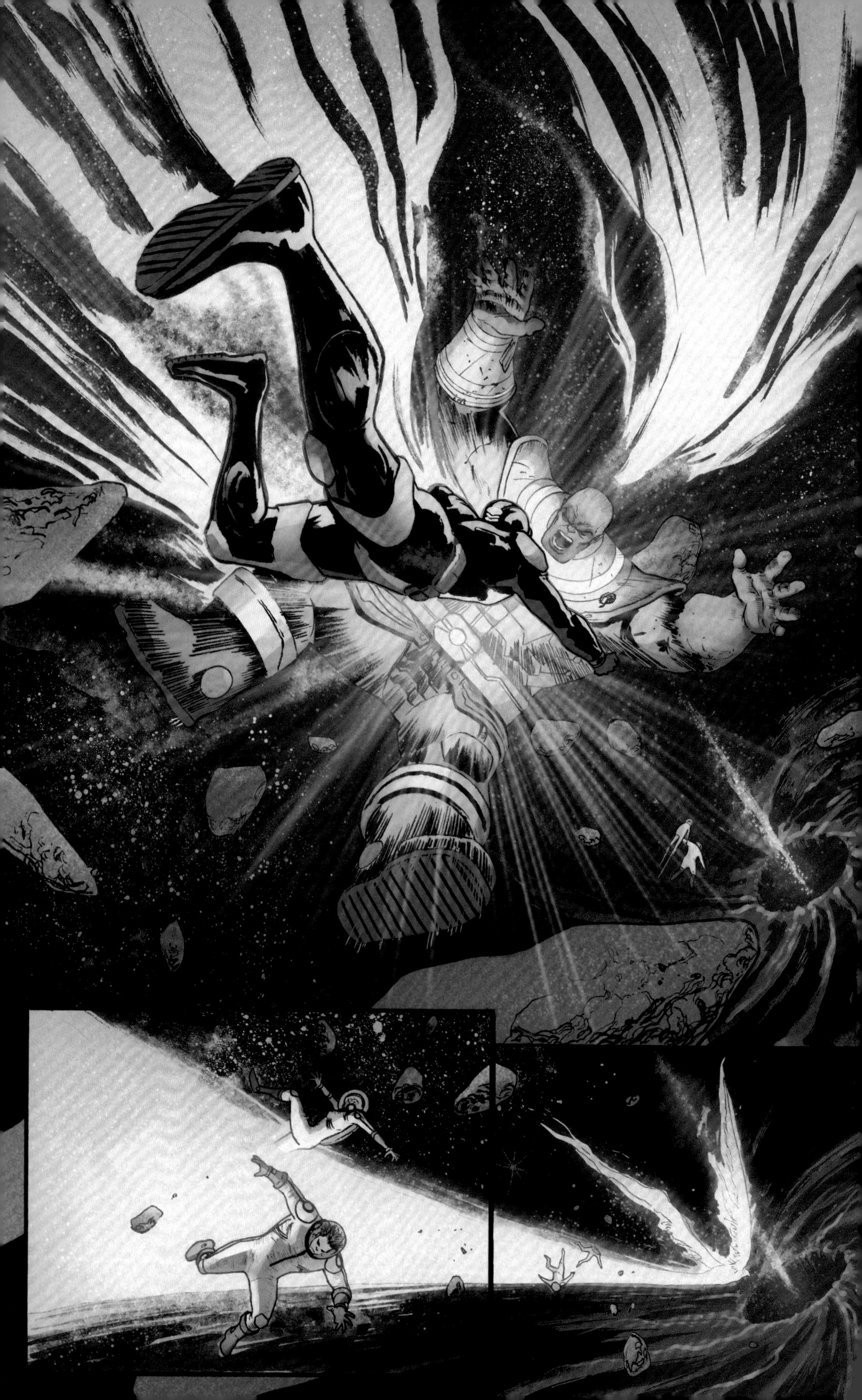

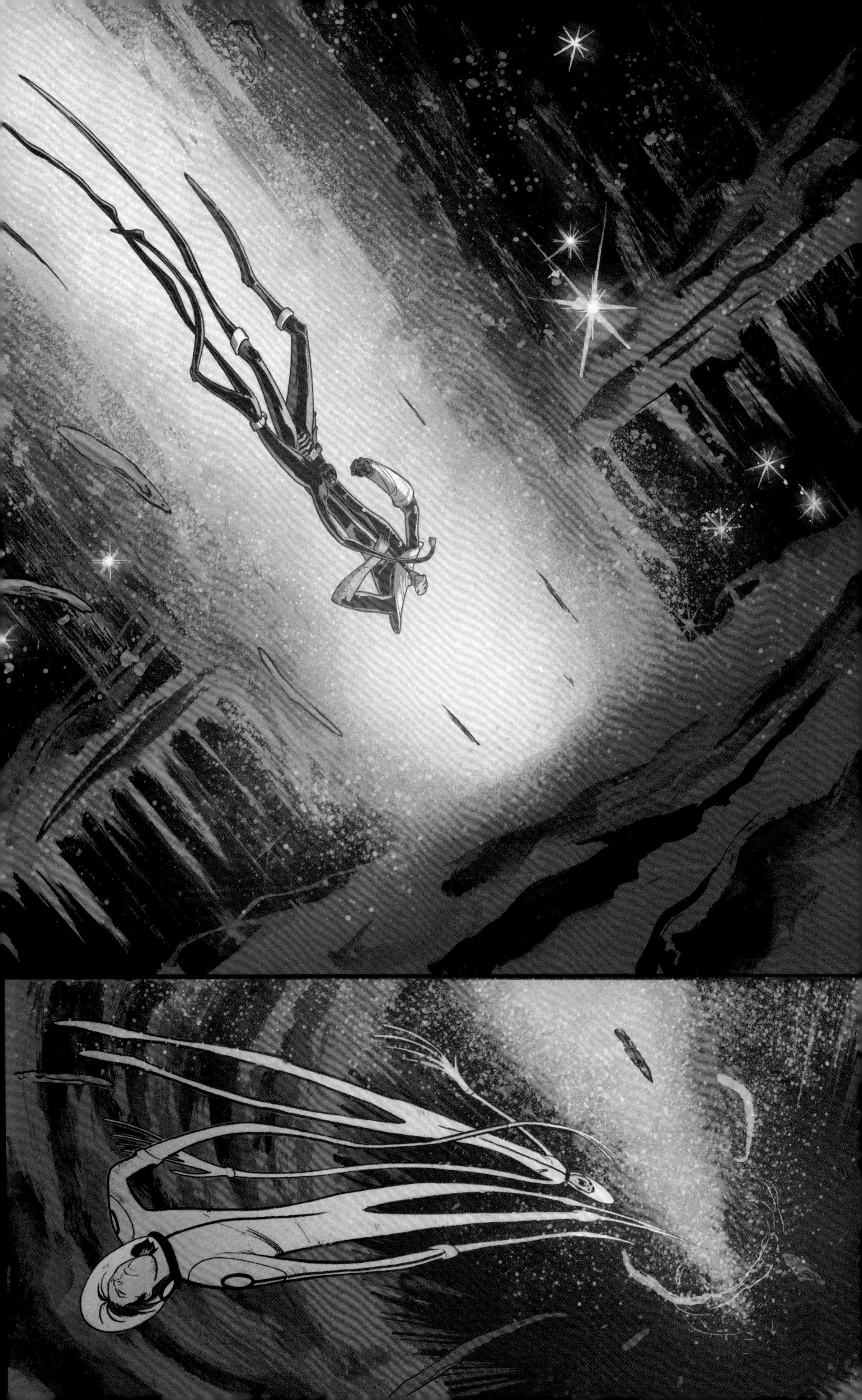

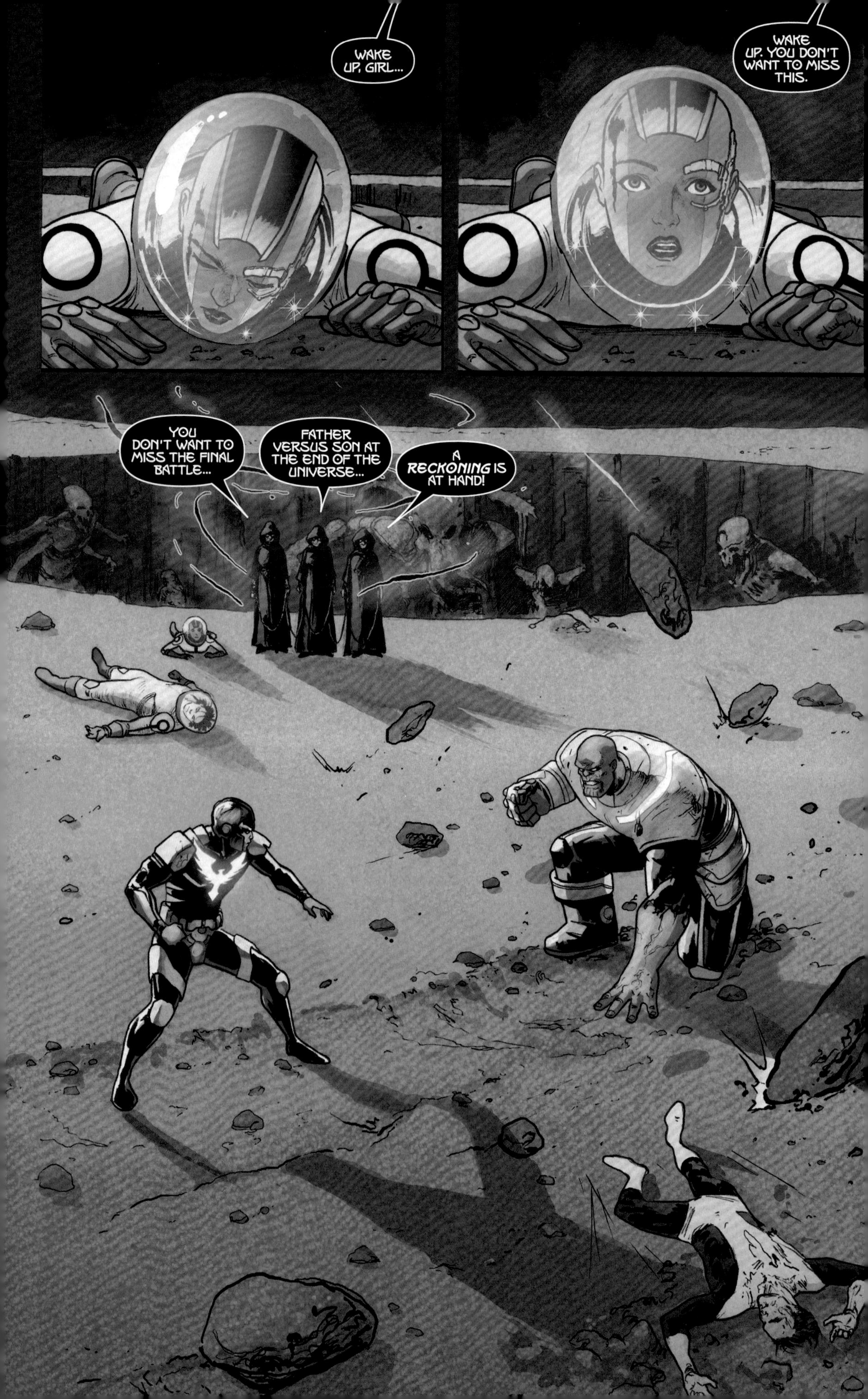
WAKE UP, GIRL...
WAKE UP. YOU DON'T WANT TO MISS THIS.
YOU DON'T WANT TO MISS THE FINAL BATTLE...
FATHER VERSUS SON AT THE END OF THE UNIVERSE...
A RECKONING IS AT HAND!

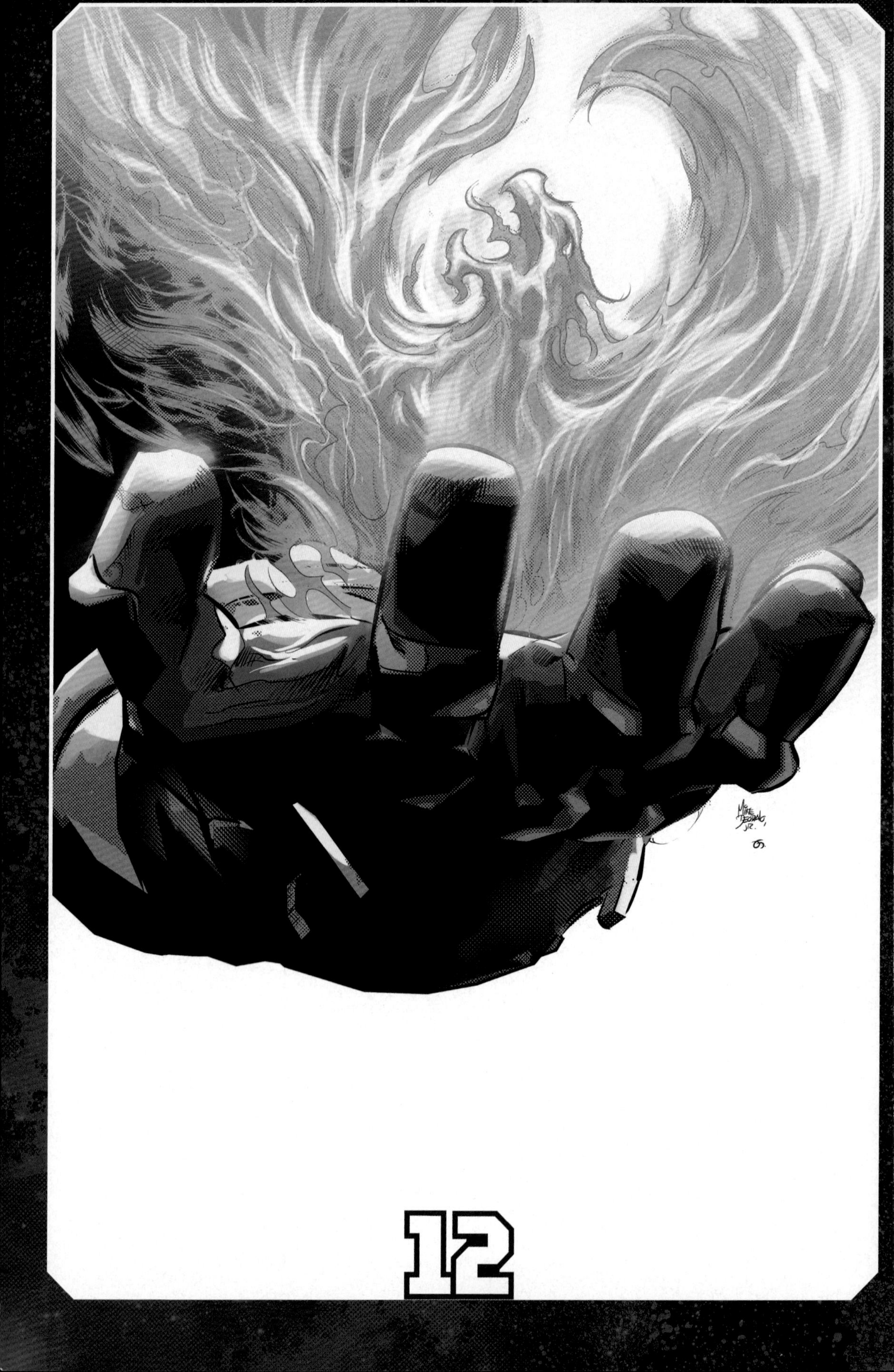

12

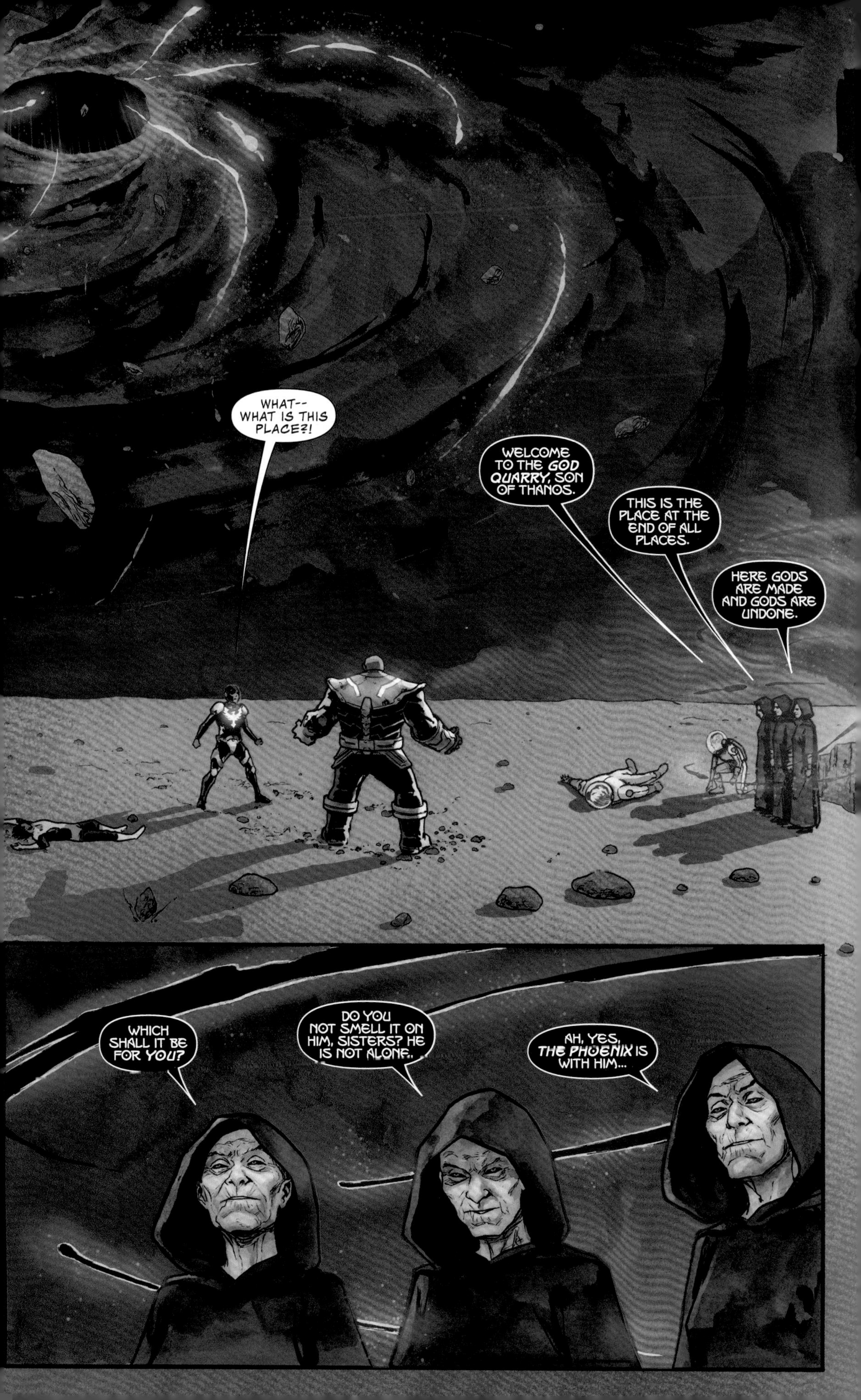
WHAT-- WHAT IS THIS PLACE?!
WELCOME TO THE GOD QUARRY, SON OF THANOS.
THIS IS THE PLACE AT THE END OF ALL PLACES.
HERE GODS ARE MADE AND GODS ARE UNDONE.
WHICH SHALL IT BE FOR YOU?
DO YOU NOT SMELL IT ON HIM, SISTERS? HE IS NOT ALONE.
AH, YES, THE PHOENIX IS WITH HIM...

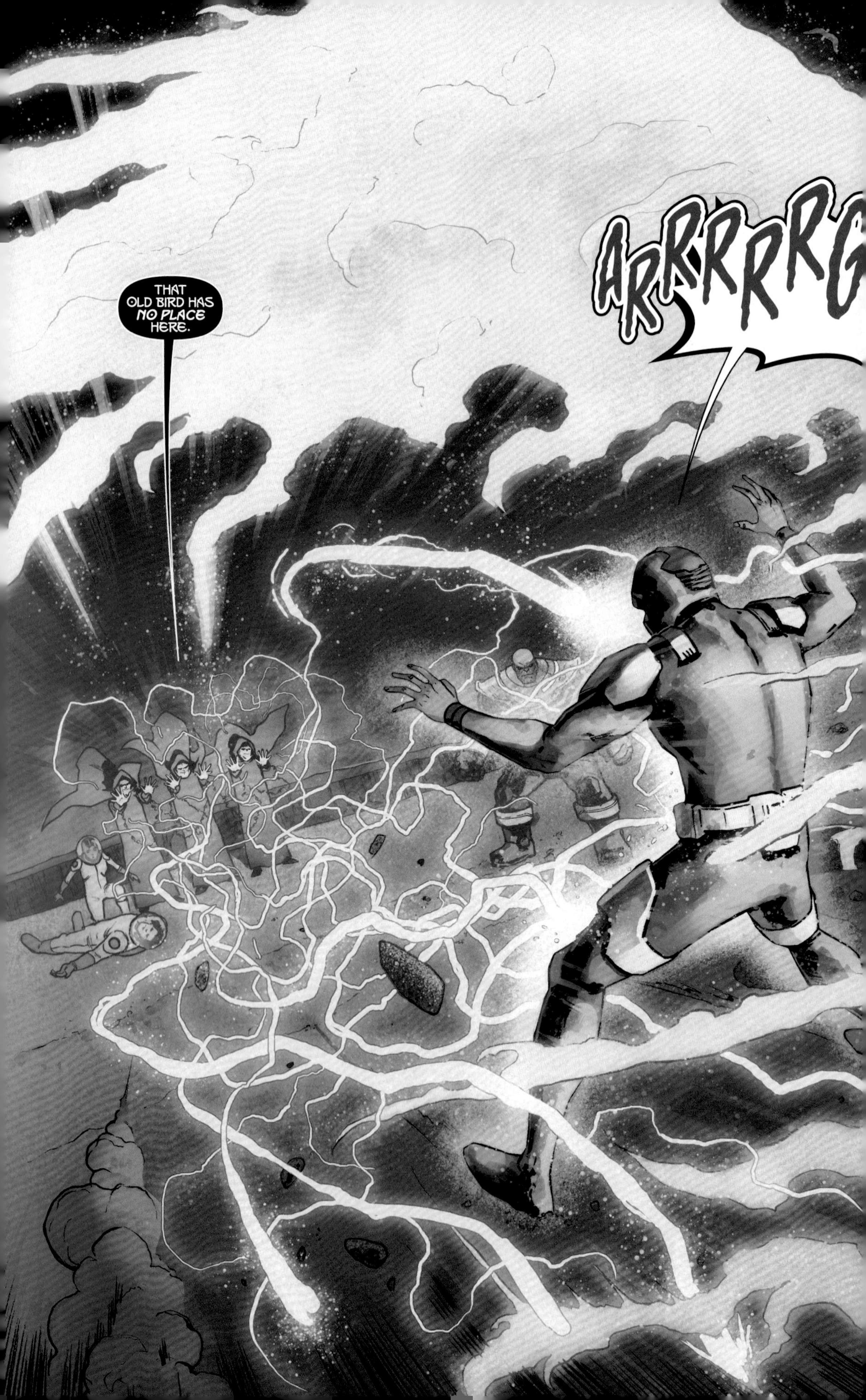
THAT OLD BIRD HAS *NO PLACE* HERE.
ARRRRRG

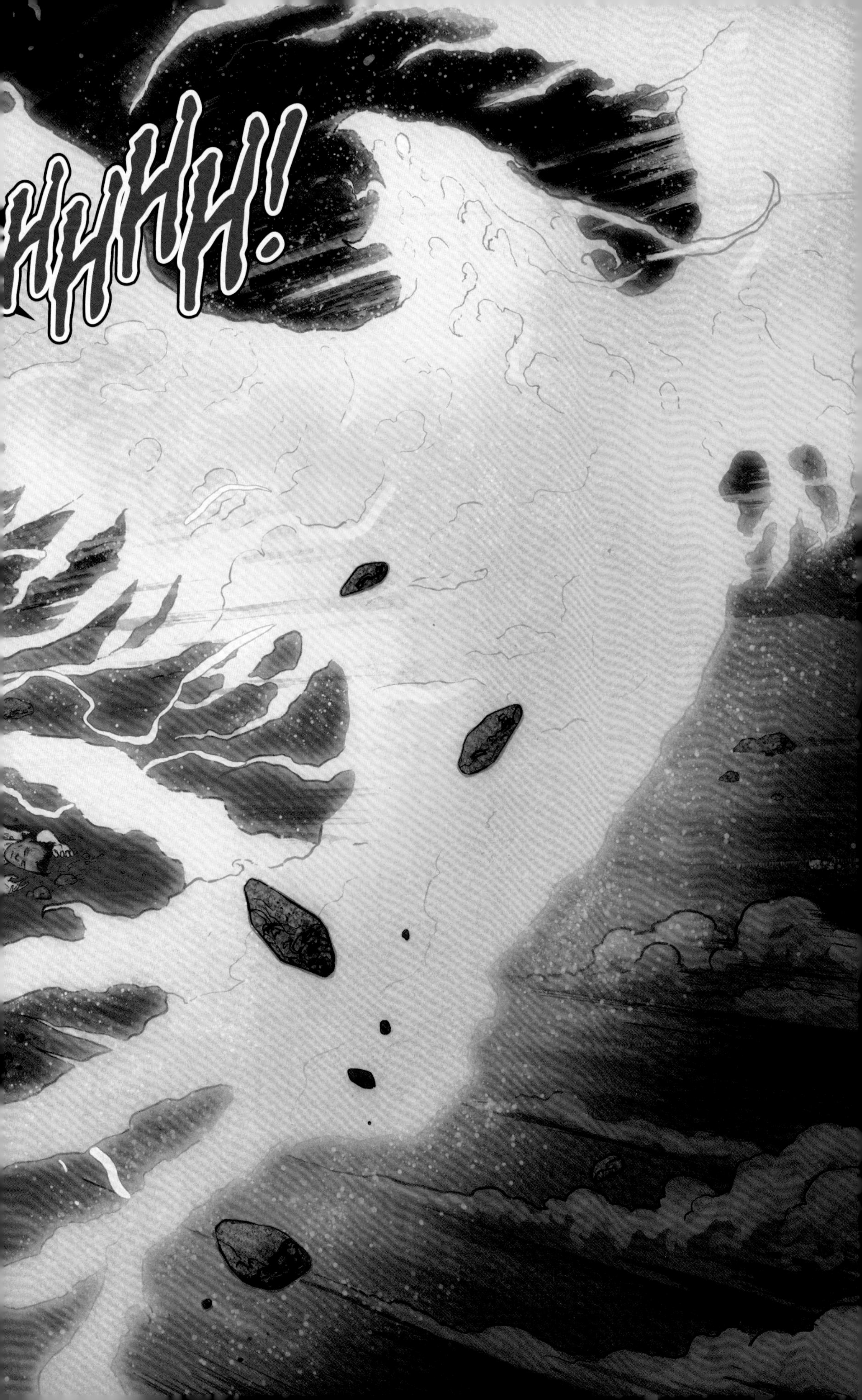
HHHH!

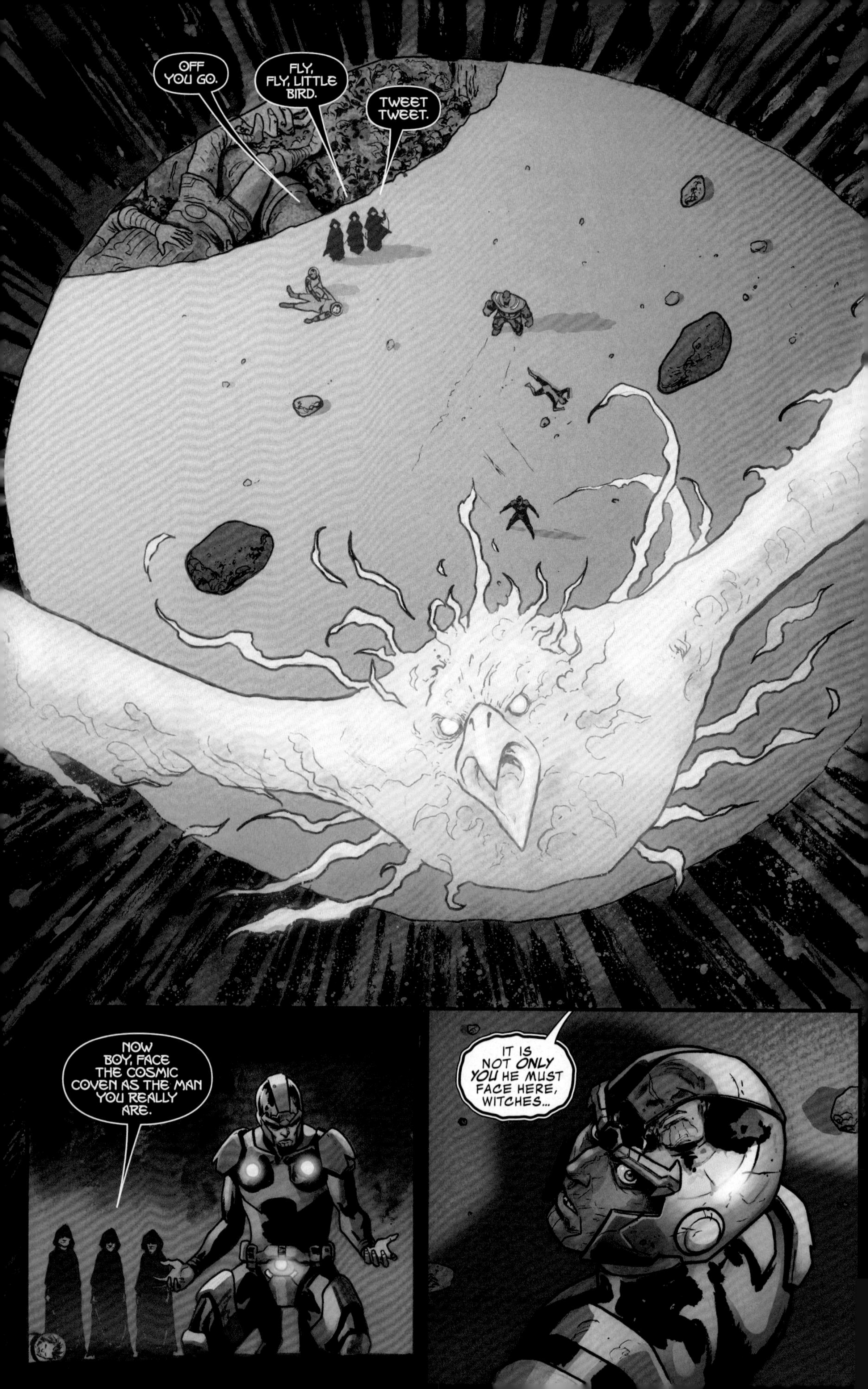
OFF YOU GO.
FLY, FLY, LITTLE BIRD.
TWEET TWEET.
NOW BOY, FACE THE COSMIC COVEN AS THE MAN YOU REALLY ARE.
IT IS NOT *ONLY YOU* HE MUST FACE HERE, WITCHES...

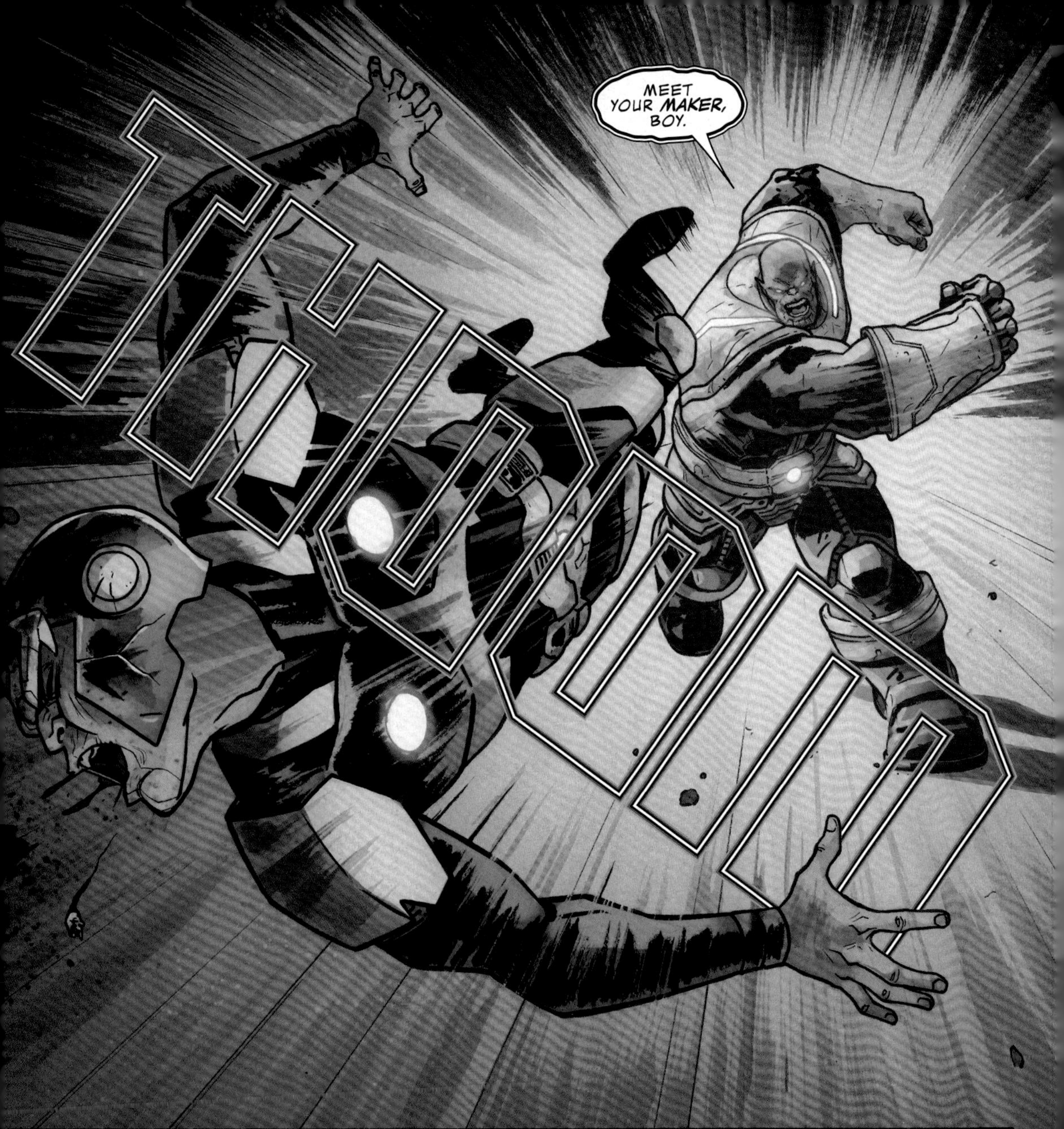
MEET YOUR MAKER, BOY.
THOOOM

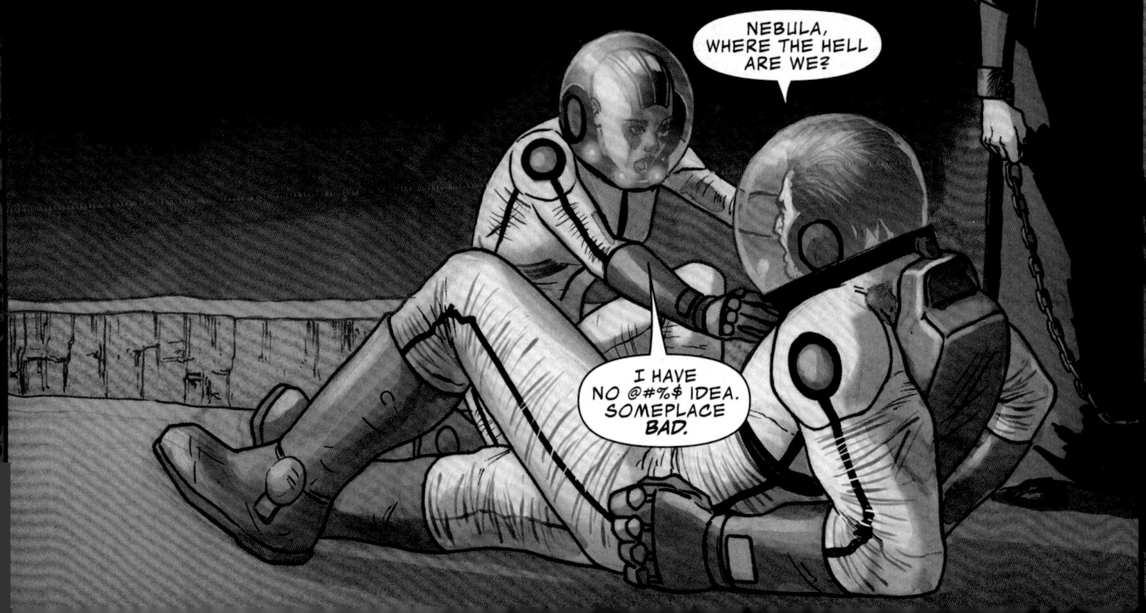
NEBULA, WHERE THE HELL ARE WE?
I HAVE NO @#%$ IDEA. SOMEPLACE BAD.

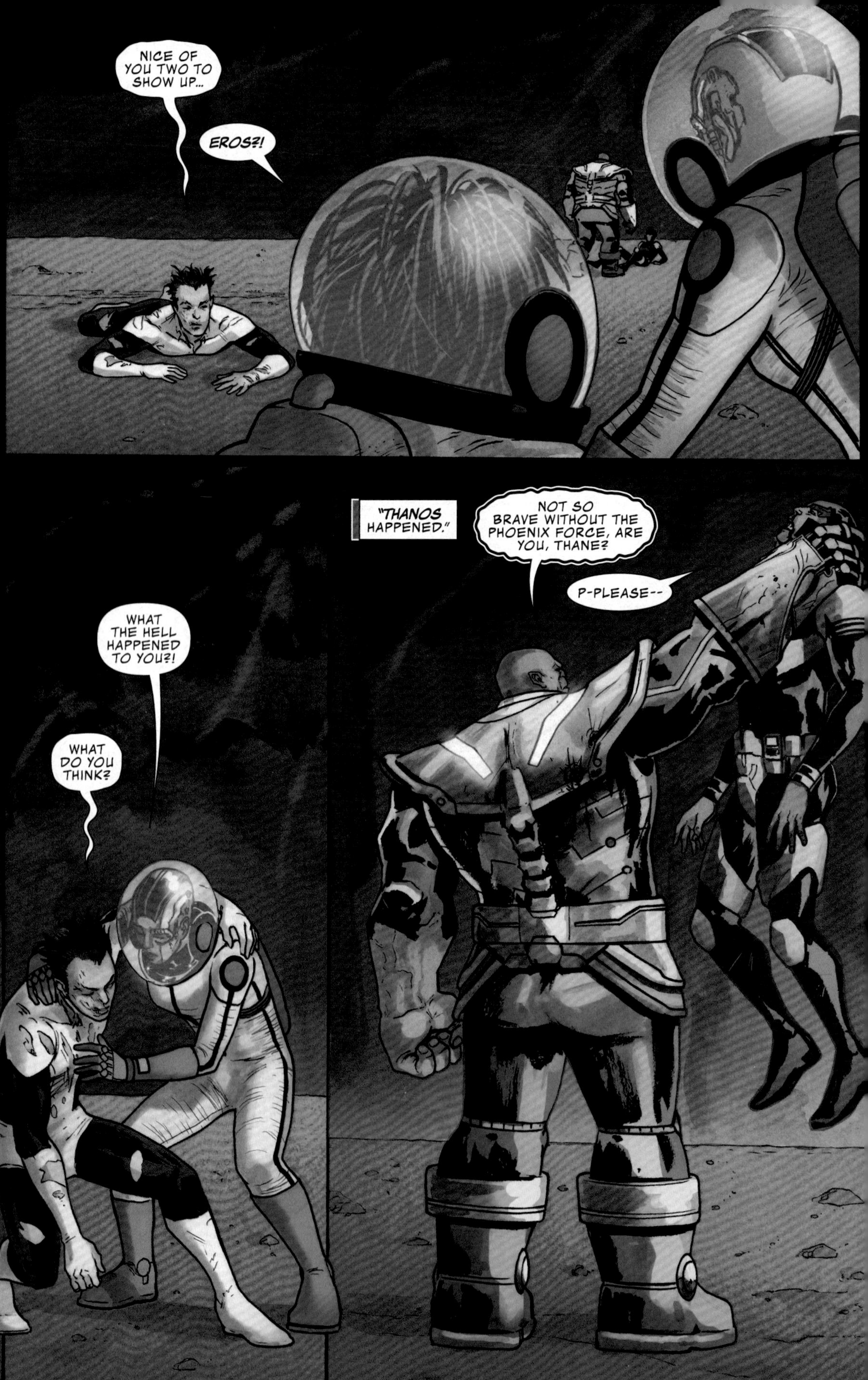

NICE OF YOU TWO TO SHOW UP...
EROS?!
WHAT THE HELL HAPPENED TO YOU?!
WHAT DO YOU THINK?
"THANOS HAPPENED."
NOT SO BRAVE WITHOUT THE PHOENIX FORCE, ARE YOU, THANE?
P-PLEASE--

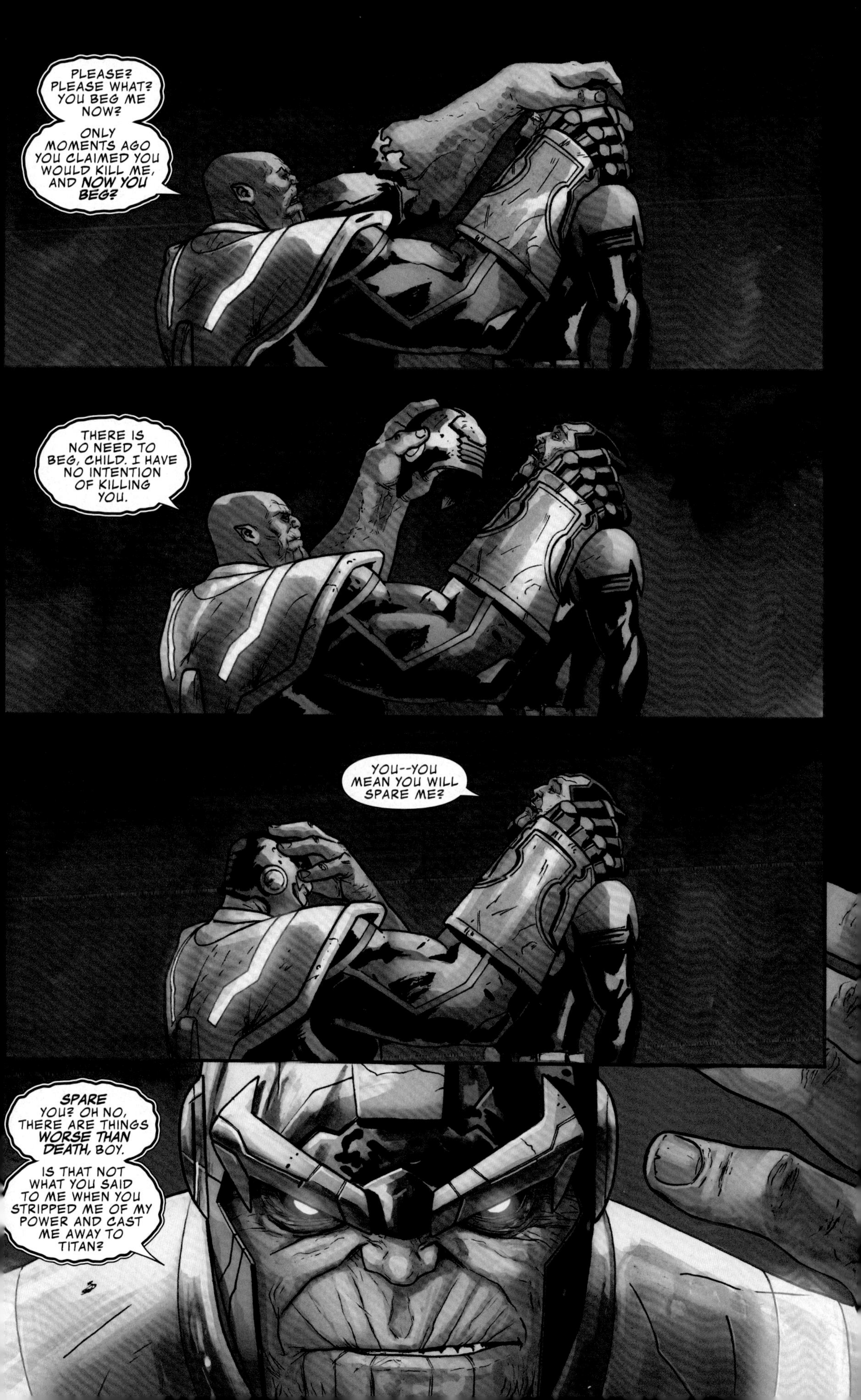
PLEASE? PLEASE WHAT? YOU BEG ME NOW?
ONLY MOMENTS AGO YOU CLAIMED YOU WOULD KILL ME, AND *NOW YOU BEG?*
THERE IS NO NEED TO BEG, CHILD. I HAVE NO INTENTION OF KILLING YOU.
YOU--YOU MEAN YOU WILL SPARE ME?
SPARE YOU? OH NO, THERE ARE THINGS *WORSE THAN DEATH,* BOY.
IS THAT NOT WHAT YOU SAID TO ME WHEN YOU STRIPPED ME OF MY POWER AND CAST ME AWAY TO TITAN?

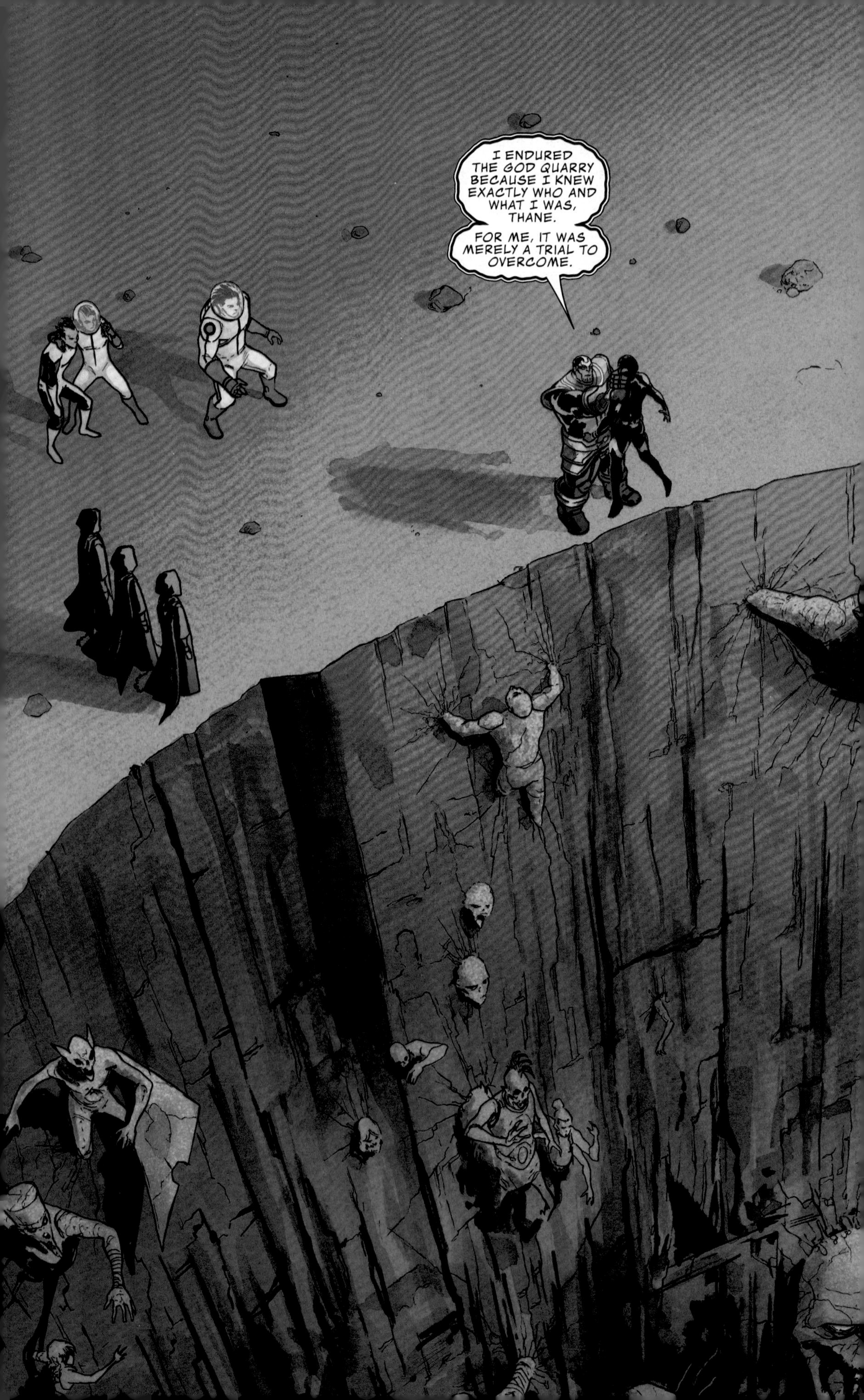
I ENDURED THE GOD QUARRY BECAUSE I KNEW EXACTLY WHO AND WHAT I WAS, THANE.
FOR ME, IT WAS MERELY A TRIAL TO OVERCOME.

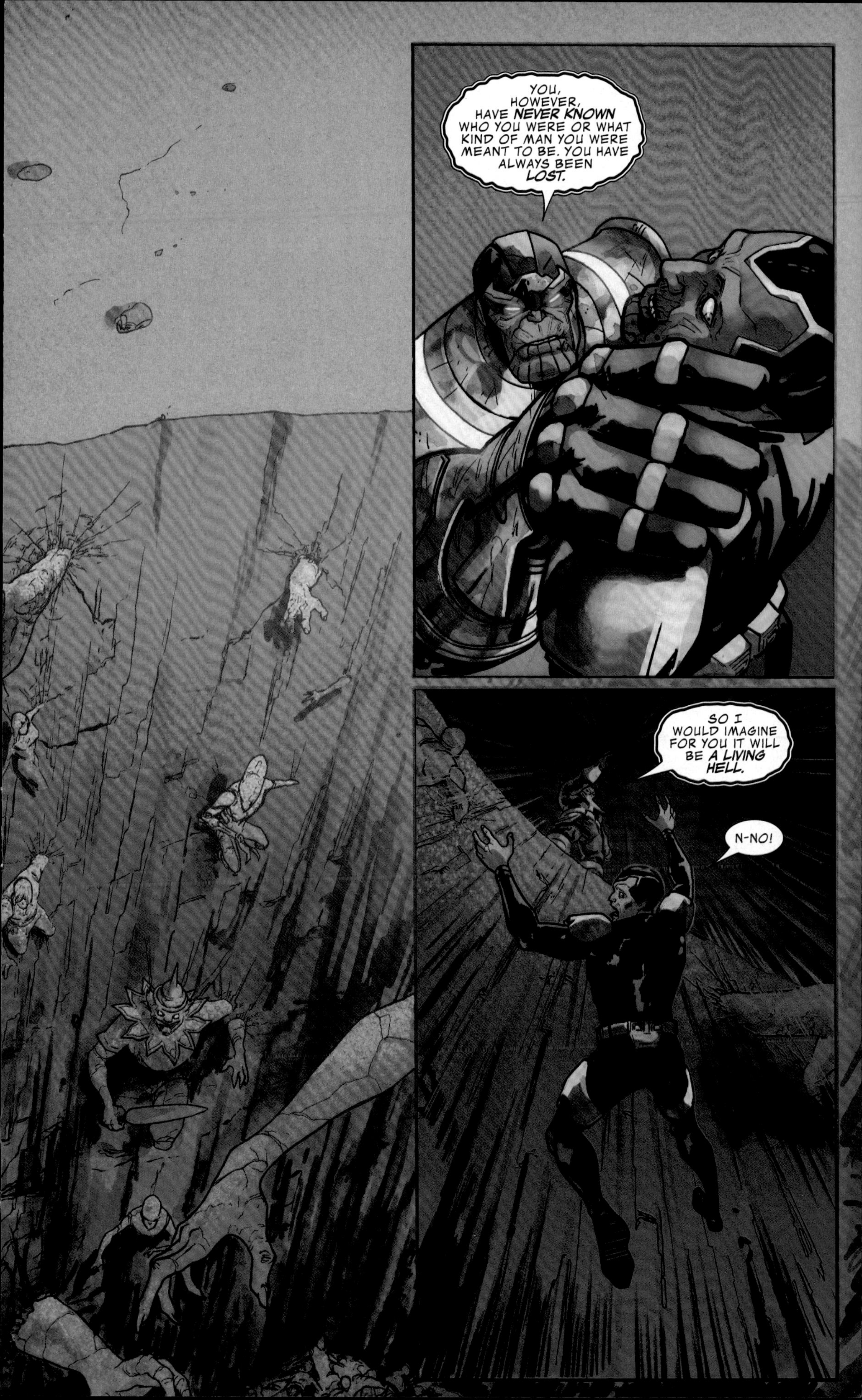
YOU, HOWEVER, HAVE NEVER KNOWN WHO YOU WERE OR WHAT KIND OF MAN YOU WERE MEANT TO BE. YOU HAVE ALWAYS BEEN LOST.
SO I WOULD IMAGINE FOR YOU IT WILL BE A LIVING HELL.
N-NO!

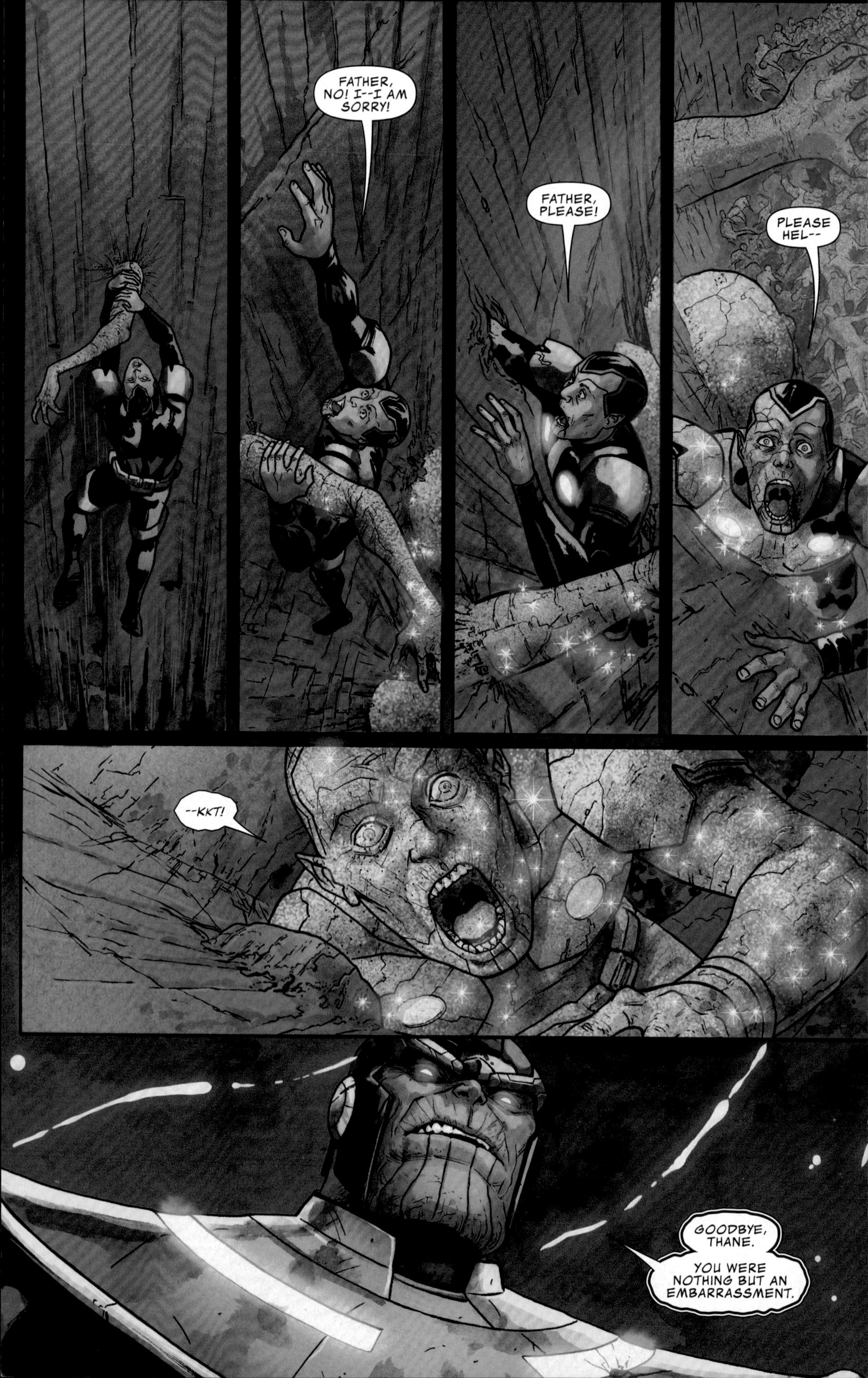
FATHER, NO! I--I AM SORRY!
FATHER, PLEASE!
PLEASE HEL--
--KKT!
GOODBYE, THANE.
YOU WERE NOTHING BUT AN EMBARRASSMENT.

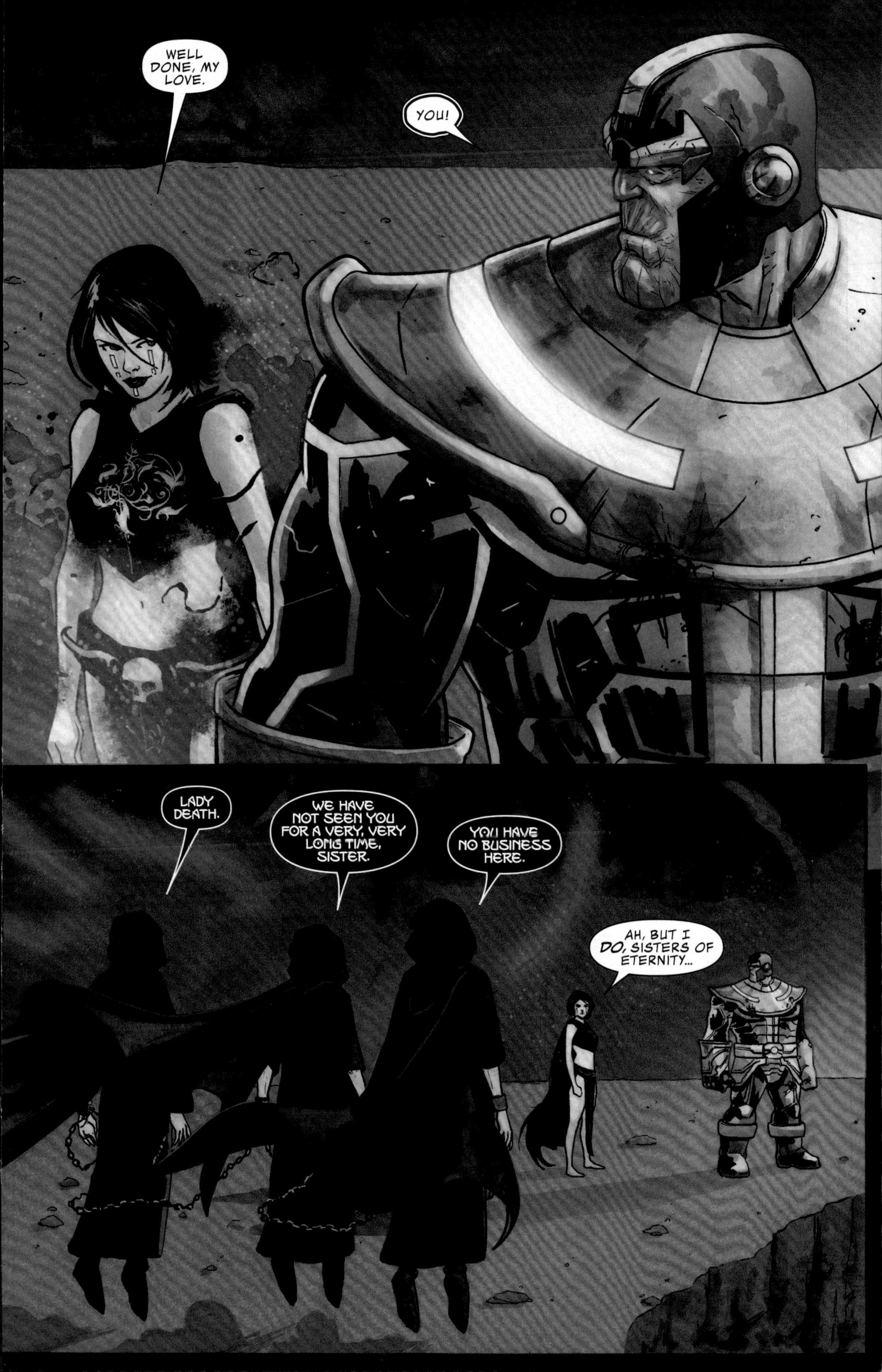
WELL DONE, MY LOVE.
YOU!
LADY DEATH.
WE HAVE NOT SEEN YOU FOR A VERY, VERY LONG TIME, SISTER.
YOU HAVE NO BUSINESS HERE.
AH, BUT I DO, SISTERS OF ETERNITY...

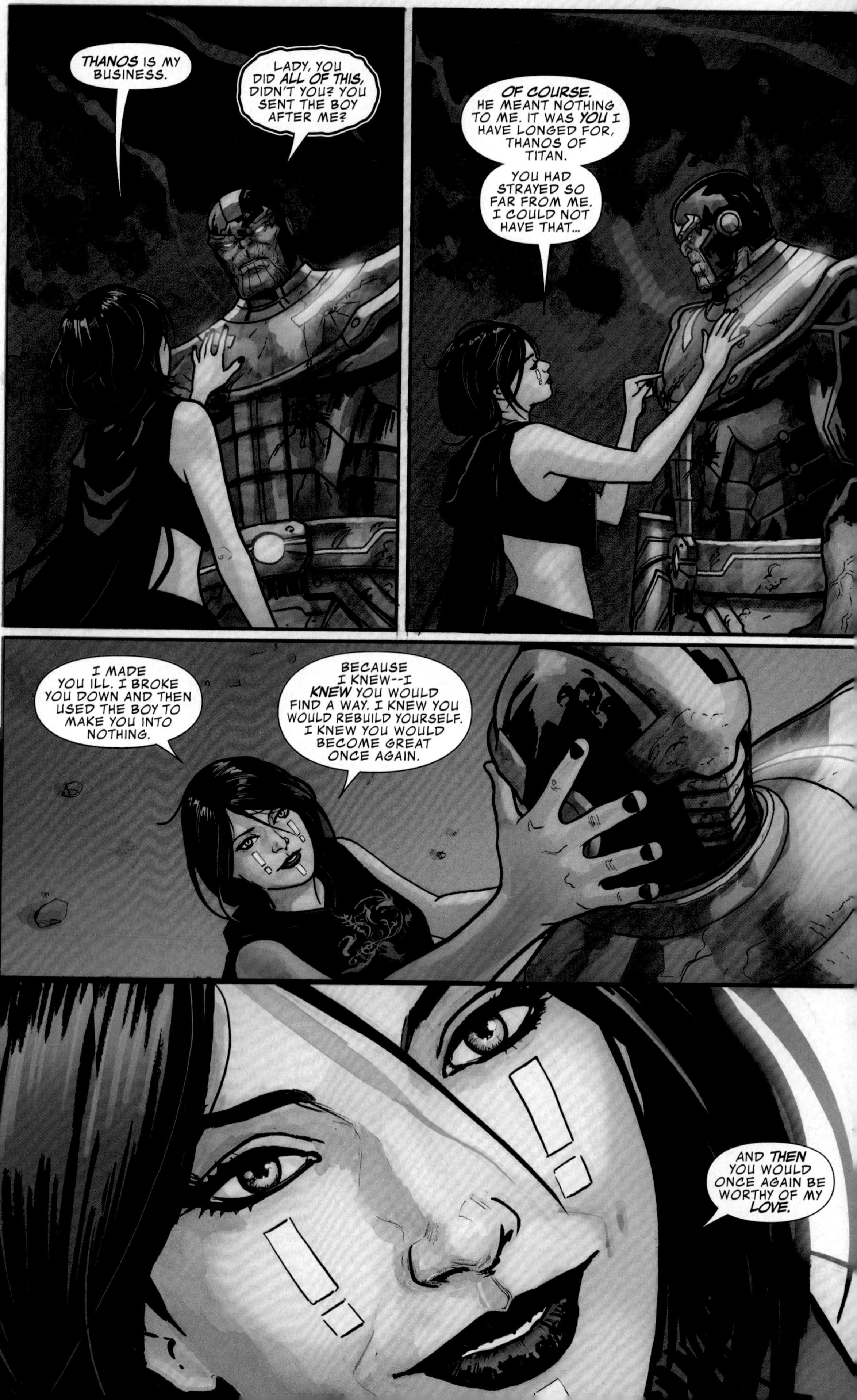
THANOS IS MY BUSINESS.
LADY, YOU DID ALL OF THIS, DIDN'T YOU? YOU SENT THE BOY AFTER ME?
OF COURSE. HE MEANT NOTHING TO ME. IT WAS YOU I HAVE LONGED FOR, THANOS OF TITAN.
YOU HAD STRAYED SO FAR FROM ME. I COULD NOT HAVE THAT...
I MADE YOU ILL. I BROKE YOU DOWN AND THEN USED THE BOY TO MAKE YOU INTO NOTHING.
BECAUSE I KNEW--I KNEW YOU WOULD FIND A WAY. I KNEW YOU WOULD REBUILD YOURSELF. I KNEW YOU WOULD BECOME GREAT ONCE AGAIN.
AND THEN YOU WOULD ONCE AGAIN BE WORTHY OF MY LOVE.

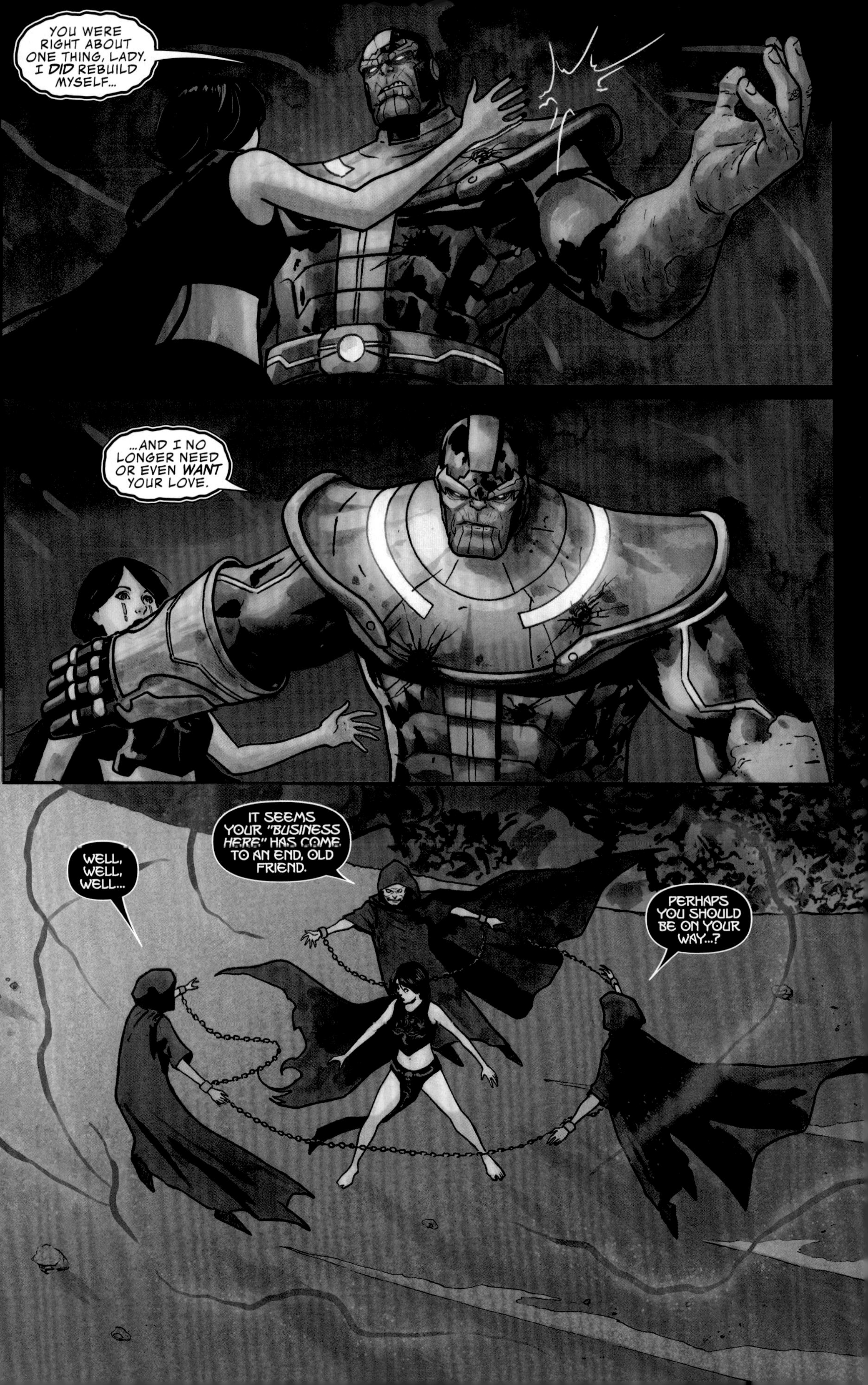
YOU WERE RIGHT ABOUT ONE THING, LADY. I DID REBUILD MYSELF...
...AND I NO LONGER NEED OR EVEN WANT YOUR LOVE.
WELL, WELL, WELL...
IT SEEMS YOUR "BUSINESS HERE" HAS COME TO AN END, OLD FRIEND.
PERHAPS YOU SHOULD BE ON YOUR WAY...?

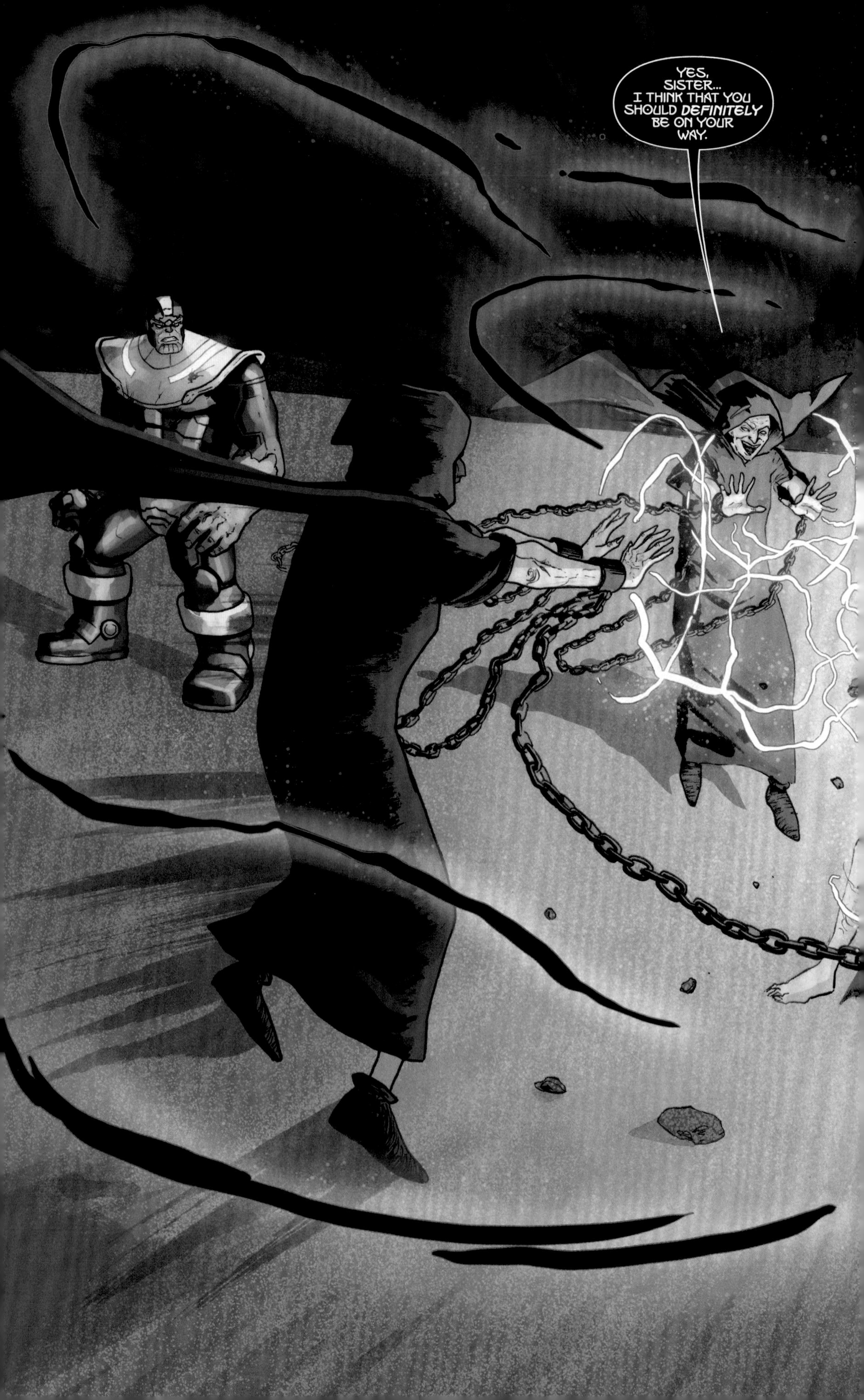
YES, SISTER... I THINK THAT YOU SHOULD DEFINITELY BE ON YOUR WAY.

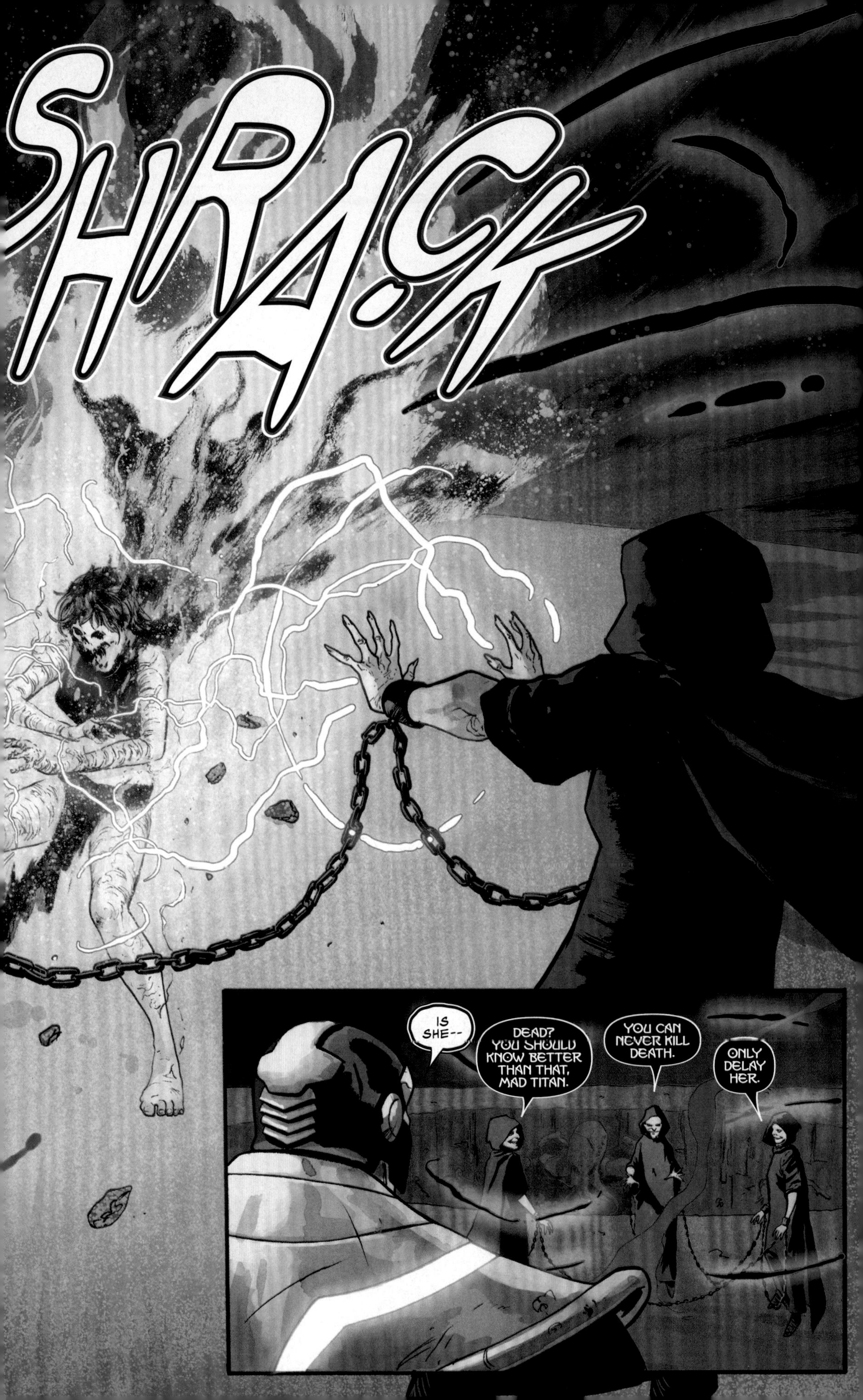
SHRACK
IS SHE--
DEAD? YOU SHOULD KNOW BETTER THAN THAT, MAD TITAN.
YOU CAN NEVER KILL DEATH.
ONLY DELAY HER.

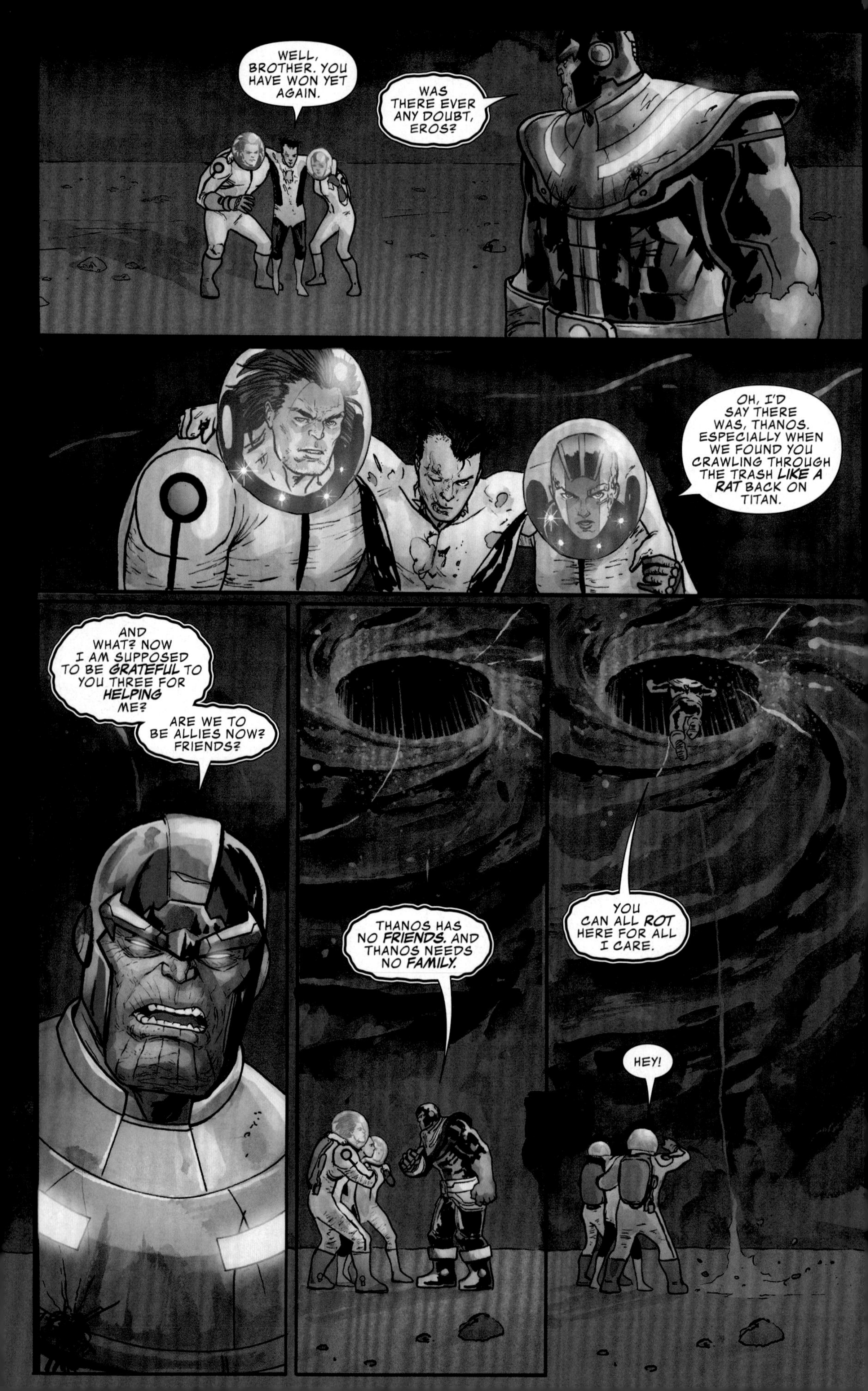
WELL, BROTHER. YOU HAVE WON YET AGAIN.
WAS THERE EVER ANY DOUBT, EROS?
OH, I'D SAY THERE WAS, THANOS. ESPECIALLY WHEN WE FOUND YOU CRAWLING THROUGH THE TRASH LIKE A RAT BACK ON TITAN.
AND WHAT? NOW I AM SUPPOSED TO BE GRATEFUL TO YOU THREE FOR HELPING ME?
ARE WE TO BE ALLIES NOW? FRIENDS?
THANOS HAS NO FRIENDS. AND THANOS NEEDS NO FAMILY.
YOU CAN ALL ROT HERE FOR ALL I CARE.
HEY!

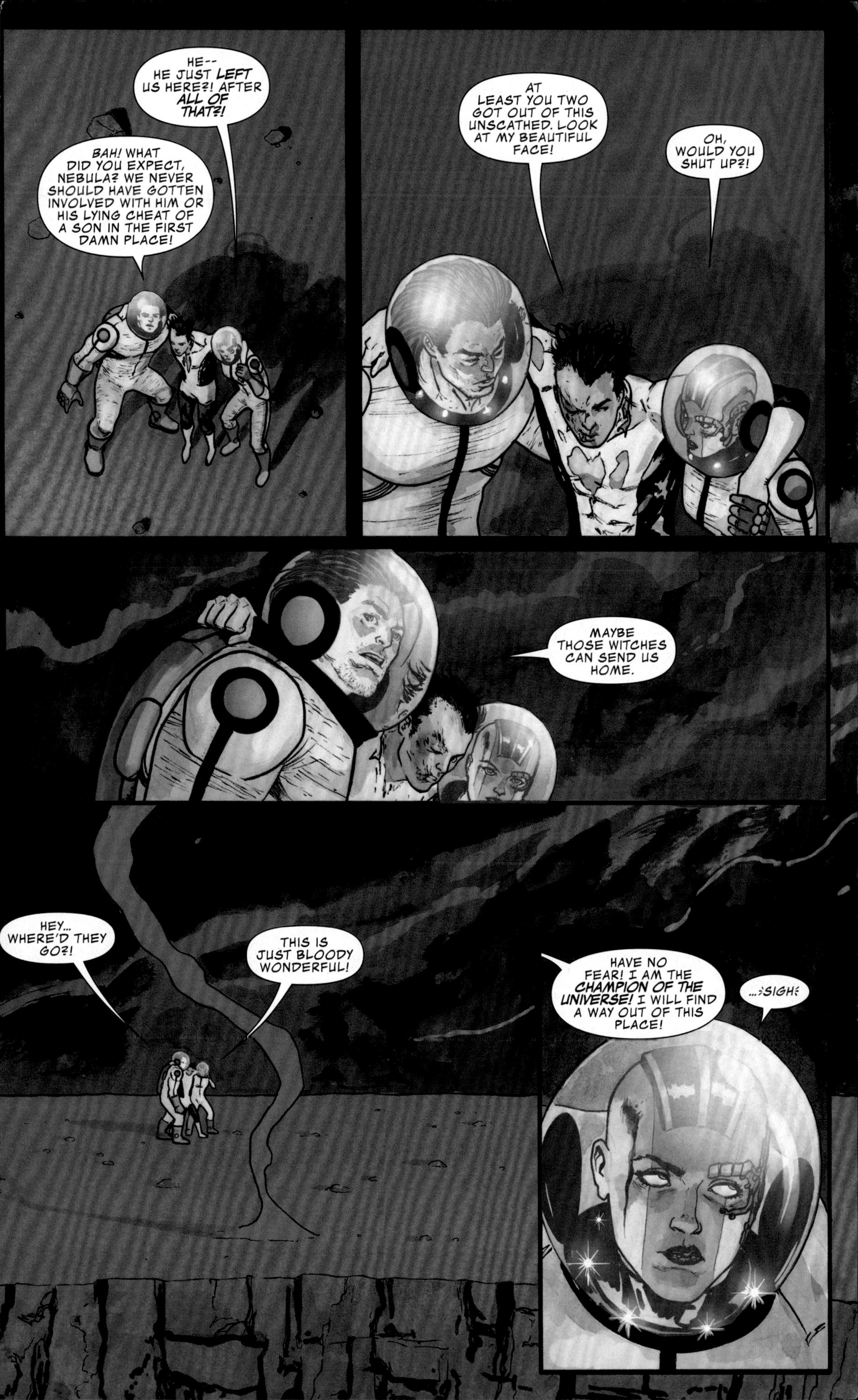
HE-- HE JUST LEFT US HERE?! AFTER ALL OF THAT?!
BAH! WHAT DID YOU EXPECT, NEBULA? WE NEVER SHOULD HAVE GOTTEN INVOLVED WITH HIM OR HIS LYING CHEAT OF A SON IN THE FIRST DAMN PLACE!
AT LEAST YOU TWO GOT OUT OF THIS UNSCATHED. LOOK AT MY BEAUTIFUL FACE!
OH, WOULD YOU SHUT UP?!
MAYBE THOSE WITCHES CAN SEND US HOME.
HEY... WHERE'D THEY GO?!
THIS IS JUST BLOODY WONDERFUL!
HAVE NO FEAR! I AM THE CHAMPION OF THE UNIVERSE! I WILL FIND A WAY OUT OF THIS PLACE!
...SIGH

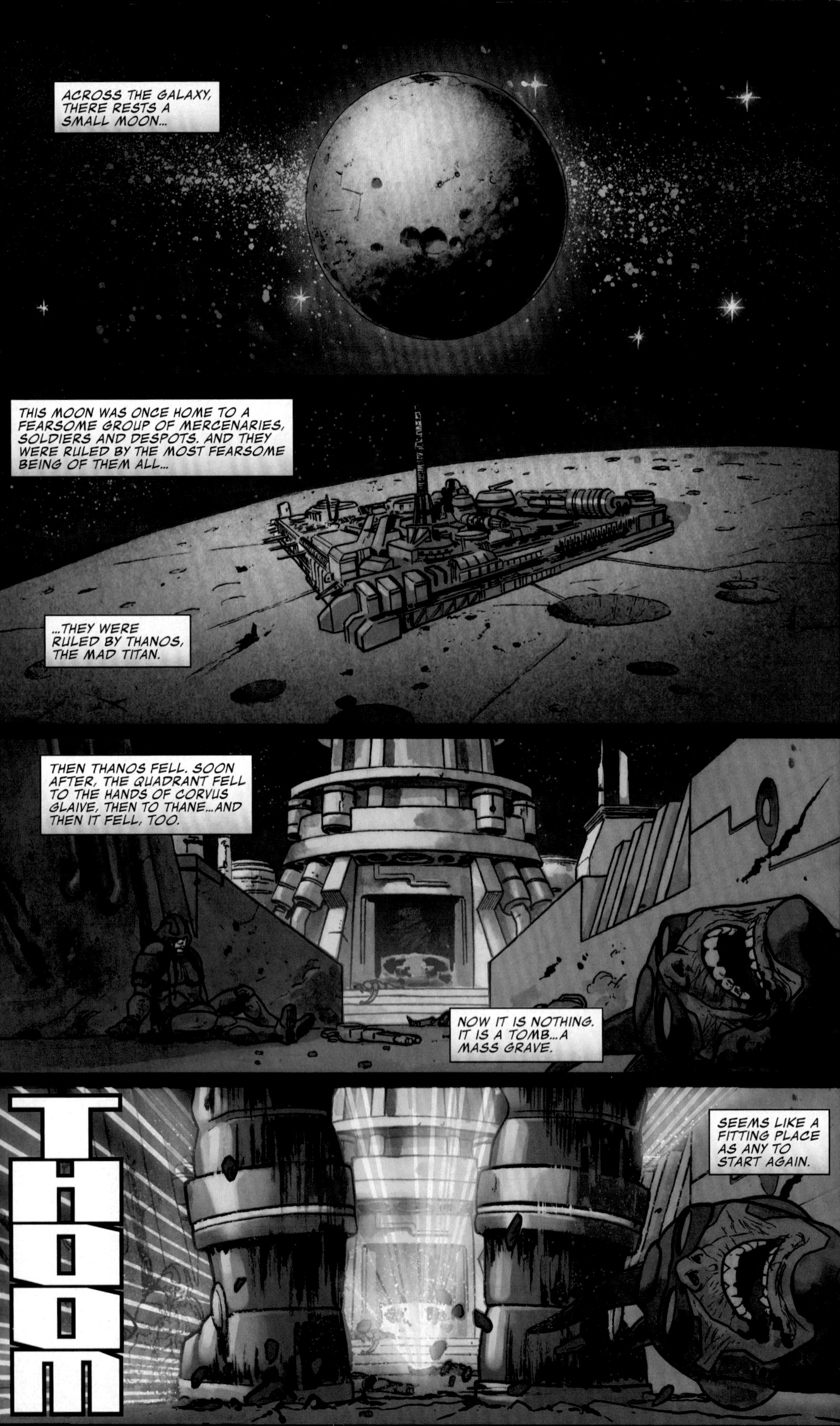
ACROSS THE GALAXY, THERE RESTS A SMALL MOON...
THIS MOON WAS ONCE HOME TO A FEARSOME GROUP OF MERCENARIES, SOLDIERS AND DESPOTS. AND THEY WERE RULED BY THE MOST FEARSOME BEING OF THEM ALL...
...THEY WERE RULED BY THANOS, THE MAD TITAN.
THEN THANOS FELL. SOON AFTER, THE QUADRANT FELL TO THE HANDS OF CORVUS GLAIVE, THEN TO THANE...AND THEN IT FELL, TOO.
NOW IT IS NOTHING. IT IS A TOMB...A MASS GRAVE.
THOOM
SEEMS LIKE A FITTING PLACE AS ANY TO START AGAIN.

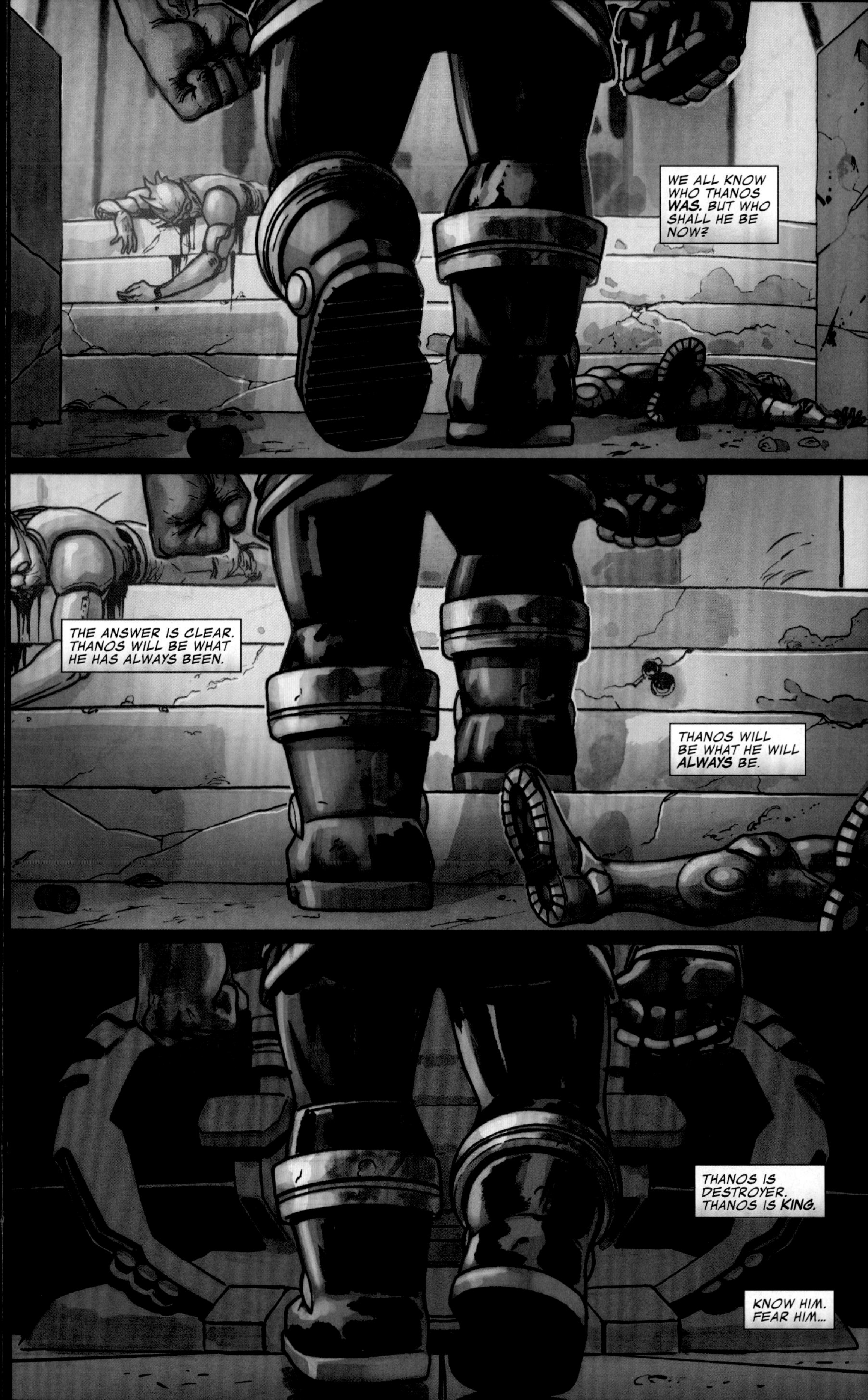
WE ALL KNOW WHO THANOS WAS. BUT WHO SHALL HE BE NOW?
THE ANSWER IS CLEAR. THANOS WILL BE WHAT HE HAS ALWAYS BEEN.
THANOS WILL BE WHAT HE WILL ALWAYS BE.
THANOS IS DESTROYER. THANOS IS KING.
KNOW HIM. FEAR HIM...

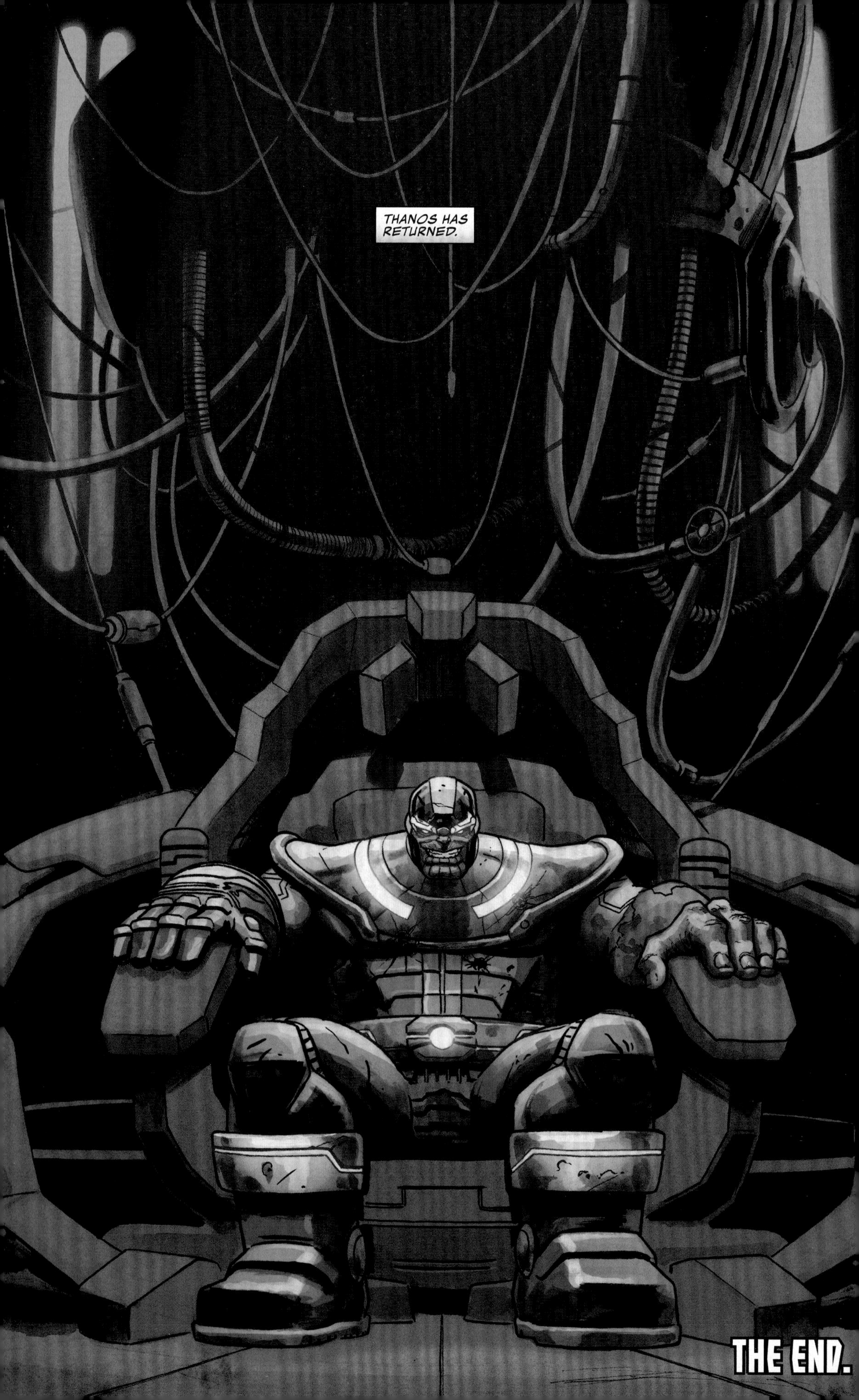
THANOS HAS RETURNED.
THE END.

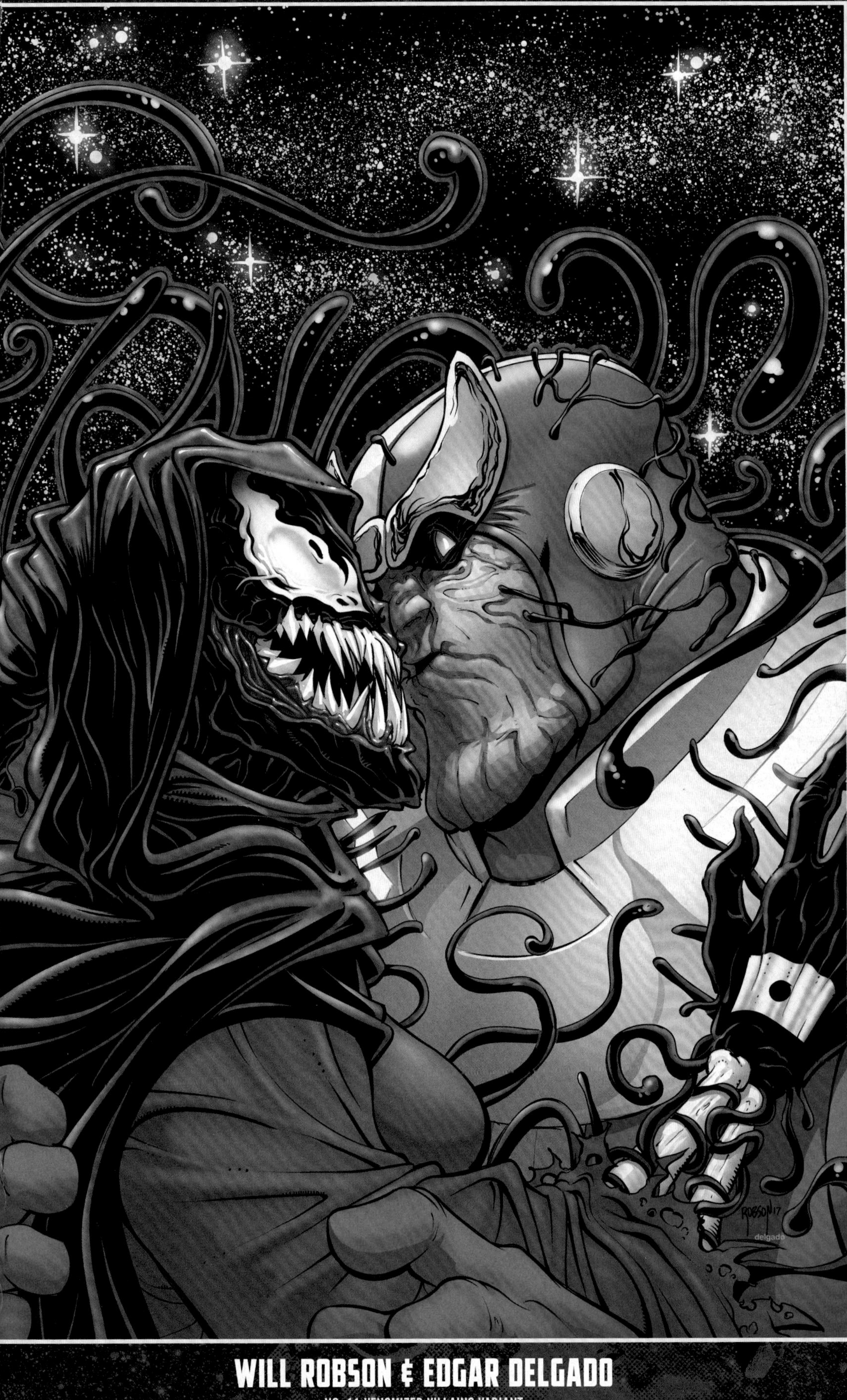
ROBSON '17
delgado

WILL ROBSON & EDGAR DELGADO

NO. 11 VENOMIZED VILLAINS VARIANT